PRAISE FOR
CAPTURED BY LOVE:

As I've written in my Mars Venus books, couples that have attained a higher love are able to grow together in passion and love for a lifetime. The riveting stories in *Captured by Love* masterfully reveal that these couples have lived this process, and the principles that they learned through such an ordeal as the Vietnam War actually brought them closer together. Read this book and be inspired to strengthen your relationship, too.

– John Gray, Relationship Counselor, Lecturer, and Author of *Beyond Mars and Venus: Relationship Skills for Today's Complex World*

Authors Lee Ellis and Greg Godek skillfully highlight the stories of these heroic men and women with empathy and historical context. Through example, the reader gains valuable lessons on the power of love and its ability to conquer all obstacles—even those of war, torture, and solitary confinement in the Hanoi Hilton.

– Heath Hardage Lee, Author of *The League of Wives*

Since I founded and publish MOVIEGUIDE®, I am always hesitant to offer to review a book, but, that said, I was totally captivated and inspired by *Captured by Love: Inspiring True Romance Stories from Vietnam POWs*, which is one of the best books about love, marriage and faith that I have read.

– Dr. Ted Baehr, Founder and Publisher of MOVIEGUIDE®

There are well over 1,000 books about the Vietnam War, but this is the only one that gathers the inspirational and sometimes heartbreaking love stories of 20 former POWs. In this book you will see that good can come out of war, and you will learn that happiness and love can arise out of the most horrifying situations. We can all learn from these stories—about love and about life.

– LeAnn Thieman, Nurse, Author, and Speaker Hall of Fame Inductee; Founder and President of SelfCare for Healthcare, and Author of *This Must Be My Brother*

I

We love this book. It's originality and freshness is stimulating and satisfying. Any couple reading this will be inspired to overcome all the challenges of their relationship for the amazing outcome that awaits them. We recommend it to all couples, whether challenged or not.

– Harville Hendrix, Ph.D. and Helen LaKelly Hunt, Ph.D., Coauthors of *Getting the Love You Want: A Guide for Couples* **and** *Making Marriage Simple*

Lee Ellis and Greg Godek have woven a moving and heartwarming story that shows readers of any age how to ensure that love endures. Given the separation they survived during the Vietnam era and the long-lasting marriages they fostered after being reunited, the POWs and wives featured in *Captured by Love* certainly know how to make love last! May we all be so lucky.

– Alvin Townley, Bestselling New York Times-reviewed Author of *Defiant: The POWs Who Endured Vietnam's Most Infamous Prison and the Women Who Fought for Them*

I am grateful for the vision in creating the *Captured by Love* that focuses on our amazing Vietnam POWs and their personal marital relationships. I believe readers will be moved to tears, laughter, and deep reflection, as well as gain new and fresh insight into their own personal relationships.

– Gen Robin Rand USAF (Ret), Former Commander, Air Force Global Strike Command and Commander, Air Forces Strategic - Air, US Strategic Command

While we have been fortunate during our careers to have heard many of the stories from our heroic POWs, until this book, we have not heard the brave stories of their spouses and significant others. As two fighter pilots married for the duration of our careers, we appreciated the perspective from both sides. Lee and Greg do an incredible job capturing the stresses of combat on both sides of relationships. A must read for military families!

– Col Kim Campbell USAF (Ret), USAFA (97), Author of *Flying in the Face of Fear: A Fighter Pilot's Lessons on Leading with Courage* **and Col Scott Campbell USAF (Ret), USAFA (95), Former 355th Fighter Wing Commander, Both Former A-10 Warthog Pilots with Multiple Combat Deployments**

What a compelling book—chock-full of romantic love stories. These are real-life relationships born out of a torturous crucible of captivity, and each chapter lays bare an abiding commitment that is sure to fortify your own relationship.

– Drs. Les & Leslie Parrott, #1 New York Times Bestselling Authors

As someone who has been professionally coached by Lee Ellis, it is great to see Lee (and Greg) apply Lee's masterful insights into the most important skill, and probably the most difficult skill, to love and support someone over the highs and lows of POW imprisonment and an entire post-war lifetime.

– Rex Adams, CEO - EyeSouth; Former CEO Payspan and AT&T East Region; USMA 1983, Army Ranger Class 84-85

This is an outstanding collection of love stories, all different and yet all similar. They all share the elements of love, commitment, separation and loyalty. This is a book that needed to be written, and if you like love stories (who doesn't?) you will be captivated.

– George E. Nolly, Doctor of Business Administration - Aviation Security, Vietnam Fighter Pilot, Retired United Airlines Captain, and Host of the *Ready for Takeoff Podcast*

What a great lesson that I learned reading the *Captured by Love* book—how the POW wives courageously led at home while their men were in captivity. These leaders at home and abroad are a great reminder that behind every great leader is someone who cheers them on, believes in them and keeps them going even when it's hard.

– Dee Ann Turner, Author, Speaker, Leader at Dee Ann Turner & Associates

Long an admirer of the POWs who returned as heroes, I was enthralled while reading their remarkable love stories! Future generations need to read these stories and learn of the traits that kept the hopes and dreams of these remarkable people alive and thriving during the darkest of times.

– Gen Mike Hostage, USAF (Ret), Former Commander at Air Combat Command

When the POWs were released, they were happy to be released but were concerned that they might face a bleak future at home. Their concerns were shared by their loved ones at home. Were loving marital and family relationships possible? Readers' hearts will be warmed by the narratives found here. They will find that love, determination, and persistence can work miracles.

– Dr. Roger Shields, Chairman of the Defense Department Prisoner of War and Missing in Action Task Group; Deputy Assistant Secretary of Defense, POW/MIA Affairs 1971-1976

What made these people different? What strengthened them? What does their love look like? These questions and more are answered in this book. 50 years later, I am thankful to hear the stories, be encouraged, and finally know the couples who made such a difference in American history!

– Pam Godfrey Younker, Air and Space Forces Civic Leader, Community Development Officer at the Children's Healthcare of Atlanta Foundation

I found these true romance stories inspiring and comforting to know the "other side" of their stories after surviving those years as a POW. To hear the role that the women served really reflected the many experiences by all that were affected during those times.

– Carol Burrell, CEO at Northeast Georgia Health System

Captured by Love provides critical lessons for joyously thriving with the lifelong commitment of marriage by turning the POW hell into a positive through the celebration of strengths and learning to be kind by forgiving the other person's imperfections and mistakes. All of the lessons can help you with every other relationship that is worth fighting for.

– Hugh Massie, Executive Chairman and Founder of DNA Behavior and Coauthor of *Leadership Behavior DNA* with Lee Ellis

The righteousness of a couple with demonstrated integrity, combined with the peace of liberation and the joy of relational rediscovery, lead to enduring romance. In this cynical age, it's so nourishing and encouraging to read stories of committed devotion. You'll be uplifted!

– Dr. Sidney A. Webb, Sharpened Focus; Leadership Coach, Conference Presenter, Pastor, Author of *Nomad's Fire: Life at the Intersection of Loss and Significance*

Every one of the 20 stories touched my heart, and I cried often reflecting on so many examples of sacrificial and enduring love. I also greatly appreciated the love lessons at the end of each couple's story and I know that I will use these lessons and the amazing love stories to be a better husband and better coach to the clients I serve. Thank you for telling these stories!

– Greg Hiebert, Founding Partner - leadershipForward; Author of *You Can't Give What You Don't Have and Changing Altitude: How to Soar in Your New Leadership Role*; USMA (81), 82nd Airborne, USMA Faculty

Captured by Love is a truly astounding book that resonated with me on so many levels! As a military officer and veteran, I ached for my comrades-in-arms who endured such brutal treatment as POWs. What a wonderful book about our brave warriors and the love stories about their wives and families. It brings a very different perspective to our Vietnam POWs. An absolute must-read!!!

– Capt William "T" Thompson, Esq, CSP, Delta Airlines Captain (Ret), USAFA (73), Former President and CEO of the Association of Graduates of the US Air Force Academy, Author of *The Flight to Excellence*

Lee and Greg are both friends, so know that I'm biased—but this book is fantastic. My wife and I are 19 years into our story, but there's so much wisdom to make the next phase even better. Thanks fellas, for a great set of stories with helpful principles.

– Clint Greenleaf, CEO of Content Capital

Seldom have I read a book that moved me so deeply on every level. If ever there was a perfect time for a book like this to be published, it is now. True love conquers all, and in these pages readers will be reminded that neither time nor distance nor division nor doubt can ever remove us from the love of Christ, or from one another. I laughed. I cried. I bowed my head in gratitude and awe. Every one of these romance stories could be its own movie.

– Laurie Beth Jones, Author of *Jesus CEO* **and** *The Path*

Captured by Love highlights the previously untold stories of romance that allow us to connect with these heroes beyond their experience as POWs. The book is artfully crafted, weaving together personal stories with historical highlights to provide perspective on the challenges these men and women faced. It presents a unique journey that left me laughing on one page and crying on the next.

– Maj Michelle "Mace" Curran USAF (RET), Female Pilot on the Air Force Thunderbirds, and Author of *Upside Down Dreams*

There is no other book like this one! The true love stories here are better than any novel! Lee masterfully weaves together the difficult histories of these incredible men and how their experiences impacted their most personal relationships. This deeply moving narrative is a must-read!

– Mary Kelly, Commander, US Navy (Ret), Author of *Who Comes Next? Leadership Succession Planning Made Easy*

The Vietnam War has faded in the memories of many Americans, but *Captured By Love* brings us back to those days of combat and turmoil, with a series of incredible true tales of the warriors and wives who endured the unendurable. It's a stunning testament to the unequaled power of soulmate support. All of them, both warriors and their mates, deserve our undying gratitude. Ellis and Godek have done an outstanding service.

– Steven Hartov is the Coauthor of *In the Company of Heroes* **and** *The Night Stalkers*, **two bestselling books about American combat aviators. His most recent novel,** *The Last of the Seven*, **is the second part in an historical fiction series about World War II.**

I served in Vietnam and saw firsthand the emotional and relational damage that war inflicted on so many servicemen and women and their families. This extraordinary collection of true stories portrays marriages that have survived and thrived despite the hellish experience of the husband's captivity in North Vietnamese prison camps. Each of these narratives compellingly counters the godless ideologies and evil forces that are destroying marriages and disintegrating God's intended order for families.

– Col Scott McCrystal, Chaplain, US Army (RET), and Executive Liaison at The Warrior's Journey

I'm from Lee's hometown of Commerce, Georgia, and I wore a POW Bracelet with "Capt. Leon Ellis, Jr. 11/7/67" on it for several years. Later in 1973 as a Delta Airlines flight attendant, I had the opportunity to meet returning POWs on Delta flights. They were anxious to talk and share stories of coming home to girlfriends, wives and families. Their enthusiasm and passion was so evident, and that is why I so enjoyed reading this book. They made me laugh and cry and fondly remember their homecoming and America's warm welcome to these heroes!

– Duff O'Dell, Retired Director of Flight Attendants, Delta Air Lines, and Councilwoman Place 6, City of Grapevine, Texas

Captured by Love is sure to capture the heart of anyone who dares to discover a brand of love that is stronger than politics, tragedy, and war. Tormented men and agonized women proved that faith, hope, and love are forces no enemy can sabotage.

– Major General Steve Schaick, USAF (Ret), 19th United States Air Force Chief of Chaplains and 1st United States Space Force Chief of Chaplains

ONCE UPON A TIME...

...there were 20 airborne warriors who were captured twice—once by force, and once by love. First, they were blown out of the sky and kept as prisoners of war (POWs) for up to eight years. Second, they returned home to create "happily ever after" marriages where they were again captured, but this time they were also captivated—by love.

I was one of them—the youngest of the bunch. The bonds we have as comrades-in-arms are deep, but our bonds of love for our wives and families are much deeper. You will see that our wartime experiences taught us lessons that have helped us achieve remarkable marital success. We believe they will serve you as well.

You will read about one wife who waited for eight years for the return of her husband, and they have now been happily married for 63! And, a single coed, though not yet engaged, waited for almost six years for the love of her life, and they married six weeks after he returned.

And while there are many great books by and about Vietnam prisoners of war, this is the only one to collect their love stories. We former POWs are forever grateful to our country, our leaders, our people, our families, and our wives. And we want to say "thank you" by sharing a few war stories, but mostly our romantic stories and our lessons for achieving lasting love.

Leon "Lee" Ellis, Colonel, USAF (Ret)
Vietnam POW 1967-1973

CAPTURED BY LOVE

INSPIRING TRUE ROMANCE STORIES FROM VIETNAM POWS

LEE ELLIS
FORMER POW

GREG GODEK
LOVE EXPERT

Copyright © 2023 Lee Ellis

All rights reserved. No portion of this book may be reproduced, stored in a retrieval system, or transmitted in any form or by any means—electronic, mechanical, photocopy, recording, scanning, or other—except for brief quotations in critical reviews or articles, without the prior written permission of the publisher.

FreedomStar Media® and Leading with Honor® are registered trademarks owned by Leadership Freedom LLC®. All rights reserved. Leading with Honor is used as a dba of Leadership Freedom LLC.

Readers should be aware that Internet Web sites mentioned as references or sources for further information may have changed or no longer be available since this book was published.

Published by FreedomStar Media | FreedomStarMedia.com | POWRomance.com

ISBN (Softcover Trade Edition) 978-1-7336322-3-2

Drawings from Prisoner of War: Six years in Hanoi by John M. McGrath, LCDR U.S. Navy, Copyright © 1975 U.S. Naval Institute, Annapolis, Maryland. Reprinted by Permission of Naval Institute Press

Cover design: Sean Allen

Interior Art and Layout Design: James Armstrong

Editor: James Armstrong

Trade distribution is provided by the Greenleaf Book Group. To purchase this book for trade distribution, contact your favorite distributor or greenleafbookgroup.com.

For media requests and interviews, go to FreedomStarMedia.com.

Publisher's Cataloging-in-Publication data
Names: Ellis, Lee, 1943-, author. | Godek, Greg, 1955-, author. | Orlando, Tony, foreword author. | Sinise, Gary, foreword author.
Title: Captured by love : inspiring true romance stories from Vietnam POWs / Lee Ellis; Greg Godek; [forewords by Tony Orlando and Gary Sinise].
Description: Includes bibliographical references and index. | Dawsonville, GA: FreedomStar Media, 2023.
Identifiers: LCCN: 2023901150 | ISBN: 978-1-7336322-3-2
Subjects: LCSH Love--Anecdotes. | Vietnam War, 1961-1975--Veterans--United States. | Vietnam War, 1961-1975--Prisoners and prisons, North Vietnamese. | Vietnam War, 1961-1975--Prisoners and prisons, Viet Cong. | Prisoners of war--United States. | BISAC HISTORY / Wars & Conflicts / Vietnam War | FAMILY & RELATIONSHIPS / Love & Romance
Classification: LCC HQ801.A2 .E55 2023 | DDC 306.7--dc23

Special Sales

FreedomStar Media resources are available at special discounts for bulk purchases for sale promotions or premiums. Special editions, including personalized covers or bookplate inscriptions, excerpts of existing books, and corporate imprints, can be created in large quantities for special needs. For more information, please contact us at

Contact@FreedomStarMedia.com.

Printed in the USA

23 24 25 26 – 10 9 8 7 6 5 4 3 2 1

1st Printing

DEDICATION

We dedicate our book to couples everywhere that aspire to keep the love-of-their-life, soulmate-relationship vibrant and growing for a lifetime. And, of course, we dedicate it to our supportive, beautiful, and long-suffering wives—Lee's Mary, and Greg's Karyn.

"Love is friendship that has caught fire. It is quiet understanding, mutual confidence, sharing and forgiving. It is loyalty through good and bad times. It settles for less than perfection and makes allowances for human weakness."

—Ann Landers, Syndicated Advice Columnist

CONTENTS

CONTENTS

FOREWORD

BY TONY ORLANDO

I am thrilled and honored to introduce this book. You see, my relationship with these couples is so special that it's almost as amazing as some of their romance stories.

When the POWs were released and coming home in the winter of 1973, my group Dawn and I had just released a new song, "Tie a Yellow Ribbon Round the Ole Oak Tree." The first words of the song "I'm coming home, I've done my time…" not only celebrated the return of the POWs, but it signified that the war was over for all veterans. As it struck a chord with hearts across the nation, it quickly soared to the top of the charts and was the number one song in April 1973.

The next month, I got a call from Bob Hope, the most famous Hollywood entertainer and host of that era, inviting me and my two backup singers from Dawn (Joyce Vincent and Telma Hopkins) to come to Dallas to perform at the Cotton Bowl to celebrate our veterans' return home. For decades Bob had been going to war zones to entertain and inspire our soldiers, so this was going to be a very special event. And believe it or not, one of the couples in this book met as we sang "Tie a Yellow Ribbon" that night. They have now been married for 48 years.

The prophetic lyrics are about a man coming home from prison hoping and wondering whether his love would be there waiting for him. Amazingly, that song captures the essence of many of the stories that you're about to experience.

What I have cherished but didn't anticipate is a 50-year relationship with these couples, especially attending their annual reunion events.

Please enjoy these dramatic and touching stories about my friends, and I hope that you're as inspired as I was long ago.

Tony Orlando

Top-Selling Recording Artist, Songwriter, Concert Headliner, Network Television Star, Motion Picture Actor, Broadway Performer, and Author

FOREWORD

BY GARY SINISE

I'm extremely blessed to be a husband and father.

For over 40 years, I've had my wife Moira by my side. We've had our share of victories and challenges, but we've experienced nothing like the couples that you'll read about in this beautiful book, *Captured by Love.*

Lee, Greg, and these 20 couples have carefully and lovingly presented their stories to help the world understand intimate relationships and how to make them stronger. Not only do our Vietnam POWs recount their experiences as captives during the war, but equally, with wonderful humor and passion, these couples highlight how they all were so joyfully and deeply captured by love. From my personal life experience and my work with our military veterans, I have witnessed how the power of love can bring hope, healing, and happiness to broken families.

Over the years, my commitment to support our military veterans and first responders has grown. And somehow, I saw that my mission in life was more than acting (which I love)—it was to serve those who serve our country. That's why we started the Gary Sinise Foundation. From all those experiences, I can see the special power of this book.

Most readers will experience a few tears here, but also lots of laughter as they engage with these stories. The stunning level of pain and sacrifice that our POWs endured is mind-boggling, but the love and romance that they have experienced is even more extraordinary!

You'll be entertained, inspired, surprised, challenged—and hopefully moved to action—by this great book.

Gary Sinise

Actor, Musician, Author, and
Founder of the Gary Sinise Foundation

Read more about Tony's and Gary's lives and accomplishments in the Biographies section.

PREFACE, PART 1

BY COAUTHOR LEE ELLIS

Over the years, as I reconnected with my old friends from the North Vietnam POW (prisoner of war) camps at reunions and social events, I got to know their wives and became enthralled with these couples' love stories. Their accounts seemed more captivating than a Hollywood romance movie. At our 45th reunion in 2018, the idea of a book about those love stories began stirring in my head. But at the time I was busy working on another book, so I put it on the back burner. Then in 2020, it hit me that if anything was going to come of this idea, I shouldn't waste another day. I felt an urgency to get it done ASAP! Why? First, because, as one of my favorite singers, Dionne Warwick, proclaimed so beautifully, "What the world needs *now* is love," and the amazing and inspiring love stories of this group reflect this so well. And second, because our storytellers weren't getting any younger. (Our ages range from 79 to 94.) I needed to "get 'er done!"

You may be thinking, "What do a bunch of elderly couples have to offer younger folks?" Apparently a *lot*—according to the people who reviewed these stories early on. We worked with each couple to personally tell their story.

Embedded in these short romance narratives are great examples of how companionship, love, honor, commitment, and deep communication—with a liberal dash of humor—can help you *survive* anything and *thrive* through most things.

Many of the POWs have spoken and written about the hardships and suffering we endured, about the role of our spiritual faith, and about the great leadership and teamwork that enabled us to resist, survive, and return with honor. But no one has compiled these fairytale romances which became great love stories that, for some, had begun *before* the war, and for others, began *after* we came home.

As Greg and I began collecting these stories, we saw that there was more than just romance here. Yes, romance is exciting and essential—and you will read some stories here that are almost beyond a romance writer's imagination. They are like diamonds—beautiful and sparkling and attention-grabbing.

But as the stories came together, it became clear that there was also gold to be mined—the principles that lay *behind* the love stories. In a very basic way, the same principles that helped us endure and return with honor also helped these couples expand their romances into love-inspired, long-lasting relationships that shine and endure like gold.

In this book, we share the romance and love stories of couples who have been happy together for more than 40 years—and several for more than 60 years. Some of these include wives who waited *years* for their MIA (Missing in Action) husbands, and when they did not return, these women met and married a returning POW whose wife had moved on.

Aside from the touching vignettes of romance and love, you will be inspired by the example set by POW/MIA wives. They were trailblazers in the emerging women's rights movement of the late 1960s and early 1970s. They stood up and led the crusade that changed the policies of the US government and the communist government of North Vietnam.

Although the idea for this book had been planted in my mind, it would never have come to fruition without the help of one of the foremost experts on love relationships, Greg Godek. Romance is his specialty. He can see it, feel it, analyze the details, and then write it in a very creative and engaging way. Get ready for Gregorian's beautiful chant.

PREFACE, PART 2

BY COAUTHOR GREG GODEK

My dad would be baffled—but proud—that I coauthored this book. He was a 1953 graduate of the US Naval Academy (a classmate of H. Ross Perot, who later was a major supporter of our Vietnam POWs), so I grew up in a military family. Dad expected me to follow in his footsteps. Alas, his son went to a liberal arts college, then later left a solid job with an international advertising agency to write a book. Dad thought I was crazy—*especially* when he learned that it was a love advice book. He finally came around when I sold the first million copies of *1001 Ways to be Romantic*.

It was a fun and helpful book, one of 17 that I've written, but *Captured by Love* is very different and impactful in a special way. My other books are filled with ideas and *tips*. This book is filled with heart and *principles*. And we were delighted—but not exactly surprised—that all the principles track very closely with the advice and wisdom of some of the best relationship and marriage experts in the world.

My work and passion revolve around love and writing. So, two years ago when a mutual friend introduced me to Lee, I was intrigued—puzzled but intrigued. What does the Vietnam War have to do with love? Well, I quickly learned that behind the *battle* stories are many truly amazing *love* stories. And as a so-called love expert and writer, I was excited to be a part of a team that would create this unique book.

My "experience" with the Vietnam War was minimal. I watched a lot of news coverage of the war. However, being younger than college age I never got caught up in the protests and demonstrations. I *did* pay all of $2.50 for the metal POW/MIA bracelet that so many of us faithfully wore in those years. I graduated from high school three months after our POWs returned home. As an accident of age, I *did* have a draft number, but it was more disquieting than worrying. And I didn't know any local soldiers. All of which is to say that my Vietnam experience was limited.

Was it coincidence—or maybe preordained—that I would partner with Lee? I don't know, but I *do* feel "chosen" and lucky.

PREFACE

INTRODUCTION

BY LEE ELLIS, VIETNAM POW 1967-1973

In the mid-sixties, when the American astronauts were beginning to orbit the earth, there was a war on the opposite side of the world from the US in a place called Vietnam. It was a war to halt the advance of communism…It was a war that went awry…It became the most unpopular war in American history…It split the American public…It was a war whose memorial is the most powerful and personal war memorial in the world. To the generations born after 1960, this war probably seems like ancient history. Yet, there are practical insights and timeless wisdom that have emerged from the experiences of the prisoners of that war. (I've written two books on leadership lessons from the POW camps.) Then, surprisingly, I learned there were also some great lessons about love and successful marriages.

Captured by Love shares the inspiring romance and love stories of 20 men who returned from the Vietnam War after five to eight years as prisoners of war. Can you imagine spending that much of your life imprisoned by communists in North Vietnam (also referenced as the "V" later in the book)? Can you imagine those long years of being isolated from your country, your family, and especially your wife and children? Can you imagine being locked up in tiny, dark cells infested with rats and mosquitoes? Can you imagine being alone and suffering torture and abuse? Can you imagine being in solitary confinement? (For some it was for a few days, for some a few months, for a few it was years.)

And can you imagine being a wife, back home in the US, not knowing if your husband was alive or dead, and facing the challenges of family, finances, and your future life…especially during the late 1960s, when the feminist movement and the anti-war movement were both surging?

These are the stories of POWs who lived through hell, and not only returned to tell the tale but returned to continue, or begin, *amazing love stories*. How did they do it? And how did the women overcome loneliness, uncertainty, and a culture that in many ways was unsupportive of "single moms" and independent women.

This book focuses on the personal stories of a unique group of veterans—stories that began in war but end in love. As you read these stories, you will learn about the struggles of the men in the prison camps and the women at home and how they both made it through. We hope you will see how all their experiences came together to help them learn to courageously adapt and grow in both confidence and humility, in character, courage, and commitment, and also to be resilient and bounce back from the challenges of life.

Additionally, we hope you will see how the men's time together in prison prepared the POWs for healthy relationships, and how that enabled them to live happily ever after. So, welcome to this journey into their lives—where they were captured by love.

Note: As we worked on this book, we encountered many interesting historical insights, but we didn't want to insert them into the love stories. So, we have created a unique format; we have inserted nuggets of history between the chapters. They are brief backgrounders that will give you a context of the war, the culture and the people involved. Also, on the powromance.com website, we share many additional stories and articles about the war, the POWs and the wives.

The following three short sections will give you some important information that will help you understand the context in which our love stories took place.

The War

American involvement began as an effort to prevent the communist takeover of South Vietnam. In many ways, it was a parallel to the Korean War, when the North invaded the South across the DMZ (Demilitarized Zone). It was also a struggle between world powers, pitting democracy against communism. Although, it was being fought on the battlefields of Vietnam, as the North covertly and overtly invaded the South, conceptually, it was a war fought by proxy with the US versus Russia and China. American involvement lasted twelve years (from 1961 to 1973).

US involvement began when President Kennedy sent a small number of troops to train and support South Vietnam's forces. In 1965 President Johnson committed US troops into full combat, and by 1968 there were 536,000 troops involved in a war that had stretched into Laos and Cambodia. With the Domino Theory in mind, America was fighting to stop the spread of communism as it began to roll down through Southeast Asia toward the vital shipping lanes of the Malacca and Singapore Straits.

It was a war begun with the noblest of intentions, but it evolved into a political football. It was a war that divided America like nothing before. While several million American soldiers cycled in and out of the war on the other side of the world, the folks back home experienced many highs (the Civil Rights movement, the expansion of women's rights, and the first manned moon landing), and also many lows (the assassinations of Martin Luther King, Jr. and Bobby Kennedy, the contentious peace protests, and race riots). The US culture changed rapidly and radically in the 1960s and early 1970s. Political activism roiled the country. "Peace, love, and rock and roll" brought popular music, hippies, pot, and other drugs to the forefront of the culture.

The radical anti-war movement made the Vietnam War so unpopular that combat veterans returning home from the war were sometimes cursed and spat on. In some places their reception was so hostile that it was dangerous for them to wear their uniforms in public. Proof that life is unfair was shown when we POWs were welcomed as heroes. After more than a decade of the divisiveness of the Vietnam War, Americans needed to celebrate some good news—and as a whole the country stood up and gave us what our brother veterans deserved but never got—a heartwarming welcome.

Despite the war that we fought with North Vietnam and our general disdain for communism, it's important to state that it did not interfere with our deep caring for the Vietnamese people. Many POWs have returned to Vietnam and have close relationships with Vietnamese in the North and the South.

The Men

Never in history had American POWs been locked up for so many years and rarely under such horrendous conditions. One thing that worked in our favor was the fact that the Hanoi POW population consisted mostly of aircrew members, and the majority were fighter pilots. This meant that we had all been screened by very high standards of mental and physical health. We had been through lots of training and were mostly experienced college-educated professionals with the average age at capture just over 30. Some of our older leaders had fought in WWII and Korea!

We fighter pilots tend to be unflappable, believing that nothing will happen to us that we can't handle. And that kind of confidence is very helpful when you are operating on the edge of the envelope, flying dangerous aircraft maneuvers and missions and getting shot at every day in combat. But at capture, we were facing a totally different kind of challenge. It would be a humbling experience that would strip away all our rights and privileges and crush our egos.

The cultural environment of our upbringing was definitely helpful. We grew up in the 1930s, 40s, and 50s—times when young people were given big responsibilities at an early age. Most of us had grown up on farms or in families where the kids had daily chores. If we wanted a car, we had to earn the money to buy it and then maintain it. This environment of responsibility gave us a strong sense of self-worth, and a commitment to ownership and accountability. If you add to that the confident, competitive, aggressive fighter-pilot mindset, you have a unique group engaged in this unusual battle. And in many ways, especially in the early years of our captivity, *every* day was a serious battle for physical, mental, and emotional survival.

There were two other crucial issues contributing to our resilience in these harsh conditions. First, we had great leaders. They were the first into the fire. They were tortured the most, they spent the most time in solitary confinement, and yet they consistently bounced back and led with honor through courage and humility. We were inspired by their example.

Second, there was also great leadership going on back home—mostly by women. As you will soon learn, the wives and family members were courageously battling on our behalf for humane treatment and a full accounting. Without that effort and their worldwide influence, our story of survival, followed by a bright future, would never have happened.

What seems almost like a miracle is that most of the POWs, against all odds, returned home stronger and more mature than when we left. And the group of POWs in this book created "happily ever after" marriages that, so far, have lasted between 40 and 65 years.

The Women

There is no way we could have these romance stories without our women. It should be no surprise that a group of confident, front-line warrior men typically had a well-trained eye for the ladies. At the same time, you will see that when we met the *right one*—the love of our life—we surrendered and were quickly captured by love. So, you may be wondering what kind of women would be capturing these aggressive guys. Let's take a quick look.

Many of these wives shared a common theme of adventure and military background. Back then stewardesses (now flight attendants) were required to be young, single, slender and attractive women who were also socially talented. The fact that they were connected to aviation and travel gave them front row attention from military men who traveled a lot. Five of our 20 love stories were launched by pilots meeting those uniformed beauties. Additionally, eight of the couples had a previous family military connection. And some couples met as kids in their hometowns or at college.

Twelve of the wives were very involved in efforts to raise awareness of the POW/MIA plight both in the US and abroad. Several of the single girls had worn POW/MIA bracelets—and two of them married "their" POW when they came home!

Fourteen of the 20 wives were waiting for their POW/MIA husbands to come home; four of those men did not return. Those four wives found their way into our book by meeting and marrying *other* returning POWs—one of whom was her husband's best friend and had been their next-door neighbor years earlier. Two of the single women met the love of their lives through their hairdressers within two weeks of our return, and they both married within a few months!

Twelve of those waiting wives had children, raising them without their dads for more than five years. And two of them were essentially single moms for eight years. One of those two had a one-month-old son, and the other bore her son soon after her husband was captured. Both of their sons were eight years old when the fathers they had never seen came home.

The loyalty and courage of these women is almost beyond belief. In the early days when women's liberation was just beginning to stir, these women stood up, stepped out, and courageously led a battle that changed the policies of two nations at war.

To wrap up...

Captured by Love brings together many inspiring stories. It also highlights the contrasts that were dealt with in their great relationships: War and love…men and women…anguish and joy…despair and hope…humiliation and honor… blunt reality and ideal romance. They are *opposites*, but they also fit together like a hand in a glove, or like two sides of the same coin, or like yin and yang.

My coauthor, Greg, and I are in many ways polar opposites. I am a "good ol' boy" from Georgia; Greg grew up in the suburbs of New York. I am a graduate of the military Air War College; Greg is a graduate of the liberal arts Allegheny College. I am a concrete, big-picture thinker; Greg is a creative writer. I have a master's degree and more formal education than Greg, but he has sold millions more books than I have. I have spoken at the Pentagon and before international corporations; Greg has appeared on *Oprah* and *The Today Show*. I was a military fighter pilot; Greg is a civilian writer. I teach the seven behaviors of the Honor Code; Greg teaches 1001 Ways to be Romantic.

And yet we are brothers. We are both deeply spiritual. We are both speakers and writers. We are both called to share a message of hope and love with the world. We have a synergy that has motivated both of us to write a book together that, hopefully, is greater than what either of us could have created alone. And we both love our wives very much!

Our wish is that you embrace your differences, especially the seemingly opposite ones in your own life and especially in your love relationship. And our hope and prayer is that you are inspired to create a "happily ever after" partnership or marriage. Remember the words of the Apostle Paul when he said, "Be completely humble and gentle; be patient, bearing with one another in love" (Ephesians 4:2).

1 | LOVE IS...

THE STORY OF
Wes & Faye Schierman

LOVE IS...MARRYING YOUR COLLEGE SWEETHEART

"He's handsome *and* a jet pilot!" exclaimed my sorority sister.

I was a junior at Washington State University in 1957. I had heard about Wes Schierman[1] several months before I met him. On the way to a fraternity party, I glanced out the car window and a handsome fellow I'd never seen before caught my eye. Later that evening I met him. We had a mutual attraction, and we chatted comfortably. We spent the rest of the evening ignoring everyone else while we talked. We were already hitting it off before I learned that he was *the jet pilot*! I was taken with his cute smile, sense of humor, and maturity I'd never seen in a college boy.

We were pinned, engaged, and married within a year!

Yes, it was a whirlwind romance, but I knew we had something special from the very beginning. I feel lucky that I fell in love with the *man* before I fell in love with the *image* of the hotshot jet pilot!

Soon after we married, we bought a home in Spokane, Washington, and soon after that our first two children, Sandra and Steve, were born in quick succession.

LOVE IS...FLYING

Back in the 1930s adventurous pilots in biplanes used to barnstorm, performing acrobatic stunts throughout rural America. When they came through St. John, Washington, three-year-old Wes Schierman watched them with wonder and exclaimed, "That's what I want to do!"

And that's what he *did*…He joined the Air National Guard at 17. Soon after we married, Wes took a job flying for Northwest Airlines; he then jumped at the chance to fly fighter jets for the Air Force; then—after an eight-year hiatus in a prisoner of war camp in North Vietnam—he wanted to go back to Northwest. When he returned, Wes visited with the president of Northwest Airlines, Donald Nyrop, who said, "Welcome back! You can have any job you want." And Wes soon was a Captain, flying airliners internationally until he retired.

It didn't take Wes long to find a new outlet for his love of flying. He took up flying Van's RV-4 homebuilt airplanes. Wes was smitten! Those little planes handled like small jets. He and some former military men organized the Blackjack Squadron. They taught new pilots the fundamentals. And, it wasn't long until they were flying in many air shows, as well as flying a 24-ship formation of Van's RVs at the EAA (Experimental Aircraft Association) airshow at Oshkosh. They loved the fun of dogfights, of course!

Wes had left his POW life far behind him, but the fighter pilot remained—and he flew until four months before he passed away.

Wes had left his POW life far behind him, but the fighter pilot remained—and he flew until four months before he passed away.

I don't know if it was genetics or Wes's influence, but we have more than our fair share of pilots in our family. Our son, Steve, and our daughter, Stacy, are both commercial pilots. (Stacy has never lost the wonder and excitement of flying that she experienced as a child. She is so passionate about planes that she chose her apartment because it has a view of the Seattle-Tacoma International Airport; she'll often drive to the airport simply to watch the planes take off and land.) And our oldest daughter Sandy, as well as our grandson Steven, both have their pilot licenses.

LOVE IS…FAMILY

Wes was the best husband and father I can imagine. Before he went off to war, he sat down with me and explained in meticulous detail how to handle the practical side of running a household, how to handle money matters—but above all he impressed upon me the importance of taking care of myself and the children and not relying upon others. It is important to note that Wes did not *tell* me what to do. He asked me questions; most of them began with "What if—?" I would think on my own, and then we would discuss each issue. He was not controlling or even managing me; he was teaching me how to make my own decisions. This preparation made my early adjustment to being an MIA wife much easier than many wives had it.

Wes was sent to fight in Vietnam early in 1965, and the children and I moved to Kadena Air Force Base in Okinawa, Japan, so we could see him during his off-duty time. A few months later he was shot down. He then spent seven-and-a-half years in captivity. After six months of waiting in Okinawa for news about Wes, I flew home to Spokane with the goal of creating a secure home environment for our children. Wes's parents met us, and the first thing that three-year-old Steve said when he saw his grandfather was, "You look just like my daddy!"

I bought a house in Spokane. This helped keep our family close and endure the painful uncertainty of not knowing when or if Wes would return. We lived there the entire time that he was away, plus six months after his release. Wes wanted as much stability as possible for the kids, and we were successful in creating as much a sense of normalcy as one could have, given our circumstances.

Wes always put me and our children first. Upon his return to America he said to a reporter, "During my almost seven-and-a-half years in North Vietnam my greatest tribulation was that of overcoming my grief at having subjected my wife and children to the painful and difficult experience that they were to undergo. However, I had great faith and confidence in my wife's ability to overcome these difficulties, and that faith has been rewarded by a strength and steadfastness that far exceeded my greatest expectations. Throughout many years of torture, exploitation, deprivation, and degradation, my will to live was sustained primarily by this faith and love for my family."

LOVE IS...WAITING

The uncertainty of Wes's fate in Vietnam was crazy-making. Even though we knew he had ejected and landed safely, the North Vietnamese did not release his name, in defiance of the Geneva Conventions.[2] So he was listed as MIA. A glimmer of hope finally appeared after several years when Kathy Risner (wife of POW Robbie Risner, who was Wes's squadron commander) received a letter from him in which he indicated that Wes was okay, and that I shouldn't worry. I hadn't felt so happy in years! However, the Pentagon would not allow the change of status.

So I lived with their decision for a few more years until...nothing changed for our POWs. This is when the "War of the Wives" began.

So I lived with their decision for a few more years until...nothing changed for our POWs. This is when the "War of the Wives" began.

LOVE IS...TAKING ACTION!

Our government was making no progress in negotiations with the enemy, so a group of dedicated wives and families set out to make the public aware of the plight of our men. This was quite a big step for many of us because most of us were stay-at-home wives and mothers. We were also upstanding, patriotic women. We didn't *want* to fight our government, but we knew we had to change their minds about their policies in dealing with the North Vietnamese government. And so I joined the National League of POW/MIA Families when it was founded in the fall of 1969. I'm a shy, reserved person. But when our fourth Christmas came without Wes, my despondency turned into fury, and I began speaking up. I found a confidence I had never felt before. I became one of the spokeswomen who gave speeches and interviews. I was also active in the letter writing campaigns and selling POW/MIA bracelets to raise awareness.

I was surprised and pleased at the positive responses I got. My next-door neighbors, the Monroes, owned a local radio station, and they joined the cause—and we *really* spread the word! Then the Spokane Chamber of Commerce decided to send three women on a round-the-world tour to help raise awareness around the globe! Some individuals and companies stepped forward to sponsor the tour, but the Spokane leaders wanted to get the public involved. So, they created a fundraiser, asking for just one dollar per person. And they raised enough money to send three of us on a 32-day, 13-country tour!

When Wes returned home, he could hardly believe what I had done. But, he was *really* blown away to hear that I had once spoken to 25,000 people at halftime of a football game between the University of Washington and Washington State University (my alma mater)! I never pursued this kind of opportunity, but people around me jumped on the bandwagon and often asked me to speak.

To make a long story short, after several years of hard work by thousands of volunteers we finally got US international policy changed. Our officials made direct demands on the Vietnamese, and this, along with the pressure of public opinion and the world press, led to better treatment for our POWs.

LOVE IS...KNOWING EACH OTHER

Wes was a romantic. He listened to me, he "got" me, and he often took action on it. For example, "our song" was "The Twelfth of Never" by Johnny Mathis. Once the singer was on a flight that Wes was piloting. For me Wes made an exception to his rule of never intruding on a famous passenger. Wes asked him for an autograph to give to me. Not only did he get an autograph, Mr. Mathis smiled, pulled out his paper ticket, and signed it! It holds a special place in my heart *and* in my favorite scrapbook.

For my sixtieth birthday Wes took me to Las Vegas. I'm not exactly a high roller, but I confess that I have lost a lot of nickels in those slot machines! Wes would sit by me all day and read a paperback book (which he always carried with him) while I got my gambling fix! (We found many ways of being together even when our interests were different.)

Our anniversaries were always very special to us. More than once Wes turned down invitations for events occurring on September 13. One year his old squadron on Okinawa asked him to be the guest of honor for National POW Day on the base. He politely turned them down because it was our anniversary. They suggested that we celebrate *there* and attend the event as their guests. In addition to showering us with gifts and treating us to a romantic dinner at a great restaurant, Wes got to ride in an F-15 fighter jet. He said it was as close to being treated as royalty as he had ever experienced!

LOVE IS…COMMITMENT

Wes was committed to his family, his country, and to his fellow military comrades. When he was shot down, he was not captured immediately. He landed on a hill with little cover, and within sight of an enemy encampment—so he knew he had little time. He made several radio calls to the pilots overhead to coordinate a possible rescue attempt, but it was not possible that far north.

Wes was aware of and adept at balancing his love of America, his military mission, and his family. He once said of his time in captivity, "I vowed that if it was humanly possible for me to return to Faye and the kids and still do my duty to my country, I would do so. Through my faith in America, in my family, and with the grace of God, I have been fortunate enough to have endured that trial."

For years I lay awake for hours at night, worrying about Wes. He had a lot of time to worry and think too. But after awhile he turned this into a positive thing. He lived in squalid cells with little change or input. But one surprising benefit was that it gave him time to think. Lots of time. And he made good use of it. Instead of dwelling on all the negatives of his situation, he became intensely grateful for all that he did have: He was alive, he had buddies to support him, he had God looking out after him, and he had me and the kids at home waiting for him.

Wes was a prisoner for seven-and-a-half years minus two weeks. He was kept in solitary confinement several times, with one stretch lasting ten-and-a-half months. He was listed as MIA longer than any other returned POW—four years and eight months. It was a horrible limbo in which all POW and MIA wives lived. When I finally learned that he was a POW, I experienced waves of mixed feelings. Mostly I was ecstatic that *he was alive*! But, I also worried about how he was being mistreated.

LOVE IS...CAMARADERIE

Wes developed a ghastly allergy to a local tree that affected his breathing. His captors ignored his suffering. It was so severe that he had to sit up at night in order to breathe. A cellmate and good friend, Mike McGrath, later told me that often at night he didn't think he would see Wes alive the next day. All of the POWs took care of each other. They cared for the sick, they encouraged the depressed, they taught each other, and they even laughed together. These fellows *really* bonded.

LOVE IS...A LETTER IN THE MAIL

I received my first letter from Wes four years and eight months after he was shot down. It would be an understatement to say that I was ecstatic! I received 23 letters during his last two-and-a-half years of imprisonment. But who's counting? Me! Each one was a lifeline to the love of my life. They were all wonderful...*except for one.*

In it Wes suggested that it might be best if I "move on" with my life, since the years were stretching on, and the future was uncertain. At first I was stunned. Then I was dismayed. Had he fallen out of love with me? Or had he just given up on our marriage? I struggled with this for a long time. But it finally dawned on me that he loved us so much that he didn't want me and the kids to suffer any more.

I cried with gratitude. This was the most selfless thing in the world! Well, I didn't consider for a *second* leaving this man!

Years later I came across this often-quoted line which has been attributed to Albert Schweitzer: "If you love something let it go. If it comes back it was meant to be; if it doesn't it never was." This is *exactly* what Wes had done.

LOVE IS...A HOMECOMING!

Wes was aboard the very first plane to leave Hanoi, as the US military decided that the longest-held, and the sick and wounded, would depart Vietnam first. (Wes fit both categories, as he was POW number 23, and he had breathing problems.) I could barely contain my excitement when Wes made his first phone call to me from the Philippines! His voice sounded familiar and unchanged. In some ways it seemed as if we had been talking all along.

When he returned to the States and stepped off the plane, the children and I smothered him with hugs and kisses!

Returning to our home (which Wes had never seen) was a curious but jubilant experience. As we entered our neighborhood a huge "Welcome Home" banner waved, along with American flags, and Wes was greeted with a red carpet on our sidewalk! Our neighbors turned out, and it was a wonderful party.

Wes suggested that we stick to our normal family routine, as the children had schedules with school and activities. Another one of his smart decisions was to *not* try to take over as "master of the house." He wanted to observe and gradually join in. For Wes it was always about our family and not about *him*.

LOVE IS...CHERISHED MEMORIES

I remember so many good times with Wes, our children, and grandchildren. Two years after Wes returned from Vietnam, baby Stacy was born. She was a joy to us all, but especially to Wes, because he hadn't gotten to experience much of our other children's childhoods. (It was tragic that he missed nearly eight years of their lives.)

Wes was *crazy* about our children! He wanted to be with them as much as possible. He would take one or more of them along when he ran errands like going to the store. He also instilled in all of them a love of the outdoors, and we all went camping, boating, and hunting.

I have scrapbooks and photo albums galore, but the one I cherish most was created by the teacher who took my third-grade class when I retired. It contains photos and newspaper clippings—*and* many "Love Is..." cartoons! I cherish that little naked couple and their endless simple expressions of love. Love was the theme of our lives, and I am so grateful that I had seven years with Wes before Vietnam, and then 41 more years after his return!

Wes made a swift departure from life. Late in 2013 he was diagnosed with stage four lung cancer, and he died four months later.

I am amazed and deeply touched that even now, 49 years after Wes regained his freedom, I still receive letters that contain his POW/MIA bracelet. People share both happy and sad memories of the heartbreak that was the Vietnam War. I don't quite know what to do with this, except to stop and cherish that amazing man, and our incredible marriage, and the great family we became.

LOVE LESSONS

LEADERSHIP COMBINED WITH KINDNESS

Each member of a strong couple takes on the leadership role when necessary, rising to the specific challenge. And when leadership is carried out with kindness instead of harshness, followers—and families—are inspired, and they thrive.

CHANGE COMBINED WITH COURAGE

Our lives are constantly changing. There are many possible responses to change. When change is faced with courage, the result is growth.

FAITH COMBINED WITH ACTION

Healthy people have faith in themselves, and also in people and things beyond themselves. Faith in God, faith in country, faith in friends, faith in family all play a role in creating great marriages. The important step is to take action on your faith.

Wes & Faye Schierman

1 Capt Wesley D. (Wes) Schierman USAF, F-105 Thunderchief, POW 28-AUG-65 –12-FEB-73, Retired Lt Col (0-5), RIP 4-JAN-14

2 The Geneva Conventions of 1949 are a series of treaties on the treatment of civilians, prisoners of war (POWs) and soldiers who are captured, wounded or otherwise incapable of fighting.

MILITARY CODE OF CONDUCT

After the Korean War, the Department of Defense realized that POW performance suffered because there was no clear guidance for POW behavior. A committee from all services then designed this six-article Code of Conduct that all military members memorize during initial training.

Article 1. I am an American, fighting in the forces which guard my country and our way of life. I am prepared to give my life in their defense.

Article 2. I will never surrender of my own free will. If in command, I will never surrender the members of my command while they still have the means to resist.

Article 3. If I am captured, I will continue to resist by all means available. I will make every effort to escape and aid others to escape. I will accept neither parole nor special favors from the enemy.

Article 4. If I become a prisoner of war, I will keep faith with my fellow prisoners. I will give no information or take part in any action which might be harmful to my comrades. If I am senior, I will take command. If not, I will obey the lawful orders of those appointed over me, and will back them up in every way.

Article 5. When questioned, should I become a prisoner of war, I am required to give only name, rank, service number, and date of birth. I will evade answering further questions to the utmost of my ability. I will make no oral or written statements disloyal to my country and its allies or harmful to their cause.

Article 6. I will never forget that I am an American, fighting for freedom, responsible for my actions, and dedicated to the principles which made my country free. I will trust in my God and in the United States of America.

2 | TARZAN & JANE

THE STORY OF
Carlyle "Smitty" & Louise Harris

[Greg's coauthor note]
As of this book's publication date, Tarzan and Jane have been happily married 62 years.

[Lee's coauthor note]
Forty-six years after returning home following nearly eight years as a prisoner of war in a North Vietnam POW camp, my former cellmate, Colonel Carlyle "Smitty" Harris[1] wrote the marvelous book Tap Code: The Epic Survival Tale of a Vietnam POW and the Secret Code That Changed Everything. *In the Foreword to his book I wrote that, upon our return to America, "most of us had a wonderful reunion and moved on. It seemed that the Harris family just stayed in the reunion mode."*

That's the kind of couple that Tarzan and Jane, aka Smitty and Louise, are.

"Louise and I started over where we had left off. It was as if I had simply taken a walk around the block."

Smitty's "walk around the block" included 2,871 days during which he endured torture, starvation, fear, and loneliness. Louise's walk included raising their three children, single-handedly taking on the Air Force bureaucracy, and fighting various cultural norms and business practices that discriminated against women. During those years she also sent more than a hundred care packages to Vietnam for Smitty. Much later she learned that he had received only two of them.

Several factors contributed to Smitty's surviving the POW camps: his religious beliefs, his family, and his cultural background. Oh, and humor.

Referring to the "Hanoi Hilton," where he spent most of those years, Smitty said, "The Hanoi Hilton: What an awful place! Room service, food, and accommodations were terrible!" After a pause he observed, "Humor helped me keep a semblance of my former self."

For example, Smitty's first letter to Louise included this: "I have started daily exercises and am sure that when I am released, I can get a job on TV with an exercise program, and I can be the idol of a million American women—what do you think of *that*?"

It was a miracle that this letter got delivered at all. It was among a handful of POWs' letters that the North Vietnamese communists showed to several foreign diplomats in an effort to prove that they were in compliance with the Geneva Conventions. The captors never delivered any of those letters. But one of the British diplomats slipped one of the letters into her bag when no one was looking, and she later mailed it to Louise from England.

Smitty related that at one point he and some other POWs were being moved to a different camp, and as usual they were all blindfolded. As he sat in the back of the hot, jolting truck, he glanced down and, through the edge of his blindfold, spotted on the floor his most prized possession: a letter from Louise that had fallen out of his pocket. He chuckled, saying that as he retrieved it, he thought, "I've always been a very lucky person—or perhaps Someone was looking out for me." (Do any of you readers think it's astounding—and funny—that a prisoner of war would consider himself to be "lucky"?)

MEANWHILE, BACK IN AMERICA...

...Smitty's wife Louise had been a very adventurous airline stewardess, but now the challenges she faced—as the first Air Force wife of an MIA—were beyond anyone's imagination. At the time of Smitty's capture, she—and their two toddler daughters (ages three and five) and one son on the way—were living with him on the airbase on the Japanese Island of Okinawa. As the first POW wife to be living overseas, she was the first person to experience some newly established, untested military procedures—which she found totally unacceptable. The US Air Force and the US government were completely unprepared for the power and influence that one determined woman could wield! They were about to learn.

Louise was eight months pregnant with their third child when Smitty's aircraft went down. The commanders on the base in Okinawa had never experienced a situation like this. They were uncomfortable with how her presence might send a message of loss and fear to the other fighter pilot wives. They were also concerned that her presence might even lower morale among the pilots as well. So, they decided to ship her back to the States to give birth.

The military was accustomed to dealing with cooperative and non-questioning military wives. They were not used to female grit and sound logic. Knowing more about babies than the military brass did, Louise informed them that she was going to stay right there in Okinawa until after the baby was born. She got her way.

And that was only the beginning.

When she arrived back in the States, she was met by a young lieutenant escort who told her that she would be receiving only $350 (less than one-third) of Smitty's pay with which to raise three children, while the larger portion would go into a ten percent savings account until his return. Louise was having none of it.

The young Air Force officer who tried to help her was rattled when she said, "This is unacceptable." She demanded that he get the Secretary of the Air Force on the phone.

The young Air Force officer who tried to help her was rattled when she said, "This is unacceptable." She demanded that he get the Secretary of the Air Force on the phone.

"Ma'am, I can't call the Secretary of the Air Force," he said nervously.

"You do the dialing, and I'll do the talking. Tell them that you are with the wife of the MIA Captain Carlyle Smith Harris, who insists that she talk to the Secretary of the Air Force. Tell them she is very upset and is threatening to call a news conference."

Her actions were all the more remarkable when you remember that this was 1965—a time when few American women broke ranks from their expected roles as good mothers and obedient wives.

On the phone, when confronted with the problem, the Secretary of the Air Force said, "Ma'am, we are just looking out for your husband."

"Well, you better think about *his children*! I expect to hear back from you by close of business today."

"Mrs. Harris, I need some time to look into this. I'll get back to you soon."

In her oh-so-polite Southern drawl Louise said, "Sir—*soon* is unacceptable. I need an answer today. I have three babies to care for. Please get back to me by five. Thank you." And she hung up.

And she got what she wanted. And she got it by five.

MEANWHILE, BACK IN VIETNAM...

In addition to his sense of humor, Smitty brought with him into captivity one piece of knowledge that none of the other POWs had, a piece of knowledge that was the key to their sanity and survival—the Tap Code. Aircrews know Morse Code, a series of dots and dashes, but you can't make a dash when your only means of communications is tapping on a wall.

In the 1960's the Tap Code was a virtually unknown method of communication that had been used by American soldiers during World War II, and it wasn't taught in any military classes. During his survival training, Smitty became fascinated with it when one of his instructors, Sergeant Claude Watkins, mentioned it in passing. Smitty reached out to him to learn more.

"As we were walking out of class I asked, 'But how did they send the dashes?' as I was comparing it to Morse Code. He took me to the chalk board and showed me the Tap Code. He explained it to me with a simple grid on the chalkboard. It was surprisingly simple and easy to memorize. I filed it away and nearly forgot about it." But just a few years later, Smitty was in a POW camp with plenty of time to reflect—and then it popped back into his mind. After a few months Smitty was moved from solitary confinement, and for the very first time was put in a cell with three other POWs. The men were overjoyed to have company! And they quickly realized that they needed a way to communicate when they were separated. Smitty, the Code Bearer, had the answer.

The Tap Code was based on a five-by-five matrix like the one below. Each letter was based on the row and then the column. For example, the word "Hi" would be composed of down 2 and over 3 for the letter "H," and down 2 and over 4 for the letter "i." Thus, tapping "Hi" would sound like this: tap tap pause; tap tap tap pause; tap tap pause; tap tap tap tap. Since there are 26 letters in the alphabet, they used C for K.

Across Second

	1	2	3	4	5
1	A	B	C	D	E
2	F	G	**H**	**I**	J
3	L	M	N	O	P
4	Q	R	S	T	U
5	V	W	X	Y	Z

Down First

H is down 2 and over 3 (tapped 2 – 3)
I is down 2 and over 4 (tapped 2 – 4)

Over time and in secret, nearly every POW in captivity in the Hanoi-area camps learned the Tap Code. It saved their sanity and built morale. In nearly eight years their captors never deciphered it. The enemy knew that some form of communication was going on, but they had no idea of how extensive and ongoing the POWs' communications were. The guards tried tapping on the walls of empty cells, but the prisoners next door never responded because they knew it was the enemy. The POWs tapped on walls and pipes. They blinked the coding. They swished code using the bamboo brooms, and they even had a slightly modified version for coughing code in the winter. They tapped on the arm or leg of the person blindfolded and handcuffed to them in the darkness of night when their captors were moving them to another camp.

MEANWHILE, BACK IN TIME...

Back in 1959, when Louise and Carlyle Smith Harris (who had received the nickname "Smitty" in grade school) first met, he was quickly smitten. But she took her time. He was 30. She was 21.

"I had been a freewheeling flight instructor for five years, flying to a different city nearly every weekend. I dated a lot. A *lot*. But I hadn't met a girl who was the Right One—until I met Louise."

As Smitty related this story, he reached over and grasped Louise's hand and said, "Now *that's* romantic."

"We shared so many of the truly important things in life: values, background, a positive attitude about life."

"We shared so many of the truly important things in life: values, background, a positive attitude about life."

"We were both solidly Catholic."

"And we both grew up in small towns."

"And we both had strong family values."

"And we both had a very strong sense of humor."

"Who, *us*?"

They both laugh.

"She's also witty and quick on her feet."

On an early date at the Officer's Club Smitty introduced Louise to a friend using a different girl's name: Jane. Without missing a beat Louise snapped back with, "Well, 'Tarzan,' you better at least get my name straight!"

MEANWHILE, BACK TO THE FUTURE...

"When I finally regained my freedom, on February 12, 1973, my top priority was to call Louise: long-distance, from the Philippines to Tupelo, Mississippi."

Louise recalled, "Oh, I was so nervous! What if we'd drifted apart? What if we simply couldn't continue on? Would we really know each other after all this time? We had not seen each other in more than eight years. My heart pounded in my chest, and I sent up the same prayer I had been praying for many days: 'Lord, please let him say something that lets me know that he remembers like I remember and still feels the way I feel.' And then the phone rang! The very first words Smitty spoke to me after almost eight years apart were, 'Hi Jane. It's Tarzan.'"

There is an aura of true fondness, humorous lightness, and deep connection around Smitty and Louise.

And *that's* how a marriage can withstand circumstances that are incredibly horrible, long-standing, and stressful.

Smitty said, "I hadn't planned on saying that, honestly! I just said it spontaneously."

Louise observed, "And in these lighthearted words I knew that God had heard my prayers. I cried with happiness and relief. Smitty remembered as I remembered. His voice was warm and filled with humor. The conversation was *us*. I knew that whatever adjustments we faced, we were going to be just fine. Much better than fine, in fact! After I hung up the phone, I let out a deep sigh of relief. It was as if I had been holding my breath for eight years."

There is an aura of true fondness, humorous lightness, and deep connection around Smitty and Louise.

"From the very beginning we knew our marriage would last. We believed that wedding vows are exactly that—vows."

"Right. I knew there was no way out!"

Louise jabs him gently on the shoulder.

"We are simply thrilled to be together."

"And apart!"

"Right. We're very close *and* very independent. I'm happy for him to spend four days away golfing with his buddies."

"And I'm happy that she volunteers for several charitable organizations."

"We trust each other completely and implicitly—always have."

Three months after the POWs' release, they were all invited to a "welcome home" gala at the White House. Louise remembers, "The evening was surreal. Dignitaries and VIPs were everywhere. Henry Kissinger and Jimmy Stewart sat at our table. Imagine that!"

Following his return home, Smitty and Louise spent a few months getting reacquainted with family and friends, and then escaped for a second honeymoon. Upon their return Smitty was assigned to the Air War College in Montgomery, Alabama, and after graduation he remained on the faculty until his retirement in 1979. They moved back to Tupelo where Louise had bought a house next to her sister when she had returned to the States. Smitty then enrolled in law school at Ole Miss and upon graduation managed a law firm for many years.

All three of their children grew up there and have raised *their* children there as well. Harris family get-togethers are frequent and boisterous, as they include seven grandchildren and four great-grandchildren!

> **[Lee's coauthor note]**
> *Many of these senior fighter pilots have continued to fly in retirement. Smitty and Louise have owned several aircraft over the years. He says that as a couple they often invited another couple to join them and they would on the spur of the moment head out for a vacation. They loved having the luxury of flying to the Caribbean, or back to the mountains of North Carolina, where Louise grew up, for a vacation. Golf has also been a fun vacation for the guys. Four couples in this book spent a week at Myrtle Beach, and the guys played every day.*

Smitty was the sixth POW to be captured in North Vietnam. He survived nearly eight years in the camps—2,871 days—and he returned home with honor. Louise survived a different battle, and her example of courage and duty is inspiring to all. Smitty recently celebrated his 93rd birthday. He remains active, he still drives, and he and Louise travel together to conduct book signings and presentations. They say they have never quarreled. Louise explains, "We have such a finely tuned appreciation of life. Why would you fight? Why would you waste a minute?"

The happy couple is still enjoying life—and they show no signs of slowing down. After 62 years of marriage Tarzan and Jane seem to be having fun just swinging free amongst the trees.

LOVE LESSONS

COMMITMENT

Smitty and Louise both take their wedding vows seriously, and their unshakeable faith in each other sustained them through their many years apart.

CONNECTION

The happiest couples have the deepest connections. And sometimes that connection can be seen in just a few words: "Hi Jane. It's Tarzan."

HUMOR

Smitty: "Humor kept all the guys' morale alive during our captivity. Humor also keeps Louise and me connected. We're very self-entertaining; our shared experiences and inside jokes help keep the spark of love alive."

Louise: "He just cracks me up all the time!"

Carlyle "Smitty" & Louise Harris

1   Capt Carlyle S. "Smitty" Harris USAF, F-105 Thunderchief, POW 4-APR-65 –12-MAR-73, Retired Col (0-6)

POW TREATMENT & RESISTANCE

Being captured in enemy territory is terrifying. You are helpless. Your hands are tied painfully tight, and usually you are blindfolded and often beaten by the locals and the militia. But thankfully, the soldiers had orders to "bring 'em in alive."

Arriving in Hanoi, a new prisoner's situation varied depending on the status of the war, the workload of the camp leaders, and the mood of the torturers. It usually started out with interrogations, torture, and isolation. Solitary confinement might last for weeks or months, and some would be alone for years. Their goal was to break the will of the POW and gain compliance.

Some of this horrible treatment was an attempt to gather military information. Some was to keep us fearful so we would obey the rules, and some was simply sadistic, but most was for propaganda. They wanted us to make statements criticizing the war and convincing Americans to turn against our government.

Locked in small cells with covered windows, we were typically miserably hot in the summer; boils were common. The overnight lows in winter averaged in the 50s—not cold—unless you have no heat and not enough blankets.

We were fed twice a day—around 10:00 in the morning and 4:00 in the afternoon. The food consisted of a bowl of thin soup and a small baguette of bread or a cup of rice. Baked bugs and stewed worms were often our main source of protein.

The "Camp Regulations"[1] were posted in English in every cell. Basically, they said "Do what you're told and don't communicate with others, or else you will be punished."

Of course, we were committed to being faithful to the Code of Conduct, so the battle lines were drawn. We were still at war—it was just our weapons and tactics that changed.

---

1 The Communist Camp Regulations for POWs are available on the book website at powromance.com

3 | A LOVE STORY THAT NEVER ENDS

THE STORY OF

Roger & Jackie Ingvalson and Wayne & Booncy Fullam—then Roger & Booncy

By Craig Ingvalson, son of Roger & Jackie

I am not a writer, but I *am* a storyteller. And some stories must be told. This is the story of my father, an Air Force jet fighter pilot…and my mother… and my father's buddy and fellow fighter pilot…and *his* wife…and how both guys were shot down over North Vietnam…and how one returned and the other didn't…and how this upended the lives of their combined four sons…and how two families became one…and, well, it's kind of complicated.

My father, Colonel Roger Dean Ingvalson,[1] was a jet fighter pilot for 26 years, from 1950 to 1976. For five of those years, he was a prisoner of war. He returned to marry the widow of his best friend. Her three sons and I grew up to be true brothers. My father was guided by the values of faith, family, compassion, courage, patriotism, and duty. This is his story and that of the many people in his circle who shared these ideals.

During his captivity, Dad's faith in God became deeply anchored, which made him tough yet incredibly compassionate. After his retirement, his POW experience led him to a special mission. He founded and directed Chattanooga Prison Ministries, later renamed Prison Prevention Ministries, to serve local prisoners and their families.

I asked the 400 people who attended his funeral to remember his firm resolve that was *hard as steel and soft as velvet.*

I asked the 400 people who attended his funeral to remember his firm resolve that was hard as steel and soft as velvet.

A wide variety of people came to honor him, including fighter pilots, ministers and local convicts he had ministered to. Dad's mix was unique. And that allowed this romance story to develop. He could have become hardened, given his situation and my mother's passing away during his time as a POW.

TOP GUN PILOTS

In the Officers Club that my father frequented as a young pilot hangs a framed quotation that reads:

> "A fighter pilot is a composite. He has the nerves of a robot, the audacity of Dennis the Menace, the lungs of a platoon sergeant, the vitality of an atomic bomb, the imagination of a science fiction writer; he is glib as a diplomat, impervious to suggestion, and is a paragon of wisdom with a wealth of unassorted, completely unrelated and irrelevant facts…"

By Ford Smartt, in the book Red River Valley Fighter Pilots

These men are a unique breed of proud, brilliant, confident, and good-looking men. (Admittedly, this is how they describe themselves, but their wives and many admiring women readily agree!)

Suffice it to say that the word "humble" was not often used as a descriptor for these jocks! These men were highly dedicated and serious about their profession. But, they knew how to have fun and blow off steam. My dad once gladly lost a $20 bet when a fellow pilot rode a Harley into the Officers Club—naked except for his helmet! (I've never been able to confirm the rumor that the wild Harley driver was Wayne.)

Dad said, "Booncy's husband, my best friend Wayne, was the best fighter pilot I've ever known. He flew by intuition!" As for me, I've always pictured him as Maverick, from the movie *Top Gun*.

AN IDYLLIC CHILDHOOD—THEN THE WAR

The lngvalson family farm totaled 600 acres about 20 miles north of Austin, Minnesota. It was a homogeneous community—all of Norwegian descent (most parents or grandparents "came over on the boat"). All dutifully attended Red Oak Grove Lutheran Church. All were farm kids, understanding that school and play came after hours of daily chores. Dad attended a one-room schoolhouse and was the envy of all the boys because he rode his horse Ted to and from school every day. All-in-all it was a solid, values-based environment that Dad embraced and practiced throughout his life and that sustained him through his five years of hell in the POW camps.

My mom, Jackie, grew up in the little town of Sanford, Maine. But her vision of her life was *not* little. She was valedictorian of her high school class. She was the top student in her nursing school class. And she later became an Air Force nurse. Friends and family described her as fiery, brilliant, and fun-loving. She and my dad met when they were both assigned to Turner Air Force Base in Albany, Georgia. They fell in love quickly and got married within a year.

Soon after I was born, Dad and his best friend and fellow pilot Wayne Fullam[2] were transferred to Eglin AFB in Florida. They and their families were next-door neighbors, and they all became quite close. My mom, Jackie, and Wayne's wife, Booncy, helped each other raise their boys. It was almost like having two mothers.

Our dads had both joined the Air Force as "peace-time" pilots. There was no hint that war was brewing in Southeast Asia, much less a protracted war or one in which they might become prisoners of war.

In 1966 the fellows were transferred, and both of them—along with their wives and four young sons—moved to Kadena Air Base on the Japanese Island of Okinawa, located about halfway between Taiwan and the Japanese mainland. Both men soon began having short temporary duty deployments to Thailand and Vietnam to fly missions over North Vietnam in F-105 "Thud" fighter-bombers. Wayne was shot down on his 36th mission, and he was declared MIA. (His wife, Booncy, didn't learn until several years later that he had died shortly after impact when his jet crashed into the jungle.)

As a close friend, my dad was assigned to escort Booncy and her three boys back to Chattanooga, Tennessee, their hometown. He then returned to Okinawa to be with me and my mom. Many years earlier, during her pregnancy with me, Mom had begun experiencing symptoms of multiple sclerosis. While in Japan she became wheelchair bound. She had good support from the Air Force doctors, but wisely, Dad returned us to Maine; just a few months later, he was shot down over North Vietnam.

I was eight at the time. I remember coming home from school and seeing the serious blue Air Force vehicle with yellow lettering on the side.

Mom was crying, and I didn't know what to think or how to handle my feelings. We were told that Dad was taken prisoner. My mom's health continued to worsen, and three years later she died.

So, by the time I was 11 years old, I had lost my mom and—maybe—my dad.

SURVIVING AS A POW

During his 85th mission, Dad was downed by enemy fire. He landed safely (that is, alive) via parachute, but not exactly secure, as he was captured immediately and hauled off to the infamous Hanoi Hilton. Because he was a senior officer, he likely had more classified information than most of the prisoners, so his captors immediately threw him into solitary confinement, where they left him for 22 months in a four-foot by seven-foot cell. How does one survive—and stay sane—in such conditions? I don't know about anybody else, but here's how my dad did it…

First, of course, he prayed. Many years later, back in America, he was often invited to speak to organizations. He always included this insight: "My captors thought I was alone—but I wasn't." Dad had communion with God many times each day. He also did mental calisthenics. He routinely calculated compound interest problems in his head and checked his math mentally. Whenever there was enough food, and he had enough energy, he would exercise by walking back and forth across his cell like a tiger in a cage (except Dad's cage had a walking space only 18 inches wide), and he would, of course, be calculating his mileage along the way. He also practiced the secret Tap Code that all the prisoners used to communicate with each other. After nearly two years, Dad's interrogators and torturers decided that he was never going to crack, and they placed him in a cell with 12 other men. Major Ingvalson was happy to be back in the ranks!

Dad was a captive for nearly five years. During that time, he received only a few letters and packages that members of his family sent to Hanoi. One package that did make it contained both joy and sorrow. The joy was a Bible that his mother sent, with this verse highlighted:

> "Yet I am not alone, for the Father is with me…I have said these things to you, in me you have peace. In the world you will have tribulation. But take heart, I have overcome the world" (John 16:32-33).

The sorrow was that she informed him that my mom, his wife Jackie, had died. Dad later told me that that night he dreamed that she was healed and happy. He had peace, and he knew he was not really alone.

BOONCY

Booncy loved her boys, she loved her husband, Wayne, and she loved what he was fighting for. She was a patriot equal to those who fought on the front lines. Following the news of Wayne's shoot-down, she rallied for the cause of the League—traveling to Paris with her sons (ages six, eight, and ten) in tow—to state their case for the support of the Geneva Conventions, which required prisoners to be identified, allowed to communicate with family, and treated humanely. The ultimate result of her efforts—along with many League members who dedicated a big chunk of their lives to the cause—was the recognition by the general public that though it may not be a "declared war," it was a real war.

Booncy worked tirelessly for her husband and for the other POWs and MIAs, not for any fame or reward for herself. But, she knew that her efforts would be "rewarded" in a higher way. Little did she know that her "reward" would be a new husband—along with a bonus son!

I've always marveled at the depth of Booncy's faith and at her many talents. Combining these two, she was a member of the Billy Graham Crusades, where she spoke *and* sang!

A NEW LIFE & A NEW FAMILY

It was natural for Booncy and my dad to connect following his release in March of 1973. It seems quite providential to me! But, their coming together was probably the easy part. The war was over, they had fallen in love, and both Dad and Booncy wanted to get on with their lives. He soon asked her to marry him. But then the question arose: how to integrate her three boys with Roger's one? Mike, Booncy's eldest, had the best understanding of the previous six years. He accepted what might become of the rest of his and his mother's life. His brothers, Mark and Gary, were equally accepting.

However, my dad's son (that would be me) wasn't so accepting. At least at first.

I felt abandoned. Dad left when I was eight; mom died when I was 11; and Dad re-entered my life when I was 13. When he first came home, I was beyond joyful! But our wonderful father-and-son reunion was interrupted just six months later when Dad told me that he and Booncy were going to get married in three months. Too much change too fast! For a while I felt especially isolated. Booncy had to work overtime to win me over.

It took me about two years to fully embrace Booncy and our new blended family.

It took me about two years to fully embrace Booncy and our new blended family.

Years later I learned that, while their romance was fast-moving and wonderfully exciting, Dad and Booncy very consciously kept their overt displays of affection to a minimum—for my benefit. I am deeply grateful that they eased me into our newly blended family. Booncy was very loving and empathic, but I admit that sometimes I would resist and be resentful because she wasn't my *real* mother. I remember one time when she resorted to "tough love" and chided me, "Listen here, young man! I used to change your diapers! There is no 'step' mom in me!" She was able to unite our families by assuring me that she would become my dad's soulmate and lifelong partner—*and* that she would never abandon me or my dad.

True to her word, what followed was 38 years of a thriving marriage that was full of romance! Dad and Booncy were great role models for me. Their daily expressions of love were comforting and inspiring to all of us. My brothers have always described my—*our*—dad as, "The greatest man they have ever known." Wow, that's a strong testament!

After Dad's retirement from the Air Force, the family moved back to Chattanooga. Booncy loved and attended to her husband and four sons with passion and strength, buoyed by the love of God. She was the model of a strong wife and loving mother, ever supporting of all of us. Dad kept himself very busy and continued to serve his God and country. He founded a prison ministry that started small but grew and spread to several Tennessee prisons.

FLYING WEST

For many years my dad spent hours every Sunday on the phone with his family back in Minnesota and with my mother's family in Maine. They shared blessings, joys, and troubles. How close was their family? One day Dad's older brother, Kenny, told him that his kidneys had failed, and that he was going to need a transplant. Dad's immediate response was, "I'm on my way." He flew to Minneapolis where his (58-year-old) kidney was transplanted, which added 15 years of healthy living to his brother's life.

When Roger and Wayne were young hotshot Air Force Top Gun pilots, they and their wives and children had lived a great life—until the Vietnam War intervened, and everything began to unravel, but then the threads of their lives were woven back together into a new tapestry. Dad's and Booncy's love story didn't end with their deaths. Their life tapestry continues. Their legacy spans 64 years and continues through four children, seven grandchildren and two great-grandchildren. Part of their legacy continues through the military. Two of my brother Mark's children, Haden and Jay, are Air Force A-10 pilots—as is Jay's wife! Haden is the lead pilot for the A-10 demonstration team's air shows, which tour the country every year.

It has been 11 years since my dad's funeral, but people still mention my statement that he was "hard as steel and soft as velvet." I am delighted that this concept has struck a chord with so many people. Dad continues to inspire people today, and his influence will continue far into the future.

Dad flew west in December of 2011. Booncy followed him eight years later. During those years, when friends would ask her if she'd ever consider marrying again, she always replied, "No way! I've been married to the two best. Why would I ever marry again?"

Their love was genuine. Following Dad's death, Booncy told me many stories about how romantic Dad had been. She taught me the lesson that romance is very important in any healthy love relationship. Her retirement home apartment was full of memories of him. Framed memories were everywhere: the wedding photos, the photos from their many trips, and the nearly life-sized oil painting of Dad that could not be missed on her bedroom wall. The most touching display of their love and romance might be the little sticky note on her refrigerator, which he had left for her 20 years earlier, saying simply…

I love you,

Roger

LOVE LESSONS

FAMILY

Happy and strong couples create nurturing environments in which they raise their children. Everyone's life is a tapestry, and everyone is unique. Craig's family tapestry is especially tightly woven, strong, and long-lived.

EMPATHY

Empathy is one of the cornerstones of all deep and strong relationships—and is especially important for couples and families. Craig's dad and his new mom were very aware of, and sensitive to, his needs as a young teenager.

STRENGTH—*AND* VULNERABILITY

Truly strong people have learned to embrace and balance their strength *and* their vulnerability. The gentleness of love, compassion, and empathy can—and should—exist side-by-side with the strength of confidence, courage, and resilience.

Roger & Jackie Ingvalson

Roger & Booncy Ingvalson

1 Maj Roger D. Ingvalson USAF, F-105 Thunderchief, POW 28-MAY-68 – 14-MAR-73, Retired Col (0-6), RIP 24-DEC-11
2 Maj Wayne E. Fullam USAF, F-105 Thunderchief, MIA/KIA 7-OCT-67

TORTURE...IN THEIR OWN WORDS

"Starting in the fall of 1965, all hell broke loose. For the next four years, men were consistently being tortured or severely punished in every camp. In one particularly painful torture, they tied you up like a pretzel. With your hands behind your back, they ratcheted your elbows together until they touched—then tied them tightly. This cut off your circulation. Then one torturer pushed your arms up and the other shoved your head down toward the floor with his foot. (The drawing shown above is one of many that I sketched shortly after our release and included in my book.)

"Sometimes these sadistic torturers would tie your hands behind your back and then loop another rope through your arms and hang you mid-air from a beam." —*Prisoner of War: Six Years in Hanoi*, Mike McGrath, pg. 79.

"The torturer...seized the end of the strap binding his arms and heaved upward. His whole upper body exploded and his eyes flooded. The pain increased. Indescribable. Pectoral muscles tore against their anchor points and his sternum pushed outward as rib ends tried to pull away from it....His muscles were being torn apart, slowly, jerking, slowly, jerking. He screamed and screamed." —*Prisoner at War: The Survival of Commander Richard A. Stratton*, Scott Blakey, pgs. 91-92.

"We were made to lie on our stomachs on the floor, no shirt, pants down to our ankles, and were beaten with a fan belt. The guard stood back and took several steps toward me, whipping the fan belt from behind his back in an arc, bringing it down across my back, flaying the skin off and turning the back of my body into hamburger. The impact was so hard that my body bounced off the floor and quivered with pain." —*The Ways We Choose*, Dave Carey, pg. 54.

"I had no socks and my feet swelled up and felt as if pins were stuck into the soles and toes...The more I dozed off, the more regularly the guards came in to bat me around, slapping and kicking at random. Forbidden to get up and use even the primitive toilet facilities, I managed to contain my bowel movements for some days, but I could not hold in my urine. The damp and soiled clothing added to my discomfort, particularly in the cold night hours. After four days of nothing but stolen catnaps, I was almost immune to their physical and verbal abuse." —*Chained Eagle*, Everett Alvarez, pg. 169.

"Interrogations were often conducted while a POW was on his knees. After several hours, his knees became flattened, red and swollen. If quicker results were desired, a small rock would be placed under each knee. I once spent 30 hours over two days on my knees as punishment because a guard had caught me peeking out of my room through a floor-level vent." —*Prisoner of War: Six years in Hanoi*, Mike McGrath, pgs. 44-45.

4 | A 58-YEAR LOVE STORY WITH AN 8-YEAR GAP

THE STORY OF
Bob & Lorraine Shumaker

Bob[1] grew up on a farm in western Pennsylvania and wanted to be a veterinarian...until his aunt Marge gave him a subscription to *Boy's Life*, the Boy Scout magazine. An article entitled "Annapolis and West Point: Where Boys Become Admirals and Generals" caught his eye. Thirty-five years later he actually *did* become an Admiral! In between he courted the love of his life with a love-letter writing campaign...he graduated from the US Naval Academy...he became an elite Navy fighter pilot...he was a finalist in the Apollo astronaut selection process...he had a baby son with Lorraine... he became the second pilot to be shot down by the North Vietnamese...he spent eight years and one day in their prison camps...he returned home, and he co-created a life-long love affair with his wife.

Their son Grant was one month old when Bob left for Vietnam. Grant didn't meet his father until he was eight.

THE CAPTURED WARRIOR

Bob had the misfortune to be shot down on the second American air attack following the 1964 Tonkin Incident, which pulled America into active fighting. After ejecting from his F-8 Crusader fighter jet, Bob's parachute opened a mere 35 feet above the ground. He suffered a broken back. "From there things went downhill," he says with a wry smile. The locals who captured him turned him over to the communists who then put him in front of a firing squad. After several terrifying minutes they shouldered their rifles to Bob's great relief.

"As the second prisoner in the camp, the communists didn't quite know what to do with me. A doctor conducted a cursory 'examination' of my injuries, then smiled for the surrounding cameras for a propaganda photo. That was the only medical care I ever got. They didn't even give me an aspirin! So much for what our captors called their 'lenient and humane treatment.' Eventually my back healed on its own. And that's why I returned home from the war an inch shorter than when I entered it."

Bob coined the nickname "Hanoi Hilton" for the Hỏa Lò camp, a phrase that has entered the lexicon. This reflects Bob's sense of humor and irony—attributes that were essential for every POW's survival. It was three weeks until the next "guest" arrived.

Eventually Bob became a member of the "Alcatraz Gang," a group of 11 of the most recalcitrant captives who received "special treatment" (meaning extreme torture and solitary confinement) for years. "I spent a total of nearly three years in solitary. That gives a person a lot a lot of time to think.

"One of our strategies for keeping our sanity was our 'mental projects' which would help us pass the time over weeks, months, and even years! One of my projects dealt with mathematics and the musical scale. I was curious as to the frequency relationship between any one note and its immediate neighbor. Without pencil or paper it took me three weeks to calculate that the ratio is the 12th root of 2, which is 1.05946. This would take your phone's calculator less than one second to calculate.

"Another was designing the house that my family and I would live in when—not *if*, but *when*—I returned home. Years later I still remembered the architectural plans, the materials, the construction plans, and landscaping. My one miscalculation was the *cost*. Inflation had increased the cost of my original $35,000 mansion to five times that amount! But luckily for me Lorraine had lived frugally and saved enough money to fund my dream home. I am one lucky man! I live in that house now and enjoy the expansive eight acres that surround it. For someone who had been confined as we were, it's important to not be constrained by space restrictions. And five years after my liberation we *did* build that house here in Fairfax, Virginia. Lorraine and I have always placed a high value on having a comfortable, stable, loving, and welcoming home."

THE QUIET CIVILIAN WARRIOR

Meanwhile, back in America…Lorraine stayed in San Diego, cared for their infant son, went back to school, and became a nutritionist. She was friendly with the other POW wives, but she preferred to do her own thing. She had a strong independent streak. In 1969, when the League brought the plight of our POWs to the whole world through highly visible publicity, Lorraine steered her own path. Shunning the spotlight she made a difference in a quiet way, by traveling to Paris—on her own—to confront the Vietnamese representatives. "Pretty damn audacious!" marvels Bob.

> **Lorraine was a quiet crusader. She wrote letters back and forth with Bob that contained veiled messages that were impossible for the enemy to detect.**

Lorraine was a quiet crusader. She wrote letters back and forth with Bob that contained veiled messages that were impossible for the enemy to detect.

All the POWs benefited from their clandestine communications.

"As I was one of the first pilots to be shot down, Lorraine holds the title of the longest serving POW wife. Not a distinction she would have chosen, but it is a testament to her resilience and love."

BACK IN AMERICA…

Bob was released on February 12, 1973, on the very first C-141 transport plane out of Hanoi as part of Operation Homecoming. After he made his first call from the Philippines, Lorraine observed that, "It was just like we had never parted!" Now *that's* a deep connection.

Having missed the mini-skirt era, Bob asked her to wear that style when she first greeted him. As Lorraine prepared for their reunion she asked Grant, who was now eight and somewhat shy, what he was going to do upon meeting his father. He shrugged his shoulders and committed to nothing. Lorraine said, "I'm going to run up and give him a big hug and a kiss!" The boy shrugged again. When the plane landed and his dad emerged, Grant broke away from his mom, raced up to him and hugged and kissed him first! The competitive youngster had won the race!

Cmdr. Robert Shumaker, is greeted by his son, Grant, and wife, Lorraine at Miramar Naval Air Station on Feb. 15, 1973.
(/ U-T file photo)

Lorraine was active as a competitive bridge player, and she knitted much of her wardrobe. "She also loved to play golf and drive her Corvette." And not to be outdone by her fighter pilot husband, Lorraine became an experienced copilot. She and Bob enjoyed traveling aboard their homebuilt Glasair airplane.

Career-wise Bob quickly made up for lost time. He earned a second master's degree and then earned a Ph.D. in electrical engineering. He rose through the Navy ranks and retired as a Rear Admiral. Along the way he held many posts, including project manager for tactical missiles at the Naval Air Systems Command, commander of the Naval Postgraduate School in Monterey, California, and he worked at the Pentagon.

In 1998 Bob and Lorraine were featured in the PBS documentary "Return with Honor," hosted by Tom Hanks. This QR code will link you to it on YouTube.

Lorraine passed away in November 2021 and was interred at the US Naval Academy Cemetery. Bob now lives alone and is comforted by his pleasant memories of Lorraine's love and laughter. As of this writing Bob, at a spry 89, is still flying planes.

LOVE LESSONS

COMMITMENT

"...Till death do us part." In our culture today, many people struggle with this vow. But some people take this very seriously. Bob and Lorraine were tested very *early* in their marriage. Eight years—and one day! That's a long time to be separated...especially when you are largely out of touch and dealing with a lot of uncertainty. But when you are 100% committed, it gives you a lot of strength, patience, and peace.

VISION

Strong people and strong couples have a vision/image/idea of what they want. A vision of your future life, a vision of your relationship. While in captivity Bob created a very detailed vision of the house he wanted to build when he returned. Lorraine was integral in making that vision a reality by saving enough money to build that home.

FOLLOW YOUR OWN PATH

"To everything there is a season..." (Ecclesiastes 3:1). There is certainly a season for joining others for a cause. But there is also a season for going solo and following your own heart and your own path. Lorraine was aligned with the League, but she did it *her* way, and in so doing, helped her husband.

Bob & Lorraine Shumaker

1 LCDR Robert H. (Bob) Shumaker USN, F-8 Crusader, POW 11-FEB-65 – 12-FEB-73, RADM USN (0-8)

KEEP QUIET!

In the early years of the war (1965 to 1968), POW/MIA families were told that the policy was to "keep quiet." It was part of the State Department's "quiet diplomacy" and the belief that publicity might bring punishments on their husbands.

This policy also meant that the military bases did not talk much about the missing men. There was little support for the wives who, in many cases, were almost treated like outsiders, especially since the people in most units turn over every 24 to 36 months. And to some degree they were seen as being a threat to morale—the presence of POW/MIA wives could be a painful reminder of the dangers of war.

Facing tough decisions when their husbands were missing was a difficult psychological battle. For example, should you move to be near your family, or should you stay near the base and the military community? And for many, their powers of attorney dates were expiring. Should you wait faithfully for your husband whose status is unknown, and he's already been missing for two or three years? Or should you move on and find another good man?

Consider the challenges that these women and families were facing. Keeping quiet meant that they were not supposed to be sharing their story with others. So, at the same time their husbands were locked up in maximum security cell blocks to keep them discouraged and isolated from their peers and team-mates, the wives were being isolated and told not to discuss their situation publicly. At a time when they most needed to be in a support community, they were often alone, facing the toughest times of their lives.

Yes, the POWs were tough and suffered, but the women stood strong and matched them in different yet painful situations. Their character, courage, and commitment were remarkable and enabled them to set a great example of leadership and teamwork that will inspire all generations.

5 | SHE BECAME HIS "DATE FOR LIFE"

THE STORY OF
Everett & Tammy Alvarez

Tammy

"I just met the man I'm going to marry!" I eagerly shared with my sister over the phone. She was skeptical. This was just after meeting Everett[1] for the first time and talking for all of 30 minutes. Seven months later we were married. And 49 years later we're still living happily ever after!

Everett

Do you think maybe we should give them a few details about the intervening years?

Tammy

Well *maybe*. You go first.

Everett

Okay. The first indication that providence was having a hand in my love life was shortly after I regained my freedom from the hellhole of a North Vietnamese prisoner of war camp. Following a press conference at the Bethesda Naval Hospital, I was scheduled to return home to California, departing the next morning from Baltimore Friendship Airport on United. At the last minute I changed my plans, which meant departing from Dulles International Airport instead. Little did I know that Fate was playing its hand, leading me to meet Tammy Ilyas, the love of my life.

Tammy

I was the United Airlines Passenger Service Representative at Dulles, which served more VIPs than any airport in the country. (There were only 20 of us nationally to hold this position at United.) My job was to provide special services to VIPs flying in and out of Washington, D.C. Times were different back in the early 1970s, and there were few private jets, so we hosted many CEOs, movie stars, sports figures, politicians, and military brass. I became personal friends with many of them. I served an informal "family" of several hundred very special people. It was quite a glamorous job, and I loved it!

That morning, as I was walking to my office with coffee in hand, I heard "Commander Everett Alvarez" being paged. I was surprised because his name was not on the flight manifest, which I always checked at the end of each day.

Everett
Because of my last-minute change of plans.

Tammy
When the POWs were released, starting in February 1973, orders had come down from the top—from Mr. Ed Carlson, the president of United Airlines—that we were to treat all returning Vietnam POWs as *extra special* VIPs. I immediately asked the ticket counter agent to page the commander again, and to then bring him to my office. I then upgraded him to first class, I alerted the United captain and crew, and I ordered champagne for him.

Everett
I was surprised and pleased to be bumped up to first class, but I was dazzled by the charming and beautiful woman who escorted me! Before my flight, we spent a pleasant half hour together in Tammy's office that seemed like mere minutes. "Nice girl," I thought. At the gate she handed me her business card and said, "Call me if you get back to Washington." I gratefully tucked Miss Tammy Ilyas's card away in my wallet for future reference.

Tammy
I want to point out that I did *not* include my personal phone number! People were more proper back then, and I also had to maintain my poise and professionalism. But *inside* I was all butterflies!

Everett and I just clicked. It was so easy and comfortable that it was like home being with him.

Everett and I just clicked. It was so easy and comfortable that it was like home being with him.

Right from the beginning our conversation was two people connecting as human beings. I was impressed by his politeness, confidence, and genuine friendliness.

Everett

Let's back up for a moment…

Eight-and-a-half years earlier, on August 5, 1964, when I was a 26-year-old pilot, I was in one of the very first squadrons of A-4 Skyhawk fighter jets sent to attack targets in North Vietnam (in response to the controversial Gulf of Tonkin Incident). I was the first pilot to be shot down over North Vietnam, and the first American to be captured and held there. I was a POW for nearly the entire length of America's involvement in the war. (Think of it as twice the length of America's involvement in World War II or twice the length you spent in high school.) I was captured at 26 and freed at 35. I missed the defining events of an era—the late sixties and early seventies—not just: the moon landings (all six of them) but also the many cultural challenges and changes that took place during those years.

When my tour began in 1964, I was a newlywed of seven months, and the dream of my reunion with my wife had kept me going for seven years—until my captors gave me a "gift" on Christmas Day, 1971: a letter from my mother informing me that my first wife had divorced me and remarried.

Tammy

Everett was blessed having the support of his fellow POWs. He also had plenty of time to process and come to terms with such a devastating turn of events before he returned home. His strong faith in God sustained him.

Everett

Right! When my plane was shot down, I found myself literally saying The Lord's Prayer when I hit the water after ejecting. On the very first Sunday I spent in the POW camp I used a rusty nail to scratch the outline of a cross into the stone wall beside my cell door to create a crude altar. From then on, prayer was my daily companion, and I regularly reconstructed as much of the mass in Latin as I could remember to worship at my altar.

Tammy

Our faith in God is the solid rock upon which we have built our relationship. I grew up in the Antiochian Eastern Orthodox Christian Church, and Everett was raised in the Catholic Church. He and I easily overcame the slight differences between the denominations. We married in my Orthodox Church. Our shared faith and values have sustained us for *decades*. Those same beliefs, tools and skills gave him a strong foundation that sustained him through all those unspeakable years of terror as a POW.

Everett

In the Navy I learned how to take things by lightening up. When really put to the test I realized that humor could be at least as important as courage. In fact, humor could be called a kind of courage, a very effective "whistling in the dark."

Of possible interest is the fact that I received especially harsh treatment from our North Vietnamese captors. As a Mexican-American, I was singled out for especially intense interrogations designed to get me to turn against America, the Navy, *and* my "white oppressors." I never did. And neither did my fellow prisoners who were African-American: Fred Cherry, Tom Madison, and Norm McDaniel.

It was a long eight-and-a-half years. I lived through many interrogations, many of which included torture. I survived a total of over 17 months in solitary confinement, near-starvation, beatings that sometimes lasted for several days, and I also spent several weeks at a time in arm and leg shackles. I was once thrown into a pit inside a cell in just my shorts, with no mosquito netting, and only one thin blanket to protect me; I covered myself with it and breathed through a tiny hole. My world contracted to the most basic concepts: food, faith, sleep, and loyalty. There was a six-month period when both my arms and hands were black because of the chains and ropes which they used to torture me. Years later back home, a team of neurosurgeons miraculously reconstructed my hands and arms. Thank God for America!

Most of us suffered through similar torture, interrogations, and abuse. I was just one of the guys. By 1973 conditions were more relaxed. We were so numbed by false alarms and false hopes, we shrugged and resumed a bridge tournament when the announcement came that we were actually going home.

How did I survive all of this? My "Plexiglas Shield," behind which I suppressed my feelings. But, while it helped me survive for all those years in Vietnam, it also held me back when I returned to America. Part of my recovery was the process of writing my first book, *Chained Eagle*, 17 years after my release. My coauthor, Anthony Pitch, said of me, "His feelings are so deep within him that they are bound up tighter than the cloth around an Egyptian mummy."

I am the luckiest man alive because Tammy stood by me through the many years it took me to unbind myself!

I am the luckiest man alive because Tammy stood by me through the many years it took me to unbind myself!

And speaking of Tammy…There was something wonderful and mysterious about the way my life and Tammy's started to become entwined. Several weeks after my brief first meeting with her, I was at the head table of a welcome home celebration dinner. I was seated next to Burt Talcott, who had been a referee for my high school's league sports teams; he also had been a WWII POW, and now he was a California congressman. He slipped me a note that read, "Call Tammy!"

How interesting. How in the world did *he* know Tammy?

"Oh, *everybody* in Washington knows Tammy. She's a *wonderful* girl," he said. What an amazing endorsement from a man I knew and respected.

Unbeknownst to Tammy and me, Congressman Talcott was one of *dozens* of Tammy's VIP "family" who were conspiring to spark a romance between the two of us! (One of the co-conspirators was none other than Vice Admiral Elmo Zumwalt, the Chief of Naval Operations, and his wife, Mouzetta!)

I was somewhat surprised that Miss Ilyas had even remembered me! But I lived in California, and she was in D.C., so there wasn't much future in that—or so I thought. It remains a wonder to me that I made any impression on her at all, considering the many important people she met every day.

Tammy

As much as I enjoyed my job, I wanted above anything else to get married and create a family of my own. But I wasn't actively *looking*. I prayed I would meet a man I could live with for the rest of my life. So, I left it up to God. On a certain level I had faith that God was sending the right man to me. And on another level, I set my own deadline. If my future husband didn't make an appearance by the end of 1973, I would consider giving up my job, going back home to Pittsburgh, opening a travel agency, living with my parents, and possibly adopting a child as a single parent.

Everett

Tammy was one very independent woman! Both of us believed then, and believe now, in the power of prayer, and nothing has so reinforced that belief for both of us as the fact that Tammy apparently saw her answer in *me* when we met. I often wonder why we met under the circumstances we did. Was it Fate? Destiny? A miracle? Or was it God's plan we meet? (Maybe it was *all* of them!)

Of course, I was pretty much unaware of all this in the months following my release. I still wasn't thinking very far ahead. I was, though, aware that the chemistry between us was right, that we had felt immediately comfortable with each other and that this feeling grew with every minute we were together. And so, when I was invited to a grand event at the White House—along with all my fellow POWs—I asked Tammy to be my date. That event, hosted by President Richard Nixon and First Lady Pat, was described in the newspapers as the "most spectacular White House gala in history," with more than 1,300 guests attending.

[Greg's coauthor note]

In Everett's second book, Code of Conduct, *he captioned a photo from that event: "Between [fellow POW] Jerry Coffee and me is Tammy Ilyas, my date for the evening who would become my date for life." Now that is an insightful and powerful phrase: "My date for life"! But wait, there's more…A wedding photo of Tammy and Everett is captioned: "The beginning of 'happily ever after.'" Everett was very positive* and *romantic!*

Everett

Both of us knew what we wanted in life and in a partner. We shared our values, and we both had a deep faith in God. We realized early on that we were a natural fit. It really was like magic, like in the movie *Sleepless in Seattle*. We were simply *meant* to be together.

Tammy

We both felt something big might be happening, so Everett stayed in D.C. the week following the White House gala. A pleasant kind of tension was building between the two of us. And then, on our third day together, on the dance floor of Le Bateau, a floating nightclub on the Potomac, the tension broke. We felt so happy that we simply couldn't stop laughing. As we were holding each other close, I simply said, "If life is this much fun, we should just get married!"

Everett

And so we did. From then on there was no turning back—although the course of true love would be far from smooth. Challenges included a reluctance of my family to accept Tammy as my wife. But Tammy and I overcame all obstacles. Heck, I had overcome all the obstacles which our communist captors had thrown at me, and that provided a unique perspective on every other obstacle that life threw at me!

For example, even though my religious beliefs and Tammy's coincided, our backgrounds did *not*. Tammy comes from an urban, upper middle-class family, her father was a doctor and a leader in their church, and she had a sophisticated job that required finesse and etiquette. My grandparents came to America from Mexico early in the 1900s. I grew up in a small, modest home. My father was a great role model of a responsible, hard-working man. Despite having only a seventh-grade education, he was industrious and upwardly mobile. He held increasingly advanced positions, starting as a welder during WWII, and ending as a sheet metal worker who also worked with computers to develop prototypes for the Food Machinery Company. From humble beginnings Dad gave us a solid foundation and made sure that my sisters and I received a good education, which led to our success in life.

Tammy

Obviously, Everett inherited his family's strong work ethic. He has always been hyper-busy and a deep thinker, which I deeply respect. The boys and I were always there to support him. After the war Everett dealt with the challenges of reintegrating into American society with our love and with his own strength and perseverance. He was determined and enthusiastic about accomplishing his dreams to continue his graduate education and achieve his goals in his several careers.

[Lee's coauthor note]

Upon returning from Vietnam Everett continued his Naval career. He requalified for flying jets in Kingsville, Texas. After that, he attended the United States Naval Post-Graduate School, where he had been accepted before he was shot down. His goal at that time was to enter the space program, and one of the requirements was to attain a master's degree in aeronautical engineering in order to qualify. (Tammy says, "Everett has always dreamed big!") But by the time he regained his freedom, he was 35 and too old to be an astronaut, so he obtained a master's degree in Operations Research and Systems Analysis. After graduation, the couple moved to Washington, D.C. where Everett was stationed at the Pentagon. While doing that, he attended George Washington School of Law five nights a week.

When he first came home to California, Everett had developed a very special relationship with then Governor Ronald Reagan and his wife Nancy. After Everett retired from the Navy in 1980, his friend, now President Reagan, asked him to join his administration. Everett served as Deputy Director of Peace Corps for almost two years, and then as Deputy Secretary of the Veterans Administration for four years. While serving in these positions he continued law school, earned his Juris Doctorate degree, and was admitted to the D.C. Bar.

After nearly six years with the Reagan administration, he decided to enter the private sector. He joined the Hospital Corporation of America as Senior Executive Vice President of Government Affairs. Two years later he made another one of his dreams a reality when he founded his own company, Conwal Inc. After building a successful business employing 400

*employees, he sold it and founded another corporation, Alvarez, LLC,
which is now being run successfully by their son, Marc, who is also an attorney. Their other son, Bryan, has a medical practice in Denver, Colorado, specializing in preventative medicine, occupational medicine, and in-
fectious diseases. He is also a doctor in the United States Naval Reserves.*

*Tammy had no difficulty living her own life while Everett studied, worked,
and traveled. She volunteered at school and kept busy with community
work, church projects, and her sons' activities. She attended art school for
four years. She and Everett assisted in establishing an Antiochian Eastern Orthodox Christian Church in Potomac, Maryland. They both were
constantly helping others and volunteering. Tammy produced a movie,*
Fighting for Life, *which told the story of military medicine and the Uniformed Services University of the Health Sciences, located on the Walter
Reed campus in Bethesda, Maryland. The film's mission was to promote
military medicine and save the school. Tammy's five-year labor of love
fulfilled her mission. She then formed a 501(c)(3) foundation to support
the university.*

Tammy

Everett and I are both independent *and* interdependent. Our personalities
are quite different, but we've never tried to change the other. For example,
he has never been what you would call "classically romantic." Because he
was so busy, I used to buy anniversary cards and gifts for myself and tell the
children that they were from Daddy! As youngsters they wouldn't have understood that a lack of romantic gestures did *not* mean that he didn't love
me. Everett and I embrace this mindset to this day. Just recently I was on
the phone, ordering flowers for our two daughters-in-law for Mother's Day.
Everett overheard me from across the room, and he called out, "Order some
for yourself, too!" And so I *did*. I also took the liberty to sign the card for
him: "I love you SO much!!!" When the flowers arrived, we both laughed
and laughed! Our respect and love for each other has never been in doubt;
we share lots of laughs.

In my opinion, strong couples have a lot of humor in their relationship.
Humor sometimes smooths over difficult situations, and it also builds intimacy. One of our funniest memories from our early courtship was the time

I decided to surprise Everett by making Mexican tacos for him.

Everett

(Laughs out loud!)

Tammy

I did try my best! I had never learned to cook while growing up, but I wasn't afraid to experiment. There weren't any Mexican restaurants near us. But I thought, "How hard could this be?" So I bought taco shells, ground beef, lettuce and cheese. I cooked the meat then boiled the shells—*without taking them out of their cellophane wrapper.*

Everett ate them without any complaints. The next evening, we were enjoying dinner with some POW friends. I proudly related to the wives my culinary adventure. They doubled over with laughter. And then, of course, they had to tell the tale to the guys. I was a little bit embarrassed but mostly proud of my adventurous nature.

Everett

Tammy has never been insecure or needy. I sure got lucky *there*! She is independent, just like me. This works amazingly well for both of us. I never poke my nose into what she wants or buys. (All I ask is that she wears what she buys at least a *couple* times.)

Also, we've had arguments like all couples, but we've always been respectful of each other.

The one thing that frustrates me is that she is *always* right!

Tammy

(Laughs out loud!)

Everett

Well, let me amend that. She is right 92% of the time!

Tammy

Through the years—*decades*—we've had our challenges, but they didn't destroy us. Our faith helps us, and our unshakable love for each other has seen us through everything. Also, we are both practical and reasonable—and we don't put ourselves first. God and family have always come first. Period. We also give back to our community. Everett is a many-faceted gentleman. He was a fighter pilot, an electrical engineer, an attorney, a government executive, and a successful entrepreneurial businessman. And he also loves Shakespeare and poetry. We both love music: classical, symphonies, Broadway. Everett's favorite "theme song" is the soundtrack from *Top Gun*. No surprise there!

The secret to creating a "happily ever after" marriage, as Everett called it in his book, "Well, there's no *one* thing, but it's very important to support each other's dreams. We have always believed in each other, and we support each other through thoughts, words, and actions. We have always been a co-equal team. If I was happy, he was happy. If he was happy, I was happy. Maybe it's as simple as that."

Everett

Looking back on our lives together I marvel at the way destiny arranged for us to meet at the Dulles Airport and set into motion our happily ever after marriage. As of this writing we've been together for 49 amazing years. One of our family rules is that we never go to bed angry, we say our prayers before falling asleep, and we say, "I love you."

— LOVE LESSONS —

CORE VALUES

Shared core values can help couples overcome nearly anything that life can throw at you. Though Everett and Tammy had different backgrounds, their values provided a strong foundation enabling them to embrace each other for *who they are.*

PRAYER

Pray for the kind of partner you want, but then be patient, keep your eyes open, and watch for the important things.

ATTITUDE & MINDSET

There are times when married couples need to think of each other as husband and wife, but perhaps if they began calling each other—and treating each other—as their "Date for life," their respect for each other and their companionship would override all the challenges of marriage. We might see the divorce rate plummet.

Everett & Tammy Alvarez

1 LTJG Everett Alvarez, Jr. USN, A-4 Skyhawk, POW 5-AUG-64 – 12-FEB-73, Retired CDR USN (0-5)

THE HANOI HILTON PRISON SYSTEM

The name "Hanoi Hilton"[1] was probably the first of many examples of sarcastic humor used to lighten the heavy load of captivity. POW number two, Navy LCDR Bob Shumaker, used a burnt match and toilet paper to make a note which he dropped at the latrine. New POW Capt. Ron Storz picked it up and read, "Welcome to the Hanoi Hilton; if you get this note scratch your balls on the way back." The name seemed to stick, even though the real name for this prison was "Hỏa Lò" and the sign on the front entrance said, "Maison Central." It was a bastille-type prison built in the 1890s by the French colonialists during their occupation. It covered an entire city block in downtown Hanoi. Its walls were about 15 feet high and three feet thick with embedded shards of broken wine bottles at the top plus high-tension electric wires. Armed guard towers were in each corner. No one ever escaped from the Hanoi Hilton.

Inside the Hilton walls were several buildings. At some point, most of us lived in the Little Vegas complex, but other areas were appropriately named: New Guy Village and Heartbreak Hotel, as they were used for isolation, interrogations, and torture.

The Hanoi Hilton operated as the hub for all the camps. The other two main Hanoi camps were the Zoo (Pigsty, Office, Stable, Garage, etc.) and the Plantation (Gunshed, Warehouse, and Corn Crib). Those are examples of how we named camps and buildings. But, we also gained a small victory over our captors by nicknaming them—for example, Greasy, Stoneface, Fidel, Groucho, Flea, Jawbone, Ichabod, Lump, Elf, Oddjob, Dummkopf, Rat, Fox, and Bug. Besides the humor of these names, they also greatly helped us communicate with clarity in covert communications.

Aerial photo of the "Hanoi Hilton"

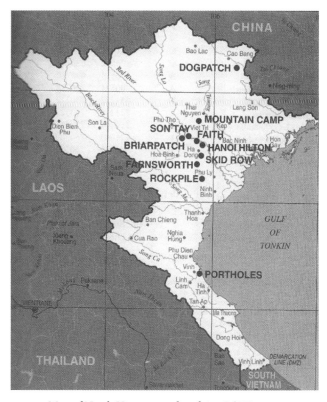

Map of North Vietnam and outlying POW camps

1   See photos and more about the Hanoi Hilton at powromance.com.

6 | TWO LOVE STORIES & A THRILLER

THE STORY OF

Carole & Steve Hanson—then Carole & Jim Hickerson

This is the story of Carole Hickerson and her two courageous warrior husbands—the first who went off to war and became missing in action (and how she became a courageous warrior wife on his behalf)—and the other who did return, after more than five years as a prisoner of war (and how the two met and lived happily ever after).

But before we get too far, we need to go back to the story of Carole's first true love.

HUSBAND NO. 1: STEVE HANSON,[1] CAPTAIN, US MARINE CH-46 SEA KNIGHT HELICOPTER PILOT

"Steve was the first—and only—boy that I said 'I love you' to! We really were 'meant to be'!

"We met in college when my roommates invited the St. Mary's College basketball team to our apartment for a little party. (Yes, we were wild coeds: We served Ritz Crackers, cheese, and soft drinks!) Steve wasn't a typical jock; he was polite, we clicked, and we talked for hours. We started dating right away and we never looked back!

"After college we both became teachers—I taught elementary school in Burbank, California, and Steve taught high school in Los Angeles. We barely made enough money to get by, but we were happy. Steve had an apartment that was so small you could sit on the toilet and fix dinner, both at the same time! We loved walking the beaches in Southern California, and Steve proposed to me on Newport Beach. We were married in 1962. At that time, like most Americans, we had next to no awareness of the secret military operations that President John Kennedy had initiated to help South Vietnam fight communism."

Steve had dreamed of being a pilot since he was a kid. He spent hours perched on a platform his dad had built atop one pole of the clothesline so he could watch planes take off from Oxnard Air Force Base in California. Steve did not come from a military family, but he was so patriotic that he left teaching and joined the Marines specifically to fight in the Vietnam War! Why did he choose the Marines? He made it very clear, "I want to succeed in the toughest branch there is." He joined in 1964.

Two years later he was sent to Vietnam, leaving behind his young wife who was nine months pregnant.

While piloting Sea Knight helicopters Steve was shot down three times. The first time he found refuge in a cave until he was recovered. The second time he landed safely in a rice paddy. His third time was *not* a charm. He was shot down on June 3, 1967, in Laos, and apparently taken prisoner, but like so many MIAs his true status was unknown.

BAD NEWS

"Imagine that you're a happy 25-year-old with a one-year-old baby boy. Imagine that your husband is a caring, loving, and—oh by the way, handsome and dashing—Marine Corps helicopter pilot. He's overseas on a mission. You trade many loving letters. Imagine that one morning while you're teaching your second-grade class in Southern California, your principal calls you to his office and you think, 'Gee, he must have something to ask me about the new second-grade curriculum.' Instead, you are greeted there by two Marine Corps officers in their dress blues.

"Fear grips you instantly. When Marine Corps officers in dress blues appear unannounced, it's *never* good news. My mind screamed, 'They're here to tell me that Steve has been killed!' But that's *not* what they said. Their exact words were, 'We are not here to tell you that Steve has been killed. We are here to tell you that he is missing in action.'

"Missing in action? MISSING IN ACTION? I can still feel the shock and fear of standing there in the principal's office. I watched my life come crashing down. I was not prepared. I had prayed. I knew that Steve was a great pilot. We had made so many plans…

"I went numb. But my protective instincts quickly kicked in. 'Oh, they'll find him! They're the Marines! It'll be a matter of days.'

But the days turned into weeks, the weeks turned into months, and the months turned into years.

> **"I went numb. But my protective instincts quickly kicked in. 'Oh, they'll find him! They're the Marines! It'll be a matter of days.'"**

"For the first two agonizing years I was a 'good girl.' Our son Todd was born two weeks after Steve had deployed, and of course being a new mom I was sharing and receiving a lot of love from this handsome little fellow. And I followed the military and government directives to not talk about the uncertain fate of my husband (their fear being that making the topic public might somehow cause the North Vietnamese to mistreat our POWs and MIAs). During those two years I received no information whatsoever about Steve.

"Over time my fear, frustration, and inaction turned into outrage, resolve, and action. Very public action. I guess I'm just stubborn."

THE FUSE IS LIT

Like most family members who lost loved ones during the Vietnam War, Carole initially bore her burden in silence. The US military had very little intel on the fates of their missing fighters, and on top of that, Department of Defense policy was to keep any information regarding them secret, even from their families. "We were met with a wall of silence."

Carole didn't even know for sure *where* Steve had been shot down until three years later when she connected with some of his squadron mates who had returned home. "One of them pulled out a big map and stealthily— without speaking a word—pointed to Laos. That's how secretive the whole thing was when he was shot down. Why? Because at that time the US had not admitted to having operations in Laos." And this is what lit the fuse. Carole was among the first MIA and POW wives to break the silence and approach the media. At that time she didn't know any other wives in her situation. She began a one-woman letter-writing campaign.

She wrote to 350 newspapers asking readers to write to their congressional representatives and to North Vietnamese communist leaders. She wrote to embassies and radio stations, religious groups, and politicians. This generated a *lot* of publicity. Some organizations generously returned the checks she had sent to pay for ads, and they ran them for free.

"I thought I was alone, but I quickly discovered that there were *thousands* of people who felt the way I did and were ready to hop on the bandwagon. I was flooded with letters from wives, mothers, fathers, sons, and daughters."

At a time when women were beginning to shatter the cultural glass ceiling, Carole was one of the first to break the wall of silence around the fate of our POWs and MIAs. Her bold action was the forerunner for women and families across the nation to band together and launch a mission to change our government's policy of "keep quiet" and begin to put pressure on the communists regarding treatment and accounting for their POW/MIA family members.

Carole's little one-woman campaign quickly connected her to the group of POW/MIA wives in San Diego led by Sybil Stockdale, wife of a known POW Commander, James Stockdale, who was the senior Naval officer in the camps. Sybil had reached the same stage of frustration as Carole and had already organized a group of wives in her area and reached out to Navy POW/MIA wives on the East Coast to collaborate with them. Carole joined this core group of like-minded wives. They soon founded the National League of Families of American Prisoners of War and Missing in Action in Southeast Asia, and a nationwide movement was born. Carole was an original board member and later served as its chairperson. She worked closely with Alice Stratton, Phyllis Galanti, Dora Griffin Bell, and Sybil Stockdale. (The first three are profiled elsewhere in this book. Sybil Stockdale's story is featured in *The League of Wives* by Heath Hardage Lee. And Sybil and her husband share their story in their own book, *Love and War*.)

Carole says, "It's important to note that ours was a humanitarian issue, not a political one. It was so frustrating that the media kept trying to politicize it, going for controversy. We knew we couldn't bring our POWs home, but we were determined to improve their treatment."

In 1971 Carole and three other wives went on an international tour to put pressure on North Vietnam. Worldwide publicity was the most powerful weapon wielded by the members of the POW/MIA organization. This small band of determined women met with Pope Paul IV at the Vatican. They sat with Indira Gandhi. They went to England, France, Norway, Egypt, Italy, Germany, and finally to the Soviet Union, where they were apprehended and locked in an airport hotel until they were deported.

"I probably should have been scared," Carole says with a laugh. "I look back at it now, shake my head, and say, 'Gosh, I was so naïve!'"

She later attended the Paris Peace Talks with a delegation of wives to confront the North Vietnamese in public.

Back in America Carole continued to be passionate, relentless, and creative. She was part of the original discussion that led to the creation of the POW/MIA bracelet campaign. More than five million people—men, women, students, and children—wore the names of all the American POWs and MIAs. "They helped keep this topic visible and widespread," she said.

Carole saw the benefits of living in Southern California and went full speed ahead to leverage the names and support of celebrities. She recruited actors, politicians, and performers. When her son Todd was three years old, he enchanted California Governor Ronald Reagan when, during a press conference publicizing the POW/MIA cause, the boy toddled over to the governor. With the press watching, Todd said, "I have to go to the bathroom!" Unfazed, Mr. Reagan took him by the hand, led him into his office, and pointed him to his private restroom.

When they returned to the main room the boy tugged on Reagan's pant leg and asked,

When they returned to the main room the boy tugged on Reagan's pant leg and asked, "Will you help bring my daddy home?"

"Will you help bring my daddy home?"

Johnny Cash also supported the League's efforts, as did John Wayne, when Carole gave him her husband's POW/MIA bracelet, which he wore for many years. They became friends, with the Duke sending gifts and letters regularly to her son, often ending the notes: "Give 'em hell, Todd!"

The wives ascended the ladders of political power, and at one point they met with Secretary Henry Kissinger monthly. Carole was one the League leaders who met in the Oval Office with President Nixon and Kissinger.

"We stated our case both rationally and emotionally. I think they were surprised that we weren't a bunch of hysterical women. We were very professional, and without saying these exact words we communicated to them that we were going to make a lot of noise, and that they were either with us or against us. We were so happy when the new administration saw things our way. In December 1969 we held a press conference with Mr. Nixon in the White House, during which he announced a more aggressive approach to dealing with North Vietnam. This further opened up the government's acknowledgment of the issue. It was an important step in the right direction, but the wheels of politics turn slowly, and the war would drag on for three more years."

THE WAR ENDS

Steve was officially MIA for six years. Carole waited. She waited patiently and quietly for two of those years. And then very actively and *loudly* for four!

Through all those years Carole wrote to Steve every night. "The letters and packages I sent were all returned to me. I never got used to the uncertainty, but I never gave up hope." Early in 1973 the Paris Peace Accords were signed, the war ended, and the surviving POWs were returned home. Steve's fate was still in limbo, as he was still listed as MIA.

"For two months in February-March 1973, I watched the TV news shows as the POWs were released and returned to their families. I cried every time a group came home, and Steve did not walk off a plane. Friends, family, and faith got me through this excruciating time."

Then in May, Carole attended the massive reception and dinner for returned POWs and wives of MIAs at the White House hosted by President Nixon. At the event she met Sergeant Frank Cius, who was a crew member aboard her husband's helicopter, who had also been listed as MIA. He told her that Steve was injured in the crash, that he was involved in a fierce firefight with enemy soldiers, and that he very much doubted that her husband could have survived.

Having some closure was a mixed blessing, and Carole was somewhat lost. Shortly after the White House gala, H. Ross Perot, W. W. Clements, and about 20 other business leaders organized a two-day celebration called Dallas Salutes to honor the returned POWs and other veterans. There was a ticker tape parade, a large dinner dance, and a rally at the Cotton Bowl attended by more than 30,000 people. The all-star entertainment included Bob Hope and Tony Orlando and Dawn, whose new song "Tie a Yellow Ribbon" had just become number one on the US music charts *and* a symbol for the POW/MIA movement.

> **"When the song 'Tie a Yellow Ribbon' was playing, I got very emotional. It was hard adjusting to the fact that Steve wasn't coming home."**

Carole was invited but, "I was so downhearted that I didn't think I could handle a huge, upbeat celebration. Especially since *the event was scheduled for the same date that Steve had been shot down!* The irony of it was crushing. That pretty much sealed my decision. But then my mother motivated me out of my sadness. And I thank God she did! And so, I went."

THE COTTON BOWL

The chances that Carole Hanson would sit next to Navy fighter pilot Jim Hickerson at the Cotton Bowl were about one-in-fifteen thousand. "It was a God-thing!" Carole was escorted by a POW and casual acquaintance; Jim was escorting a female acquaintance.

"When the song 'Tie a Yellow Ribbon' was playing, I got very emotional. It was hard adjusting to the fact that Steve wasn't coming home."

Unbeknownst to Carole, Jim was in the midst of an unexpected emotional upheaval himself. He explains, "Immediately upon leaving Vietnam and landing in the Philippines I phoned my wife. After being separated for five years, anything could have happened, but I was looking forward to being the Best Husband Ever. But I did have the thought, 'If she doesn't cry when we talk, I'm in big trouble.' She didn't cry. We'd had a good marriage, but I understood that the waiting and the uncertainty could be truly unbearable for anyone. Yes, I was upset, but I have to admit that the positive high from regaining my freedom was much bigger than the negative low of losing my wife. Hey, I may have lost my *wife*, but I had regained my *life!*"

Back at the Cotton Bowl…Carole remembers that "Tears were running down my face. And Jim, who is a very soft-hearted soul, leaned over and just gave me a little kiss on my cheek."

Jim jokes, "That was the most expensive kiss I've ever given!"

Carole and Jim created a friendship of mutual support, as they shared the Vietnam experience of pain and uncertainty, albeit from the different lives of an MIA wife left behind in America, and a POW in the Hanoi prison camps.

HUSBAND NO. 2: JIM HICKERSON,[2] CAPTAIN, US NAVY A-7 CORSAIR II FIGHTER PILOT

Back at the Cotton Bowl Jim did a double take. "You're *the* Carole Hanson?" You see, Carole had become famous among the POWs for her 1972 interview on *60 Minutes*. Most of the POW wives interviewed on that program shared an attitude of, "I want my husband home in any way, under *any* circumstances." But proud Marine wife Carole Hanson said, "I want him to come home with his head held high and return with honor." Because most of the women chosen for that program displayed attitudes more aligned with the anti-war perspective, a recording of that interview was played over the camp radio for the POWs.

At a time when Jim was under great duress at the hands of his captors, Carole's statement about wanting them to come home with their heads held high was like a shot of adrenalin. It reminded him of the importance of embracing the mission to *return with honor* which the camps' POW leadership had long promulgated. This gave him great hope that there was this kind of feeling and support back home. "Who *is* this amazing woman?" wondered Jim and the guys throughout the prison camps.

Carole had struck a chord. The concept of honor is held in high esteem among professional military people. Carole was somewhat embarrassed by the thankful calls and letters from many of the guys after they returned home. "I'm just glad that I could help."

Jim smiles, "She's so modest! But she was so right. The men who survived the camps in the best shape were those who held honor to be one of their core values, along with love of country and faith in God."

HAPPY IN HAWAII

Jim's simple gesture of an empathetic kiss on the cheek showed understanding, connection, and support, and from that one act, a friendship developed. They talked often, shared their sorrows and their stories, and supported one another. And this quickly evolved into love…

"Jim's playful nature and his kindness toward my son Todd soon won my heart." They were married less than a year later, shortly after Steve's status was officially changed to Killed in Action (KIA).

Jim continues, "One of our biggest blessings was that Todd, at seven years old, was very excited to finally have a dad. And on top of that, he was as eager to have brothers and sisters as we were to make some! And so, we tried. Lord knows we tried!" (Carole gives him a friendly jab.) "But it just didn't 'take.' So, we decided to adopt. Well, the adoption agencies informed us that we were too old to adopt. "Too old?" We were in our early forties!

"But being resourceful and well-connected, we went through other channels. And we are so blessed that we did. We saved our first adopted child, little Jim, from abortion just 12 hours before the surgery was to take place. We got our second, Jenny, when she was five, and abandoned in a South Korean bus station. At that time the only English words she knew were 'Ronald Reagan,' 'Donald Duck' and 'Popeye.'"

Carole believes that a big part of their long and happy marriage is that they remember the little things. "We start every day with a good-morning kiss. We still hold hands and touch like we did when we first fell in love.

I appreciate Jim's willingness to always help me, no matter what the task is. He never forgets important dates. And I have more meaningful jewelry than any girl deserves. This is the only area where Jim *doesn't* listen to me! I tell him, 'I can't wear it all, Honey!' but he always finds another piece of jewelry that is beautiful *and* meaningful."

Jim observes that they love the same things, have the same outlook on politics and religion, and love doing things together. "We travel together nearly always, whether it's for meetings or pleasure. I have no need to escape to poker nights or fishing trips with the guys, and Carole doesn't need a 'night out with the girls.' We simply enjoy doing most things together, even going to the store."

"Actually I don't let Jim go by himself because he finds lots of 'goodies' that we don't need!"

"One of my favorite memories is that, during our first Christmas together, Carole decorated my Christmas tree with 100 yellow ribbons!"

"While we enjoy an occasional grand gesture, our greatest joy is our family. We are blessed with children who keep in close contact with us. Even though we live in Hawaii and the three of them live in three of the four corners of mainland America, we have contact with each other more than many families that live in the same city!"

Thinking back to the war Carole adds, "Even though our lives have been filled with tears and fears, the love and joys more than outweigh the negatives. I feel so blessed! I've had two wonderful marriages. I have three incredible children plus seven beautiful grandchildren."

Jim notes, "I'm just a man who feels blessed to be alive every day. I'm just a man of faith. And I am so thankful to have Carole as my Commander-in-Chief!"

The two 80-something lovebirds smile at each other.

LOVE LESSONS

AUTHENTICITY

Being your authentic, genuine self is essential for creating and maintaining a strong relationship. "While dating neither of us tried to impress the other. We just shared ourselves and got to know each other," Jim observes.

CHEMISTRY

Great couples have great chemistry. It's hard to define it, but you know it when you feel it. It's a reflection of many connections that reside at a deep level, a place where core values, trust and personalities click, and result in an effortless bond.

EMPATHY & SPONTANEITY

If you can feel what another person is feeling, and you combine that with being courageous enough to act on it, magic can happen. When Jim kissed Carole at the Cotton Bowl, he had no hidden agenda, he was simply communicating, "I understand."

Carole & Steve Hanson

Carole & Jim Hickerson

1 Capt Stephen P. (Steve) Hanson USMC, CH-46A Sea Knight Helicopter, KIA 3-JUN-67
2 LCDR James M. (Jim) Hickerson USN, A-7 Corsair II, POW 22-DEC-67 – 14-MAR-73, Retired CAPT USN (0-6)

THE LEAGUE OF WIVES & FAMILIES

As the years dragged on with almost no information about their men, the POW/MIA wives and families became impatient, then angry, and then motivated to take action. They felt that their men were being put on the back burner, with no concern at all being expressed by our government that the North Vietnamese were violating the Geneva Conventions, which require humane treatment of POWs and release of the names of captives. Most families were living in a horrible limbo, not knowing if their husband, son, or friend were dead or alive.

In late 1968, Sybil Stockdale, the wife of Commander James Bond Stockdale, the senior Naval POW, began to express her concerns. She began to connect with other POW/MIA wives in Southern California. Also, she reached out to her military contacts in D.C. and questioned the policy of keeping quiet. Soon, she connected with wives in other Naval aviation communities across the country.

It began as the League of Wives, but very soon families of POW/MIAs joined in. Their efforts grew rapidly, and in June 1970 the organization was chartered as the National League of Families of American Prisoners and Missing in Southeast Asia. The League was a humanitarian cause and not in any way funded by the government. With the strong efforts by the League and many organizations supporting their cause, they were able to bring great pressure on Hanoi through millions of letters sent to Hanoi and their envoys at the Paris negotiations. (For more, see the books *League of Wives* by Heath Lee.)

Thirteen of the wives in this book were involved with the League, and two of them were National Chairpersons. And three of the POWs here were not married but had family members involved in the League.

Ultimately, this amazing organization, mostly women, changed the policies of two nations: the US Government (got them to speak up and pressure our communist captors) and the North Vietnam Communists (got them to stop the torture and improve our treatment). Their courageous leadership and teamwork changed our lives forever.

7 | GOD IS OUR PILOT

THE STORY OF
Ralph & Bobbi Gaither

By Bobbi & Ralph Gaither
As told by Bobbi with some excerpts from Ralph's book *With God in a P.O.W. Camp*

Bobbi

To start, I wore Ralph's[1] POW/MIA bracelet for several years before we met. When we finally *did* meet it was on a blind date! I had no idea that it would be him. Shortly after he regained his freedom, our date was secretly arranged by his cousin Judy (my hair stylist) and his sister Shirley. During that date this handsome, rugged fighter pilot recited poetry to me. "Is this guy for real?" I wondered. Yes, he was. Eighty days later we married. Forty-six years after that—during which we had the happiest marriage I could have imagined—Ralph passed away in 2019.

Here is one of many poems Ralph composed during his imprisonment in North Vietnam:

Your Face

Like a new day's dawning
Your face comes to my mind;
With the fresh breeze of spring
And fall of summer's rain
Into this standing time.

Your face is like a light
Bursting through the dim fog

Giving this lost man sight
Through these lonely nights
To Freedom, home and God.

Whatever fate may be,
I face it without fear;
For in this tempest sea
Shines the dream to be free,
And meet with you, my dear.

This love poem wasn't written for a specific woman. It expressed Ralph's yearning for a love partner, and the depth of his faith. I like to think he wrote this touching poem for me—years before we met!

I think that great couples are built on shared values and, often, on parallel experiences. Ralph and I both grew up in Miami but went to different schools. We both flew for a living—he as a fighter pilot and me as a stewardess (admittedly a much calmer career). We both grew up in loving families, in the Christian faith, and in a patriotic environment. Oh, and when we met, we both owned Corvettes: His was a silver, 1963 split window, and mine was a 1964 red hardtop convertible. How's that for being in sync with each other?!

But, for the first three decades of our lives, Ralph and I followed different paths. I married at 23, had a beautiful daughter, Nikki, and was divorced at 30. When Ralph was 23 and single, he was an Ensign in the Navy, and then, as a Naval Aviator, began his Vietnam tour in 1965, flying F-4B Phantom jets off the *USS Independence*. He was shot down by the North Vietnamese and spent 2,675 days—more than seven years—in captivity. As he was among the first captured and longest held, he was among the first to return home after the Paris Peace Accords were signed in January 1973.

[Lee's coauthor note (Lee was a POW cellmate of Ralph's.)]
I find it fascinating that the first line of Ralph Gaither's book, With God in a P.O.W. Camp, *is "When I left North Vietnam, I had not planned to write a book"—and yet his book was the very first written by any of the many members of our Vietnam POW brotherhood. Ralph had a burning desire to share his story—and his testimony—with the world, even*

though he was rather humble. (He didn't even include a biography in his book.) His first paragraph shown below clarified his motivation...

Ralph

...The other prisoners had so much more to tell. But I knew I had a story to tell about Christ. As a Baptist, I believe in personal witnessing for Christ. I had seen His love and felt His hand in many difficult times. I had come to know and understand God in a way that should be told to others so that they, too, might understand Him...I told myself, "Ralph, you have two of the greatest things in the world going for you. You have, first, the love of God, and He will never let you down. You have, second, the United States of America, with a President and a people who will never forget you or let you down."

Bobbi

When Ralph returned home from Vietnam in 1973 after more than seven horrid years, I was recently divorced, had a two-year-old daughter, and the last thing on my mind was meeting someone on a blind date! Exactly one month after Ralph regained his freedom, we met at his cousin Judy's in Miami and drove (in his Corvette) to Ft. Lauderdale. After a surprisingly fun and comfortable dinner, as we were driving home, Ralph reached over and held my hand. Outwardly I remained calm—but inside I jumped! It had been a long time since I had been on a date, and I wasn't expecting things to progress so quickly—and easily! We came to a stop light, we gazed at each other, he reached over—and kissed me!

While the kiss was a bit of a surprise, the big surprise was that, for the very first time ever, I felt sparks flying!

While the kiss was a bit of a surprise, the big surprise was that, for the very first time ever, I felt sparks flying! (I'd thought that only happened in the movies.) I was thrilled—and a little scared. But not too scared to willingly throw myself into a whirlwind of dating him!

It wasn't long until the deal was sealed when my daughter Nikki and I met Ralph's family in the Florida Keys for a weekend. His family embraced us. They were all warm and kind, and we felt like family right away. Nikki loved his parents. Ralph's mom, Frances, was a lovely lady and the strength of the family. I miss her chocolate pie but especially her warm smile and hugs.

Later that evening, after scuba diving together, Ralph and I took a walk in the moonlight. We sat under the palm trees and started talking about how fast our relationship was going. He reached over, tenderly brushed his fingers through my long blonde hair, and kissed me again. He asked me to marry him. I knew it was genuine and spontaneous because the ring he gave me was not a pre-planned classic diamond engagement ring; it was a nearby scuba gear rubber ring! I still have it today.

We decided not to tell anyone right away because we thought it was a bit early for them to accept it. After all, he had been imprisoned for more than seven years in North Vietnam, and I had only recently divorced after seven years. How could anyone be ready to marry after only a few weeks of knowing each other? You've heard the old saying, "You know when you know"? Well, it's true. Ralph and I connected on many deep levels—spiritual values, family focused, genuine, loving—not only on a romantic, infatuation level.

SNAPSHOTS OF LIFE AS A POW

Ralph

The years were very short. The days were longer. The minutes were even longer. The moments were longest. Time functioned in that inversely logarithmic manner. If a man could make the minute, he could make the year.

> **[Lee's coauthor note]**
> *One of Ralph's worst experiences was "The Hanoi March," in which 50 of the POWs were marched down the streets of Hanoi, through a frenzied crowd of tens of thousands of people...*[2]

...The North Vietnamese officer in charge ordered us to march with our heads down...but we would not. Guards grabbed our hair and jerked our heads down. We raised them up again...We were determined. We were Americans...Women and men hammered at our shoulders and bodies with their firsts, and hit us with rocks. The children kicked our legs and flayed at us with their fists as high as they could reach. Women removed their shoes and beat on our heads with the wooden heels. Men broke into our paths and spat into our faces.

> **[Lee's coauthor note]**
> *The prisoners were handcuffed together in pairs. They bled, stumbled, and fell many times during the harrowing hour-long walk…*

…We took turns supporting each other. Jim Bell [whose story is told elsewhere in this book] repeatedly said to me, and I to him, "Stand tall, you're an American." [At one point the two of them spoke aloud the entire 23rd Psalm.]

> **[Lee's coauthor note]**
> *The parade was filmed by the North Vietnamese and other international media. The spectacle was designed to generate worldwide sympathy for the suffering of the Vietnamese people. But their propaganda backfired, and instead generated sympathy for the suffering of the American POWs.*

A few days after my first Christmas in captivity I was taken in for *interrogation*. I had been in handcuffs for several days, and they told me that my handcuffs would be removed if I would give them a biography. I refused, and they kept me in handcuffs. They were always seeking information from us that they could use as propaganda, and we always resisted. I agonized over the decision to tell them the least little thing about myself. I felt I would be betraying my country, my God, my honor, and my fellow prisoners. But then I recalled that some of the guys had told them all kinds of wild things, such as that aircraft carriers have wheels so they can drive on dry land, and the North Vietnamese had believed the story. The lower-level soldiers running the prison camps were pretty naive, so I figured a fabricated story would be pretty easy to sell to them.

So finally, I decided to give them my biography. My father, I said, was a Big Foot Indian who belonged to the Foot-Washing Baptist Church of America. My grandfather was Chief Crock-a-gator who lived in the Happy Hunting Grounds and hunted alligators and mudfish for a living. My wingman, I continued, was Dave Brubeck; my briefing officer was Walter Winchell. The interrogator obviously was pleased with himself. During my three previous months as a prisoner, I had given only the stock regulation answers. Now here I was "spilling my guts." They still weren't exactly nice to me, but they sure were proud of making progress.

My captors removed the handcuffs, and I was especially grateful for many little things that everyone takes for granted. I could go to the bathroom in a normal manner. I could scratch when I itched. I could sleep on my back with my shoulders straight.

It being the Christmas season I began missing having a Christmas tree. The camp, what little we could see of it, was overgrown with vegetation, but we were not allowed to go anywhere near the growth; we were not allowed to bring a stick even the size of a match into our cells. Outside, we were not even allowed to make a bending motion as though we might pick up something from the ground. Nothing was allowed into our cells, and frequent searches guaranteed the barrenness.

I prayed. Then one afternoon after washing my dishes, I turned to take the one step back into my cell. I looked down, and on the threshold of my door was a tiny leaf blown by the wind. I picked it up with my toes and carried it inside. The door slammed behind me. I carefully took the leaf from between my toes and looked at it for a long time. I held it to my nose. The perfume of freedom raced up my nostrils and infused my mind with its power. I fondled the leaf. It was real. I held it in my hand. God had not forgotten me! I set the leaf on the little ledge by the window. Its greenness stood out in stark contrast to the dull, gray bars. Tears rolled down my cheeks. God had given me a Christmas tree.

Years later when our four-year-old grandson, Wyatt, heard this story he finger-painted a leaf for his Pop's Christmas gift. This cherished gift is framed and hanging in our living room."

BACK IN AMERICA

Bobbi

Returning to an American culture that had transformed radically between 1965 and 1973, Ralph was slow to adapt to some things. He had slept on concrete so long it was an adjustment sleeping on a comfortable bed. He was fascinated with the change in clothing styles, and he liked the miniskirts he had heard about from the new shoot-downs.

Ralph was not a stereotypical rugged, macho fighter pilot. I know it probably sounds overly romantic to say, but he was sincerely a very kind, calm, poised person. He was creative, sensitive, and attentive. He was a gentleman, and soft-spoken. God only knows how he retained all these qualities and was able to express them immediately after seven years of inhumane treatment. I'm certain that, literally, "God only knows" how he did this!

Ralph and I thanked God every day of our four decades as husband and wife.

Ralph and I thanked God every day of our four decades as husband and wife.

Ralph embraced fatherhood and loved his girls. They grew up learning to love poetry. He recited poetry for bedtime stories, played guitar and sang for them. It wasn't until they were much older that they were surprised to learn that their friends' fathers didn't sing and make up their own bedtime stories but read from books instead! Ralph adjusted easily to the advances that women in America had made in eight years, and he taught the girls how to use all the tools and machines in his wood shop. To this day they can still fix a leaky faucet, a toilet, change the oil filter in a car, and confidently tackle any mechanical challenge.

Ralph continued to serve in the Navy for 14 more years. His ongoing military career took us from the East to the West coast. He was a flight instructor at Miramar, California, in charge of training in Land Survival at North Island, and Water Survival in Pensacola, Florida.

Now let me tell you about Ralph and his "toys": planes, boats, cars and the many tools and heavy equipment necessary to keep everything running smoothly. He used to say, "If a man made it, I can fix it." And he was right! He was an artistic craftsman of many talents. Besides writing and doing artful calligraphy, he made beautiful furniture, hand-carved doors and many other things. My favorite is a baby cradle he made for our daughter Amy, who was born two years after we met. Decades later her children were lulled to sleep in that same cradle.

Yes, our life was an adventure! I never knew what he would do next. One day he bought a sunken sailboat for $500. Yes, sunken. He and his buddies scuba dived for hours to attach the mechanisms for raising the wreck. They raised it and towed it with *Gator* (his fishing boat). It sat in the canal behind our house for nearly a year. I'm surprised the neighbors didn't run us out of town from the smell of dead fish and seaweed. After he refurbished it, he sold it and made a small fortune!

Ralph loved flying. Over the years he rebuilt several VariEze airplanes. They were high-performance homebuilt aircraft that were invented shortly after his return from Vietnam. The "EZ" has been described as "a little airborne sports car" that was designed by the company's creators' desire to have their own little fighter plane. Nothing could have been more perfect for Ralph! He often buzzed the house when he flew locally. He especially got a kick out of flying over the Gulf when he knew his buddies were fishing. He would check their coordinates and tease them later about having discovered their secret fishing spots.

Once, when we were flying cross-country together, we had traveled through (what I thought were) dangerous clouds in dangerous and disorienting whiteout conditions. At first I was scared, but then I said to Ralph through his earphones, "If you can fly an F-4 in the middle of the night that is dark as the inside of a cow and land on a postage stamp in the middle of the ocean, you can get me down out of these clouds. He responded, "Sweetheart, I'm doing the best I can." I heard a click…then silence…He had turned off my mike.

When we were stationed in San Diego, Ralph and his POW buddy George Coker bought a 27-foot sailboat, the *Thursday's Child* (apropos, as the nursery rhyme states that "Thursday's child has far to go"). Now here's the crazy thing: Neither of them had ever been sailing! But they confidently announced, "We learned how to sail through the Tap Code while in prison!" George's wife, Pam, and I looked at each other and declared that when they go out—and if they make it back—we'll go the next time!

Our biggest challenge was in the fall of 2004, when Hurricane Ivan ravaged Pensacola, Florida and destroyed our home. We found our baby grand piano upside down in the front yard, our refrigerator across the street, and some splintered furniture down the road. The most heartbreaking thing is that we lost most of our family photos and baby books. But miraculously Ralph's toys survived unscathed! His airplane "Freedom" was safe in a hangar, his boat, the *Gator*, rode out the storm in the canal, and his heavy tools stayed put, although full of saltwater, in our demolished garage. At first we were in shock. But faith and love held us together. You've heard the saying that "God is my co-pilot." Well Ralph and I were able to set our egos aside, and we turned the piloting of our lives over to God.

We were happy with our supporting roles as co-pilots. I can't speak for anyone else, but this certainly worked wonderfully well for us! A small but profound miracle just for me was a small, silver cross that I had laid on a closet shelf. After the severe wind and rain had destroyed our house, I found that cross hanging on a nail on a still-standing section of wall. Seeing it gave me strength, and I knew we would get through this.

Our last 12 years together were challenging and painful, as Ralph suffered from Parkinson's and Lewy Body dementia. It was a long, sad descent for the war hero, adventurer, poet, father, and lover that I married. His final day was bittersweet and full of fond memories for me, as I sat by his side, and we were holding hands when he died peacefully in his sleep.

Here is a poem that Ralph wrote about a year before he was freed. I still marvel at how this man could maintain a positive mindset while being in prison. (I have italicized two lines that foretold *our* love story.)

I Thank Thee Lord

I thank Thee Lord for blessings big and small;
For spring's warm glow and songbird's welcome call;
For summer's lease with clouds that dance and rain;
For autumn's hue and winter's snow-white shawl.

I thank thee for the harvest rich with grain;
For tall green trees, a park with shadowed lane;
For rushing streams, for birds that love to fly;
My country's land, the mountains and the plain.

I thank thee for each sunset in the sky;
For sleepy nights, the bed in which I lie;

A life of truth and peace, a woman's love;
Her hand in mine until the day I die.
I thank Thee Lord for all these things above;
But most of all, I thank thee for thy love.

A good friend, Larry Zimmerman, set Ralph's poem to music, and arranged to have it performed. If you want to be inspired, please watch it on this YouTube link:

LOVE LESSONS

EXPRESSIVENESS

Love isn't really love until you take action on it. Communicating your deepest feelings is absolutely essential for creating a lifelong, loving relationship. Choose your own methods for expressing your love: gifts or activities that touch his/her heart; a simple touch; poetry (yours or someone else's); or just plain sitting and talking together.

GRATITUDE

If you can remember to be thankful for what you do have, you have a superpower that can get you through the worst of circumstances. (See the poem above.)

TIME TOGETHER

People who are living "happily ever after" marriages all share one characteristic: The happiest couples spend time together. Quality time. Fun time. Intimate time. Whether it's going on dates, or playing board games, or just sitting side by side while watching TV, it's those shared moments that are important.

Ralph & Bobbi Gaither

1   LTJG Ralph E. Gaither Jr. USN, F-4B Phantom, POW 17-OCT-65 – 12-FEB-73, Retired CDR USN (0-5), RIP 17-JUN-19

2   The 2022 book *The Hanoi March* by Gary Wayne Foster covers this march in greater detail.

THE ESCAPE, THE TORTURE & THE MIRACLE

In May of 1969, there was an escape at the Zoo camp in Hanoi. The two bold men were captured within 48 hours, and all hell broke loose. They were tortured severely—one of them to death—and the North Vietnamese immediately began a torture campaign in *all* the camps.

At the same time the communists were feeling increasing pressure from the US and from many previously neutral countries around the world. They were criticized for not following the Geneva Conventions, which require humane treatment of POWs. With the negative press gaining momentum, the communists wanted to counter that bad PR. Their response was as insane as it was cruel. Their *goal* was to get the POWs to sign statements saying that we had received "lenient and humane treatment." Their *strategy* was to *torture* us into signing those statements! When we confronted them with the fact that we could not sign a statement with a lie, they responded "No, not so. The truth is that which most benefits the *Party*." In other words, the end justifies the means. (A major difference between True Democracy and Communism.)

The heinous treatment continued until September of 1969 when their leader, Ho Chi Minh, died. In October when the new leaders took over, they stopped the torture for the most part. And life in the camps for our final three years became more live-and-let-live. We assumed this change was tied solely to Ho Chi Minh's death, because we had no awareness of the National League of POW/MIA Families and their powerful impact. But their efforts seriously rattled the communists, which led to our improved living conditions. This allowed us to strengthen our physical, mental, and emotional selves—and this helped us to not only return home, but to *return with honor*.

8 | LOVE CONQUERS ALL–TWICE

THE STORY OF
Gene[1] & Rae Smith—then Gene & Lynn

I didn't *choose* to stop smoking on October 25, 1967. I was floating three thousand feet above the ground, dangling from my parachute when I remembered that I had a pack of Salems in my flight suit, so I lit one up. My F-105 Thunderchief fighter jet had just been blown out of the sky by flak from the North Vietnamese. I looked down and saw what seemed like 5,000 people running toward me. One of them had an AK-47 and he ripped a burst through me. Two bullets came through my left thigh and out the other side. It didn't hit the femoral artery, didn't hit the bone, and didn't come up through my groin. So, I guess I was lucky—but my first reaction was, "Hey, that SOB just *shot* me!"

What followed was five-and-a-half years that included torture, deprivation, isolation from my family, the loss of my freedom, and lack of medical care for my badly wounded legs. I got one shot of penicillin, and that was it. Yes, being a POW was every bit as bad as the stories you've heard…Hung from the ceiling, somebody beating the hell out of you. Making you sit on a low stool for seemingly endless days and nights trying to get you to make a confession or something. All that stuff.

But let me back up 63 years, to the beginning of my two love stories!

A WHIRLWIND ROMANCE

I was a groomsman for a buddy—my aircrew training classmate—Larry Tibbets. At the wedding rehearsal I was awestruck by one of the bridesmaids, an absolutely stunning, beautiful brunette in a red dress. Her escort was a friend and pilot Larry Griffin. I turned to him and said, "That one's *mine*." (That might sound a little aggressive and egotistical, but fighter pilots tended to talk like that with each other in a friendly way in those times back in 1958.) I really did feel a connection that went deeper than just looks. I was happily single, and as I said to my buddies, "I'm interested in finding some quality female companionship."

Unfortunately, I had been assigned to escort one of the *other* gals. But, during the reception I made my way over to Rae, and we spent the rest of the evening together. I guess you could say we hit it off. The next day I drove her from Waco to Dallas, Texas, which wasn't *exactly* "on the way" to my home in Tunica, Mississippi, but the detour was worth it! Rae shared an apartment with three other Braniff stewardesses. I got to sleep on the couch that night…while all four gorgeous girls walked around in their nightgowns. That's what I call cruel and unusual punishment!

I soon had several weeks of leave and was headed back to northwestern Mississippi to visit my parents. I invited Rae to visit me if she had any free time, and if Braniff flew into Memphis. She said, "In two days I've got three days off, and yes!" She flew into Memphis, I picked her up, and we had a fabulous dinner and dance evening. Then, we drove back to Tunica and headed to my parents' home where I was staying.

We got home about one o'clock in the morning. We slipped into the house, being very quiet so we wouldn't wake my parents. Rae tiptoed into my bedroom to say goodnight. Yes, just to say goodnight. (But I couldn't help noticing that her nightgown was quite short!) Suddenly, here comes Dad in his shorts and an old undershirt—being the bashful individual that he was. Ha! And a minute later here comes Mother to join us.

And that's how Rae met my parents. They loved her instantly!

Over the next few months, we fell in love. We saw each other rarely, but we sure talked a *lot*. I called her from a pay phone in the Officers Club, and we talked till my

It soon dawned on me that I loved her and wanted to marry her. I proposed over the phone, and she said, "Yes!"

change ran out. She visited me at the base and got a small taste of my military life.

It soon dawned on me that I loved her and wanted to marry her. I proposed over the phone, and she said, "Yes!"

When I called to tell my mother we were getting married, she said, "You *can't* marry her."

"Why? You guys love her!"

"Yes, but it would be a mixed marriage! She's Catholic and you're Presbyterian."

(Remember, this was down South back in 1958. Quite a different world!)

Believing with all my heart that love conquers all, I replied, "That doesn't matter. I'm going to marry her. We'd love to have y'all celebrate with us."

I give my parents credit for overcoming their reservations. They joined us, and they loved her all the more. So, Rae and I met in June, we married five months later in November, and 11 months later our first child, Kelly Ann, was born in October. I guess we were in a hurry to get on with living life to its fullest!

And that was the beginning of our journey of love that would last for 45 years, one month and one day. (But who's counting? *I* am! And I thank God for every day of it.)

SNAPSHOTS OF A NEWLYWED COUPLE

Shortly after we were married, I discovered that Rae didn't have a driver's license. I was absolutely floored! She had occasionally driven one of her Dallas roommate's cars…and was stopped a couple times—but talked her way out of getting a ticket. (I guess there is great power in being both beautiful *and* quick on your feet! I'm proud to say that I saved her from a life of crime and illegal activities by helping her get her license!)

Rae and I lived in a remote little house in Oscoda, Michigan, where previously my buddy Larry and I had lived for a while. He and I loved to hunt, and we had a freezer full of squirrels we had killed in the woods around us.

One day I suggested that we invite Larry over for dinner.

"Hey, let's cook up those squirrels!" I said.

"How do you cook squirrels?"

"Just like fried chicken."

"How do you cook fried chicken?"

Uh-oh, I thought. But we worked it out. And Rae became quite an accomplished cook!

Throughout our marriage Rae was 100% supportive of me and my military career. Through dozens of moves, and caring for our three kids, she stayed positive. Of course, we had our "moments"—but we never had major disagreements or heated arguments. During my years as a POW, she handled our finances brilliantly, and she cared for our kids lovingly. Yes, it was hard on her. She once said, "Even though every day has 24 hours, some of them are longer than others." That insight is also a good description of my years in captivity.

THE LIGHT AT THE END OF THE TUNNEL

Curiously, I was shot down on my daughter Kelly's eighth birthday. And coincidentally, I was shot down in 1967…and I was in captivity for 1,967 days. I don't know if this *means* anything, but I find it fascinating.

Thanks to the intense pressure brought to bear on the North Vietnam government by the National League of POW/MIA Families (called the League of Wives by some), plus a change of leadership in the North Vietnam government, conditions in the POW camps improved greatly during our last two or three years of captivity. The torture stopped, the food improved, and best of all we were moved into larger rooms that held around 50 of us. Yes, it was crowded, and there was zero privacy, but we loved it because we could communicate freely and enjoy each other's company. We discovered so much talent and knowledge among us that we held classes in everything from mathematics to poetry to Spanish, and French, and we held church services and stage performances.

[Lee's coauthor note: Here's an excerpt about Gene from my book *Leading with Honor*.]

"Gene Smith treated us to an innovatively orchestrated rendition of the movie Grand Prix. *(Gene knew it scene-by-scene and line-by-line!) Just prior to deployment several of us had given this movie "two thumbs up" for its beautiful women and fast cars with powerful engines that roared around the track in first-of-its-kind surround-sound realism. Gene secretly recruited and stationed men around the room to imitate the movie's sound effects. The real movie opened with a screenful of race car engine tachometers revving up in sync with room-shaking roars coming from the surround sound. For a similar impact, Gene told us to close our eyes and as he described those tachs on the screen, he signaled for his sound effects. The room came alive with the surround-sound roar of engines. It was an unforgettable moment. The performance was a big hit with everyone—everyone except the guards."*

FREE AT LAST!

I regained my freedom on Wednesday, March 14, 1973. Our reception at Clark Air Base in the Philippines was amazing! Thousands of people lined the streets from the landing strip to the hospital. Minutes after I arrived in my room I heard a tapping on the wall. I smiled broadly. The guy in the next room was using our secret Tap Code to say, "Hey Gene, want a drink?"

I tapped back, "Sure where's the bar?"

"My room." A buddy of his had sneaked a bottle of Jack Daniel's into his room.

So, I walked over and had a drink with former F4 pilot Red Wilson—within an hour of being back! Now *that's* what I call a taste of freedom!

I don't remember exactly what Rae and I said during our first phone call in five-and-a-half years, but I *do* remember the feeling of unconditional love in Rae's voice. Our oldest daughter, 13-year-old Kelly, came on and said, *"Buenos días, Papa, cómo estás?"* She memorized this after hearing Rae say that I had learned some Spanish at the "Hanoi University." Our 11-year-old son, Rick, came on and said, "I learned to play golf—and I'm ready to beat you!" I was one proud father! It brought tears to my eyes when they told me that they had set a place for me at the dining room table during the entire time of my imprisonment.

I had a curious and humorous experience before we left the hospital at Clark Air Base in the Philippines when my military handler, Armstrong, took me shopping for civilian clothes. They were the wildest things I'd ever seen! Bright colors and paisley patterns and bell bottom pants? "Are you *sure* this is what guys are wearing?" "Yes," he smiled patiently, "If you don't wear these you'll stand out!" It took some getting used to, but *anything* was better than the prison pajamas I'd worn for years!

When our group finally landed in America, Rae and the kids ran toward me as I ran toward them. As Rae hugged me, and the kids swarmed around us, I thought, "I feel like my life is beginning again."

My most delightful discovery was that Rae and I remembered how to make love! (I think that's all the detail you need!)

A surprising and funny thing happened when I returned home and shooed our little poodle, Andre, off "his" spot on our bed. "You get off there, and out of the bedroom! I'm home now!" As I backed him down the hall, he growled at me the whole way.

TIME TO PUT FAMILY FIRST—A WISE DECISION

During my first three years back in America I explored several career paths in the Air Force, and in 1976 I was on the War College list, which thrilled me—until I thought about uprooting my kids, all of whom were in high school; and until I realized how much time I would have to spend away from them and Rae. Finally, I chose family over flying. We settled back in Mississippi and built a house on a new golf course. I soon became the general manager of the Golden Triangle Airport near Columbus, Mississippi. Being close to Columbus AFB made it easy for me to stay involved with the Air Force Association, and I eventually became National President and Chairman of the Board.

TWO WIVES AND THE IMPORTANCE OF CHOCOLATE CHIP COOKIES

Rae and I were great friends as well as husband and wife, and the decades slid by happily until—to make a long story short—in August 2002 Rae discovered that she had a tumor on her kidney. It was renal cell carcinoma that had metastasized. We were all in shock and very sad, but Rae's upbeat personality was undaunted. She said, "God's got this in His hands." Now *that's* faith. Rae passed away just over a year later and for sure she was in His hands.

Early in our marriage I was surprised when she instructed me, "Whatever happens to me, I want you to be happy. So, if I die first, I want you to get remarried. And if you *don't*, I'll come back and haunt you!"

Being the good soldier that I am, I always follow orders—but it took me awhile.

After Rae's funeral my daughters came home to help me pack up her clothes. We all cried, but it was cathartic. They understood that I just didn't want to go in that closet and see her clothes, knowing she was not here anymore. Later, they were greatly amused that I needed some help learning to live solo. (I *did* know how to use the dishwasher, but I *didn't* know how to operate the clothes washing machine.) Emotionally I felt a gaping hole in my life. Several times a day it would hit me very hard that Rae was never going to be back. I would let myself grieve for about half an hour and then I would say, "Gene, that's enough. Rae wouldn't want you to do this."

Sometimes I would be driving somewhere and be so overcome with grief I would have to pull off to the side of the road until the feelings passed.

Sometimes I would be driving somewhere and be so overcome with grief I would have to pull off to the side of the road until the feelings passed.

I kept myself distracted by playing golf, going fishing, and visiting my son Rick and his family in Phoenix. Then I returned home and kept busy with church activities. I was an elder in our Presbyterian church and a bass in the choir.

I had some very helpful talks with our minister, and I prayed a lot. At one point I said to him, "I feel that I'm close to being open to dating." His wise response was, "This is *your* timetable and *God's*, nobody else's."

Soon after that I came home from choir practice on a Thursday night to find a message on my answering machine. The next day I listened to it. It was from Gail Glenn, the wife of a hunting buddy. She said, "I have a tennis friend who lost her husband about a year ago, and she finally gave me permission to give you her phone number. I want you to call her and ask her to dinner!"

At first, I thought I would call her the next week. Later that evening I was about to make dinner, and I was sticking with my "No Drinking While Home Alone Rule." (I didn't have a problem, but I thought, "Why fall into bad habits?") And I thought, "What the heck, I think I'll call her!"

I really had no idea of what to say. The beginning was somewhat awkward, as we struggled to make a connection. But then we discovered that we had grown up just *35 miles* apart! (Me in Tunica, and her in Clarksdale, Mississippi!) As we played the "Who do you know?" game, we discovered many people we knew in common. Also, we both attended Presbyterian churches, and we had the same values and positive outlook on life. We talked for a *long* time. I asked her out to dinner for the next week, and she said, "Yes." When I hung up the phone, I could feel joy coming back into my life. I celebrated with a Jack Daniels. (Hey, they're my rules so I can break them!) Then I asked myself, "Why wait until next week?" So I picked up the phone, called Lynn back, and asked, "How about dinner tomorrow night?" She said, "Yes!" We clicked, and we've never looked back.

I met Lynn in March and we married seven months later in October. It was *also* seven months between my meeting Rae and marrying *her*. Cosmic coincidence? I think not! God had put Lynn into my life pretty quickly. This seven-month period was fairy tale–like. We had instant chemistry. Another good sign was when my 12-year-old grandson Tyler exclaimed, "Pop, you *have* to keep her! Miss Lynn's Famous Chocolate Chip Cookies are the *best*!"

At one point I said to Lynn, "If you really want to get to know me, you need to attend one of our annual POW Reunions." She accompanied me, and she clicked with my fellow POWs instantly. Lynn has the wonderful ability to connect with people she's just met. Afterward I said, "She has more POW friends than I do!"

Lynn and I have a lot in common. We both like popular music from the 1950s and 60s; I like country and western. (Lynn stops at Willie Nelson, but I don't hold that against her!) We often sit on the porch together, listening to music (with a glass of wine, of course). We both love to travel. We have three couples that we often travel with. We guys refer to ourselves as "The Traveling Rednecks." (Our wives aren't crazy about that—but hey, a guy's gotta draw the line somewhere!)

We're both very demonstrative, and I tell Lynn that I love her at least once a day, and she does the same. A quirky little thing we share is that neither of us ever remembers our anniversary. On one occasion Lynn's daughter Erin called us and asked, "What are you doing for your anniversary tonight?" We looked at each other and said, "Did you know it was our anniversary?" This has become a source of humor for three generations of Smiths! Lynn and I keep our love alive every day, so one particular date just doesn't stand out for us. We have our wedding invitation framed, and we have photos of our families all over our home. We are very aware of how blessed we are with our blended family. We are very close to each other's families and their kids.

Back when we were dating, I remember overhearing Lynn say, "If I get married again, he has to make me laugh." Well, I'm no comedian, but apparently I'm funny enough.

Lynn smiles, "We laugh a lot and we don't take anything for granted."

LOVE LESSONS

GRATITUDE
Have an attitude of gratitude, and don't take the good things for granted.

COMPANIONSHIP
In the strongest marriages the two are not only *lovers*, but they are *friends*, too. Camaraderie sustained the POWs for *years*, and it sustains marriages for *decades*.

HUMOR
Humor helped the POWs survive with their sanity intact. Humor can provide social attraction and strengthen a relationship. It helps friends *and* lovers survive and thrive.

Gene & Rae Smith

Gene & Lynn Smith

1   Maj Richard E. (Gene) Smith USAF, F-105 Thunderchief, POW 25-OCT-67 – 14-MAR-73, Lt Col (0-5)

IT'S TIME TO GO PUBLIC

In early 1969, it became clear that the incoming Nixon administration would stand beside the POW/MIA wives who were stepping up and speaking out. By March the new Secretary of Defense, Melvin Laird, began addressing the POW/MIA issue. President Nixon joined in and very shortly our government began working on initiatives to encourage the wives and families and to hold the North Vietnamese accountable for their non-compliance with the Geneva Conventions.

Within a few weeks Laird's staff was meeting with the POW/MIA wives to hear their concerns. And by late spring he and his team held a press conference to clarify a new DOD and State Department position regarding POW/MIA treatment.

There was a new game in town—to the delight of the wives and families, it was no longer unofficially "Keep Quiet." It was now officially called "Go Public."

Dr. Roger Shields was appointed Chairman of the DOD POW/MIA Task Group, and he immediately developed a strong bond with the National League of POW/MIA Families. His leadership contributed greatly to the success of the Go Public efforts to get awareness and support for our cause.

As the Paris Peace negotiations dragged along so did the war, but by 1972, US troop strength was down from 535,000 to just 25,000. At this point, the wives and families had a mounting concern that the war might end without their men coming home.

So, in 1972 when the negotiations stalled, Sybil Stockdale, Phyllis Galanti, and MIA wife Maureen Dunn met again with the president to reinforce the need for POW/MIA release to be one of the highest priorities in any negotiations.

Fortunately, President Nixon listened and agreed. When negotiations did not work, he launched the Christmas bombing campaign of 1972…and 11 days later the communists agreed to end the war and release the POWs.

9 | LOVE & DUTY

THE STORY OF
Ben[1] & Anne Purcell

By their daughter Joy Purcell

Even after Dad started slipping away due to Alzheimer's, when he could no longer engage in conversation nor remember anyone's name, at least once daily he would take my mom's hand, look her in the eyes and say, "I love you." Except for a few rare lucid flashes, those were the only words he could speak with absolute clarity to his dying day. When all else was lost, their love remained.

In 1992, 24 years after Dad was taken prisoner in Vietnam in 1968, he and Mom wrote a book titled *Love & Duty*. Notice that the word "Love" comes first. One year after that I traveled with Dad to Vietnam to film a documentary about our prisoners of war. I was scared, but because of our parents' example, I wasn't angry or hateful. All five of us children grew up without hate in our hearts.

I'm going to share some highlights from Mom's and Dad's amazing life together, from their wonderful book, and I'll chime in with some thoughts of my own.

SNAPSHOTS OF MY DAD...

My mom and dad had been dating nearly a year when, on Thanksgiving Day they visited the beautiful Tallulah Gorge in the edge of the Appalachian Mountains in North Georgia. Mom wrote, "There we stood on the legendary Lovers Leap at the precipice, overlooking the seven-hundred-foot-deep canyon. Well, neither of us had any intention of jumping, but I had no idea we were about to take a leap! Ben asked me to marry him, I immediately said, 'Yes!' and we married two months later!"

Dad was born on Valentine's Day. (Maybe that's why he was so romantic!)

And, 40 years to the day later, he was interrogated for the first time by the North Vietnamese (whom we called the V). He later commented, "From this point things went downhill fast." My dad's sense of humor was one of his qualities that kept him alive and sane. And that certainly was a struggle because, as the senior ranking Army officer in his prisoner of war camp, he was treated especially harshly. He was kept in solitary confinement for fifty-eight of his sixty-two months as a prisoner of war!

> **Dad was born on Valentine's Day. (Maybe that's why he was so romantic!)**

Even though his captors confiscated his wedding band, he made a new one—out of bamboo and thread. "I knew I had Anne and the children at home waiting for my return," he said. Despite the inevitable doubts, Dad never gave up hope that he'd return home.

During his five years of imprisonment, he wrote *thousands* of letters to Mom. In their book he wrote, "Every day I wrote a letter—not on paper, but in my heart: 'Anne, find solace and strength in the Lord and in my love. If you do that, we won't be apart. Not really.'" In my opinion Hallmark has *nothing* on my mom's husband!

LOVE AND HEARTACHE

My parents had more than their fair share of heartache. Just as she was about to give birth to their first child, David, Mom's father passed away. She couldn't travel to his funeral because of her pregnancy. A few years later, when the family lived in France, she gave birth to their fourth child, Clifford Alan. Then just 12 days later their *second* child, four-year-old Clarice Ann, died from severe rheumatoid arthritis. Mom had to stay in France to care for their new baby and their two other children…and missed a *second* family funeral while Dad again made a sad journey back to Georgia alone, this time with Clarice's body, for her funeral. Can you imagine the emotional struggle between joy and sadness of not being able to attend your father's and your daughter's funerals because you are giving birth to long-awaited sons? We could never have suspected that these two almost unreal crises were forerunners to the bad news that was yet to come.

I was two years old when Dad left for Vietnam. Obviously, I didn't know that he was such a genuinely patriotic American who not only had served in the Korean War 15 years earlier but had just *volunteered* for duty in Vietnam. The night before he left, Mom and Dad gathered us children around and we prayed, and then they explained that he was going on a very important job to protect America and that he would be away for one year and one month. None of us could have dreamed that we wouldn't see Dad for more than *five* years.

TALES FROM THE POW CAMPS

Dad was a senior Army officer in the northern district of South Vietnam for less than one year when the helicopter he was riding aboard was shot down. He endured torture, solitary confinement, and inadequate food for many years. But Dad persevered with the help of his brothers-in-arms, and through faith, fortitude, and humor.

Dad was tremendously courageous, endlessly creative, and relentlessly persevering.

He opened his portion of his and Mom's book *not* with his shoot-down, but with his thoughts about his duty as a captured soldier, which was to escape. During his five years as a POW (mostly in solitary confinement) he spent countless hours devising ways to escape. For his first attempt he decided to create a key to unlock his cell door. This involved analyzing the keyhole and the inside tumblers and creating his own tools from scraps of paper, aluminum from an empty toothpaste tube, pieces of wire he had removed from a broken neon light bulb, and the rib bones from the dog meat in his soup. On the eve of success, as he was making a quick adjustment to the key, a new guard who wasn't following the routine of his predecessor caught him.

Undaunted, during the subsequent years Dad managed to escape from the camp twice! His ingenuity knew no bounds. His woodworking hobby came in handy when he decided to drill hundreds of small holes in the lower wooden panel of his cell door. He created a drill from bits of wire. He devised a kind of "wood putty" from breadcrumbs, toothpaste and soot, (for hiding the holes). He created a chisel out of a nail. (The full story in wonderfully intricate detail is told in his and mom's book, *Love & Duty*.) To make a long and exciting story short…the first time he escaped, after being lost all night, he was finally offered a ride on the back of a bicycle by a young North Vietnamese man who was riding into Hanoi. Speaking French, Dad asked him to drop him off at the French Consulate, where he planned to request asylum. Instead, the fellow dropped him off at the police station. So close yet so far!

Of course, Dad was disappointed, but he was not demoralized—on the contrary!

Dad explained: "There was a benefit to my escape. For the first time since my capture, I felt alive! While I was planning and working on my escape, the hours were consumed, and the days didn't seem to drag as badly. I had regained much of my self-respect. That was vitally important to me because it had all but vanished when I surrendered after the helicopter crash. And I'll admit that it didn't hurt that it aggravated the dickens out of the V!"

How many people could bounce back that way?!

AND HERE'S A TIME WHEN GOD CAME THROUGH FOR MY DAD…

Ben

"After several years alone in the POW camps, I was struggling to stay positive. Yet, it always seemed that when times get tough, God always showed up in some way to remind me that I was not forgotten. One of the most amazing interventions happened when I was being confronted by my camp officer, Crisco. He snapped at me, 'You will *never* get out of here. We will charge you with crimes against the Vietnamese people and you will stay in our prison for the rest of your life!' He accused me of being like a Nazi war criminal, yelling, 'You are like Rudolph Hess—and we will keep you forever!'

"He stood up and pounded on the table, then leaned over so that his face was just inches from mine. He yelled, 'Do you think your government *cares* about you? Do you think they even *know* you are here? Look around you. What do you see? You see Vietnamese soldiers, that's who you see. The only other Americans here are helpless criminals just like you. If your government is so concerned, why isn't someone here to help you right now?'

"At that very moment came what seemed like a divine intervention. As if it had been a player waiting offstage for his cue, an F-4 Phantom jet flashed by overhead at near treetop level. Both afterburners were lit, yet for a second there was eerie silence, because it was supersonic—the jet was traveling faster than the speed of sound.

"And then the sound exploded over us. Ten times louder than the loudest roar of thunder, it broke windows and rattled the very walls of the prison! Crisco literally screamed in fear and surprise. All over the compound guards turned ashen-faced and dove for cover. I sat perfectly still and didn't say a word—but Crisco could read the expression on my face. 'Where are they now?' My expression said, 'They are *right here!*'

"When Crisco finally regained his composure, he stared at me, and then in a subdued voice said, 'Go—go back to your cell.' I laughed about that incident for over an hour. It sure felt good to laugh again. I hadn't realized how much I had missed laughing until that very moment."

SNAPSHOTS OF MY MOM...

My mom is the strongest, most patient woman on the planet! Here she is, talking about her amazing adventures in what was sometimes described as "The War of the Wives" and also about our lives after Dad's return home.

Anne

"The POW/MIA movement was growing in 1969. In December the children and I were asked to join 147 other dependents and relatives of Vietnam POWs and MIAs on a trip to Paris. Our goal was to confront the North Vietnamese delegation at the Paris Peace Talks about the fate of our husbands, sons, and fathers. The trip was sponsored by the organization United We Stand, and it was financed by billionaire Ross Perot, a true patriot who had taken a personal interest in the POW problem.

"Our chartered airplane was christened *The Spirit of Christmas*. It was with exactly that hope in our hearts that we arrived in Paris on Christmas Day—the second Christmas of Ben's imprisonment.

"When we arrived in Paris, however, the North Vietnamese delegation refused to meet with us. Eventually our persistence paid off, and the North Vietnamese agreed to meet with three representatives of our group. Our appeal was answered with a 25-minute lecture on North Vietnamese history and policy.

> **"Most touching were the faces of the children as they asked about their fathers. The world was watching, and North Vietnam had no choice but to respond."**

"Despite this treatment, we had at least forced them into giving us an audience. And this brought us to the world's stage in front of an international array of news people. And here, before the eyes of the entire world, were wives and children seeking word of their loved ones. Most touching were the faces of the children as they asked about their fathers. The world was watching, and North Vietnam had no choice but to respond. We had won a moral and publicity victory."

Joy

Unbelievably, despite a series of victories and increasing worldwide attention, it was more than three long years later before the war finally ended.

REUNITED

Anne

"I was exhilarated when the Paris Peace Accords were signed on January 27, 1973. But in the previous five years I had learned to be cautious. It was exactly two months later when I got the call. It was 2:30 a.m. The familiar voice was that of our Army Casualty Assistance Officer, Colonel Gluck. 'Anne, Ben has cleared North Vietnamese air space. He is on a plane to Clark Air Base.'

"At that moment, and not until that moment, I knew for sure Ben was on his way home! I went running through the house screaming repeatedly, 'Ben is free! He's coming home!' I shook the children until they were all awake, and we cried and hugged and danced all over the house.

"True to the scripture in James 1:2-5, God had given me strength to face my problems, helped me grow in patience, and led me through these years with his wisdom."

Joy
While Mom was ecstatic to have Dad back, it was sometimes a bumpy ride.

Anne
"Ben arrived back home in March and his reception was wonderful, and for a couple of weeks we were walking on clouds while trying to get our feet on the ground. Then we began to settle in. Ben had returned home from the war, and we just assumed that our lives would fall back into place—how naïve! In the euphoria of the moment none of us fully realized how difficult it would be to put our war-torn family back together again. Reunion was easy. Reconnecting was hard.

"Our family made some great memories that summer. We were out from under the clouds of war and uncertainty, and it was freeing. Still, an undercurrent of tension was building as we tried to weave Ben back into our lives. For almost six years the children had me all to themselves, and it was difficult now that my attention was divided between him and them.

"Many adjustments had to be made, and sometimes power struggles ensued. The children automatically came to me whenever they needed something. This caused Ben to feel left out, so I started sending them to him for permission and advice. They did not like it, but it was the best way I knew to start integrating their father back into their lives.

"I, too, had to adjust. For nearly six years I was the family's sole caretaker, decision maker, and disciplinarian. Now suddenly Ben was back in the picture, and he wanted to help. More precisely, he *needed* to help. He needed to reclaim his role as head of the household and, although part of me was eager for him to do so, another part was lost without all the responsibility. The things I once thought impossible had become part of my daily routine. It was tough stepping back, but I knew that I had to if we were to survive as a couple and family. Ben's return forced us to realign our home and the roles we played in it."

Joy

After the initial excitement and happiness, Mom slipped into depression. Neither Dad nor the rest of us realized this until Christmas. None of us had anticipated how difficult our first Christmas together in six years would be. It became clear that Mom was in crisis.

But then, right after we returned from Christmas with our families in Georgia, a miracle began. Our chaplain asked the two of them to share their experiences with a couples group at the chapel. Somewhat reluctantly they began preparing. Each evening Mom and Dad sat down and told each other their stories—of their current and past battles, doubts, fears, and their suffering.

Through that process of dialogue Mom's spirits rose quickly. And two months later, when it was time for them to tell their story, she was back to her old self. Those very vulnerable and often painful conversations, as they openly shared their feelings, helped them reconnect on a deeper level and brought healing to Mom.

Mom and Dad had private jokes and secret signals. While holding hands they would often squeeze hands three times in quick succession. It meant "I-love-you!" We siblings eventually discovered what they were doing—and we started doing it with Mom and Dad, too! They used creativity and humor to offset the pain and challenges of life, and Dad's talent for those two seemed unlimited at times.

After he retired Dad wanted to be his own boss, and for many years he ran a Christmas tree farm in our hometown of Clarkesville, Georgia. It was there, in 1992, that they coauthored their book, which was both a joy and a sorrow for them. Revisiting the bad memories helped bring them closure, and reliving the good memories enlivened them. To this day I am still amazed by their bravery of tackling such a challenge.

Ben

"My ability to play my part as well as I did was due to the strength I received from an abiding faith in God and my country, from the ever-present hope within my heart, and from the matchless love Anne and I had for each other and for the Lord. So then, it was these three: Faith, hope and love—but the greatest was love."

Joy

When Dad talked about love it came from a place deep inside him. His humbleness and his faith are an inspiration to me every day. His obituary described him as, "…a soldier for peace and a warrior for the Lord."

And this brings us full circle, many years later, and I'll end where I began…

Even after Dad started slipping away due to Alzheimer's, when he could no longer engage in conversation nor remember anyone's name, at least once daily he would take my mom's hand, look her in the eyes and say, "I love you." Except for a few rare lucid flashes, those were the only words he could speak with absolute clarity to his dying day. When all else was lost, their love remained.

LOVE LESSONS

TRUST

Trust in each other. Trust in God. Trust in America. Trust on many levels is necessary for intimacy to grow and relationships to thrive.

PERSEVERANCE

Perseverance in the face of uncertainty. Perseverance in the face of outrageous unfairness. Great marriages require perseverance through good times and bad, through the sorrows and the joys.

FORGIVENESS

Forgiving yourself (for weakness). Forgiving your partner (for not being perfect). Forgiving your enemy. Ben even forgave his captors! "I have never found it in my heart to hate Hooknose, Goldtooth, or Spit. We were all players upon a larger stage, and each of us had to act according to the roles written for us."

Ben & Anne Purcell

1 LTC Benjamin H. (Ben) Purcell Army, UH-1D Helicopter, POW 8-FEB-68 – 27-MAR-73,
   Retired Col (0-6), RIP 28-MAR-13

HUMOR IN THE CAMPS

Immediately after capture, humor was the farthest thing from our minds. We went from outright shock to survival mode, and it was usually several months before we had enough bandwidth and perspective to appreciate humor. But once it started it didn't take much. It was clear that our psyches were looking for an escape from stress.

Guys began telling funny stories from the past. Dry humor was a favorite. Then we began to look for funny ways to pull the chain of our captors. One fellow was tortured until he agreed to read political BS over the camp radio (the "Bitch Box"). While reading an article about their communist leader, Ho Chi Minh, he pronounced his name as "Horse Shit Mend." You could hear guys up and down the cell block in Little Vegas cackling. That was a huge morale booster during a dark era.

After we moved into the Hanoi Hilton big rooms in 1970, we turned to humor often. I'll never forget the night we celebrated Smitty Harris's sixth year as a POW (shoot-down dates were very important anniversaries). A group of us got together and planned a "This Is Your Life" show honoring him. One of his earlier cellmates in our room knew about Smitty's old girlfriend, "Birdlegs Bradley." We got one of our tall, skinny mates to dress up with a black t-shirt wrapped around his head like a scarf, and some socks stuffed under his prison shirt to give him a feminine busty chest. When the emcee told her story and Birdlegs stepped out, the crowd went wild.

Humor is a great survival mechanism, and we survived—and thrived—with our senses of humor intact. And, interestingly, humor also was a key player in many of our love stories.

10 | FOR GOD, COUNTRY & MAGGIE

THE STORY OF
Ken & Maggie Fisher

[Lee's coauthor note]

I knew Ken Fisher[1] because we were in the same squadron, but I had never flown with him until November 7, 1967, the day our F-4 Phantom jet blew up, and we had to take the nylon letdown into the hands of the enemy waiting below—literally for Ken, as they caught him as his feet hit the ground. I knew that he was an experienced and highly qualified pilot. What I did not know were the deep qualities of character and courage in this man who would be my cellmate for the next five years. For three of those years he was my SRO (Senior Ranking Officer)—in other words, my boss. Can you imagine living locked up 24/7 in the same tiny, crowded room for five years with your boss—or your spouse—or anyone for that matter?

In this book it's obvious how important good character, shared values, and a strong commitment are to a successful marriage. Likewise, the importance of respecting the other's differences as a person. But those same qualities and criteria were crucial to a strong companionship in the POW camps. I admired Ken's character and courage so much that living locked in the same cell with him all those years was never a problem; in fact, he had a profound positive influence on me. He was a great leader, teammate and friend then, and still is to this day.

Ken and Maggie had only been married a couple of years when we were captured. Several years after we regained our freedom, I ran into the two of them at a social event. Maggie smiled at me and said, "Now, Lee Ellis, I've lived with Ken longer than you have!"

Ken

Maggie and I met at the Officer's Club at Elmendorf Air Force Base in Anchorage, Alaska. I was a fighter pilot and Maggie was an Air Force nurse. She had just returned from a vacation in Hawaii, and when I first saw her, she was beautifully tanned and wearing a classy blue sheath dress. I can't say it was quite love at first sight, but she certainly caught my eye! We clicked right away, and after five months of dating, one night at our favorite bar, The Birdhouse, I said, "I think we should run off and get married!" Well, after she stopped laughing, she said—

Maggie

—"Ken, we're both 29, we're both officers in the Air Force, and we're stationed in Alaska. Just where did you plan to run off *to*?" I loved Ken's spontaneity. And I was soon to learn that he was also persistent!

A few months later I was reassigned to Tyndall Air Force Base in Florida. That's a long stretch—from the icy waters near the top of North America to the warm Gulf on the Florida Panhandle! I thought that might be the end of our relationship. But when Ken started "commuting" the 3,500 miles by snagging empty seats on southbound Air Force flights, I realized that he was serious about marriage!

Soon afterward I resigned my commission, and I was able to join Ken back at Elmendorf AFB on Christmas Eve. He said it was especially good to see me because he was wearing his last clean, ironed shirt. I've been telling people for years that the only reason he married me was because I could iron!

> **Ken and I kid around a lot, and we share a very active sense of humor.**

Ken and I kid around a lot, and we share a very active sense of humor.

Ken was born in the Bronx and grew up on Long Island, learning hard work at an early age, earning his spending money doing manual labor in construction. In high school he was the New York State wrestling champion in his weight class, and at the University of Pennsylvania he wrestled for two years, which earned him tuition. He was the fifth son in his family *and* the fifth son to see combat.

Maggie was a farm girl from Indiana. During her early childhood the family's home had no electricity or running water. Life was simple and hard, but as the Great Depression ended and World War II re-engaged the nation, there was a big need for farm products. Her father had been a banker, who decided to go into the cattle business. He raised and sold purebred Angus cattle. Maggie and her brother were active in the 4-H Club, showing their prize pigs and cows that they were raising on the farm. When she graduated high school (with only 36 students in her senior class) the only local career roles for women, other than homemaker, were as secretaries, teachers, and nurses.

Maggie

Of *course*, it was a difficult and stressful five-plus years when Ken was a POW. For a long time, I didn't even know if he was dead or alive. But I happened to have one advantage over most of the POW/MIA wives: First, growing up in the 1930's and 40's era on a farm, living a survival-focused life, I had learned many practical skills. Also, I'm sure it was helpful that I was already an Air Force officer when Ken and I met—so I knew from the inside what military life was like. Plus, I was a nurse. Most nurses face tragedy on a daily basis and have learned a lot about resilience; we have to keep bouncing back. So, I was already used to being independent.

Most of us had experienced our husbands' TDYs (Temporary Duty Assignments) or being on cruise for a few months to a year, but in those situations the big decisions, like moving to a new location or buying a car or a house, could be postponed until the soldier came home. But surviving as an MIA wife for several years meant making tough decisions and running the household all alone; I'm guessing that my somewhat harsh background made it a bit easier for me.

Ken

On the day I departed for Da Nang, Vietnam, our baby Susan was nine months old, and she said, "Dada" for the very first time *and* she took her first steps! It was a wonderful memory that helped sustain me as a POW.

Before I left, my mom requested that we have Susan baptized. Maggie wore that eye-catching blue sheath dress to the church. The image of Maggie and Susan at the baptism was burned into my brain, and that was one of my fondest memories that helped me survive those difficult years. My rocks were God, country, and Maggie. Before I left, she asked me what she should do if I went missing. I said, "Take good care of Susan and remind her of me."

Maggie

During the long years that Ken was away I learned to literally take life 24 hours at a time. Otherwise, I would have worried myself to death. What might Ken be going through right now? And what about *tomorrow*? I just plowed through each day, with my focus on the here-and-now. I remember clearly coming to this way of thinking. One night I was, as usual, awake long after midnight, and I worried obsessively about how I was going to pay for Susan's college education alone, if Ken didn't return. I suddenly realized that I should probably potty train her *first*—and take care of college when the time came!

Ken

One day my cellmate, Lee, and I were together, communicating with the guys in the next cell (by this time we had learned to talk through the walls using blankets as mufflers), when a message came through about the ongoing "peace talks" in Paris. It was reported that one of the American wives had shaken her fist in the face of a Vietnamese delegate! I said to Lee, "That sounds like something Maggie would do!" And guess what? Three years later when we returned home, I learned that it *was* Maggie! I was *so* proud of her!

Maggie

Believe it or not, I considered myself to be one of the lucky wives, as I got my first letter from my husband two years and five months after he had been shot down. I knew he was alive! I didn't have any details but...*I knew that he was alive.* That was more than many wives and families knew. We who were left behind were kept in the dark for *years*—until the wives and families got organized and took the lead to make the POW/MIA cause a national and international cause. I decided to get involved.

On Christmas Day, 1969, the great supporter of our troops, H. Ross Perot, chartered an airliner to take a planeload of us wives and our children to Paris to address the delegation from North Vietnam. Somehow, I was selected to be one of three of wives to speak for our group. To say it was a stressful meeting would be quite an understatement. I remember being lectured by four agitated communist men on how my husband was murdering their women and children.

Sure, I was intimidated—but I also knew that I would never get another chance to state our position, so I rudely interrupted the propaganda lecture, and spoke my mind.

> **Sure, I was intimidated—but I also knew that I would never get another chance to state our position, so I rudely interrupted the propaganda lecture, and spoke my mind.**

I guess my farm girl upbringing and my nursing training to "tell it like it is" took over. Actually, I don't remember it very clearly, but after the meeting one of the other wives told a reporter that I shook my fist in the man's face. I assumed that she remembered it more clearly than I did!

Back home I began traveling and speaking about the POW/MIA issue. I had never done anything like that before. But when you are really mad at the way things are managed in Washington, D.C., you find you have the energy and courage to take action! This was the first-time military wives had ever gotten organized—and had the education and the finances to travel and speak out. We all felt we had nothing to lose. Some of our husbands had been gone for six years or more. We were a force to be reckoned with, which soon became apparent to the media, the politicians, the country, and the world!

I managed to balance my public life and my private life. Raising a child by yourself is not an easy task. I tried to keep Ken in our lives every day. For a while Susan slept with her daddy's picture and wished he would come home soon. Several people had told her that if she was a good little girl God would answer her prayers. One day when she was five years old, she told me she had made a decision: Either she had no daddy or there was no God—because he hadn't come home after so many years. Shortly after that she overheard that her daddy was in prison—and she asked me what bad things he had done! A kindergartener should not have to struggle with dilemmas like these.

Susan Lopez, the former kindergartener

When the war finally ended, I was six. I remember Dad getting off the plane at Maxwell Air Force Base. I kissed and hugged him like crazy and said, "Now I have a daddy just like all the other kids!" I took him to school for show-and-tell for my second-grade class. But something was bothering me. I doubted that my mom and dad were really married! Why? Because Dad didn't have a wedding ring! They immediately went to a jewelry store in town and found an exact replica of the wedding ring that was taken from Dad by his captors. I was *very* satisfied that they were properly married.

Our transition back to a complete family was smooth and easy. Mom and Dad simply picked-up where they'd left off. To me it was just natural, but as I grew up, I came to realize just how deep and special their love was. Many returning veterans and their families had a lot of trauma and heartache. Mom and Dad are both strong personalities—"Type A's." Dad simply knows that he is always right. And Mom knows when he isn't and just lets it slide by. It's clear that they both trust and accept each other just the way they are. And that's why their love always shines through.

I have a vivid memory of the time Dad gave Mom an iron for Christmas. It sounds awful, but it was actually a creative, loving, and uplifting gesture. The electricity had gone out, dinner was ruined, and Mom was pregnant. She was very distraught. Dad added levity to the situation by wrapping all kinds of household items as Christmas gifts. I remember Dad dressing in a suit, and me in a pretty dress. It was actually quite magical!

Mom laughed when she read this piece I'm writing, and she added, "Getting my own iron wrapped as a Christmas gift was something I will never forget! *This* Christmas, things were a little better. I gave Ken half of a whole-house generator, and Ken gave me the other half. Now don't laugh! Gift-giving has never been a big thing in our family. Ken and I have the gift of each other and 56 years of memories, and that is a great blessing."

Ken

When I returned home Maggie and I simply picked up where we had left off. Our deep connection had never wavered. We were still young (sort of) and in love (definitely).

Maggie

We always agreed on money matters. Ken was home less than 24 hours when he asked me how much money I had saved. After living in a mobile home, driving a VW and sewing most of our clothes, I proudly answered, "$40,000!" He grinned at me and said, "I thought you would have at least $50,000." I quipped, "Next time stay at home and take care of your own finances!"

Ken

Like many of the younger married POWs, it didn't take long for nature to take its course...and Michael Fisher was born on February 16, 1974. That same day two other fellow POWs became fathers again, too! I guess that nine months earlier, May 12, was a busy and fun day for all of us! Our son Mike has turned out to be a great combination of his mom's and dad's strong traits of adventure and independence.

★ ★ ★ ★

Ken requalified for flying and continued with his successful Air Force career as a senior leader. After he retired from the Air War College faculty as a colonel, he transitioned into a new role as a financial planner, focusing mostly on helping military couples learn how to plan for their financial future and retirement. Maggie was always a highlight when speaking to the students at Air University in Montgomery, Alabama, where they lived until a year after Ken's retirement. They now have six grandchildren, some in high school and some in college.

Maggie and Ken both read a lot, they enjoy their Texas grandchildren and miss their Florida grandchildren, and Ken plays golf three times a week. And even though he is now 85, he is the senior champion of his local golf club, consistently shooting around 80. He's still as competitive as ever! Maggie is enjoying the great ladies who live on their street, and she visits their daughter, Susan, and her family frequently.

Maggie and Ken have been married 56 years, and except for Ken's little trip to Vietnam, they have been side-by-side the whole time. They agree that the ups far outweigh the downs.

LOVE LESSONS

ACCEPT AND RESPECT EACH OTHER'S PERSONALITY

Love often supersedes logic. Some couples are quite different, and they complement each other; and other couples are cut from the same cloth. There is no one "best" way for two people to live and love together. The strongest couples accept and respect each other's unique talents and style.

CELEBRATE AND APPRECIATE

Celebrate and appreciate *everything*, from the big to the small…from a grand homecoming on St. Patrick's Day after five years of imprisonment, to a used iron as a Christmas gift! The happiest couples don't focus *only* on the big and grand things—like birthdays and anniversaries—but also on the little, everyday things like watching a sunset together or just enjoying coffee.

FAITH AND PATIENCE

Strong couples have faith—faith in each other *and* in something bigger than themselves. This gives them the strength to have patience when the going gets tough.

Ken & Maggie Fisher

---

1   Capt Kenneth (Ken) Fisher USAF, F-4C Phantom, POW 7-NOV-67 – 14-MAR-73, Retired
    Col (0-6)

POW/MIA BRACELETS

Nearly five million people sported POW/MIA bracelets (including John Wayne, Ronald Reagan, and Sonny & Cher) between 1970 and 1973. They stood in solidarity with the ongoing tragedy of our downed warriors.

The idea for the bracelets was the brainstorm of two southern California college girls—Carol Bates Brown and Kay Hunter—as a way to remember POWs and MIAs in Southeast Asia. In late 1969, television personality Bob Dornan (who later was elected to the US Congress) introduced them and several other members of VIVA (Voices in Vital America) to three wives of missing pilots. One of those MIA ladies was Carole Hanson, wife of MIA Steve Hanson (his bracelet on the next page). We have captured her story in this book.

Dornan showed them a bracelet made by mountain people in Vietnam that he was wearing in honor of the POW/MIAs. This led to the idea to use bracelets as a way to garner public support for POW/MIA awareness, which was VIVA's mission. A local engraver designed the bracelet, and VIVA member Gloria Coppin's husband financed the first 1200 bracelets. They launched with great success, selling them at $2.50 each (raising approximately $12 million while also rousing public attention).

These bracelets played an important role in the daily awareness of the POW/MIA plight. On average, there were 1,500 people wearing a bracelet for each POW/MIA. Typically, people wore them constantly and prayed for their bracelet partner daily. Most were silver, but copper ones were also available. In the stories here, you will read of one young lady who wore a bracelet of a stranger, James Bailey. Yes, Suzanne Long learned from his mom that they called him "Bill." So, Suzy thought of, and prayed for, that stranger for many days and months—*Oh won't you come home Bill Bailey*. And one day he did, and it did not take long before she was his wife—Suzy Long Bailey, bearing his name and his children.

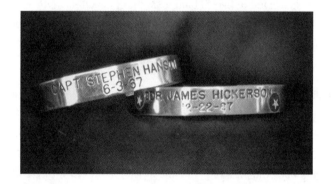

11 | DREAMS & SONGS & POEMS OF LOVE

THE STORY OF TWO MARRIAGES:
Dave Carey[1] & Karen—then Dave & Sandy

By Dave Carey

[Greg's coauthor note]
How long would you *wait for your boyfriend or girlfriend to return from a trip—a dangerous trip during which you didn't know if he or she was alive or dead? (Would you wait* five-and-a-half years?*)*

LOVE & MUSIC

The Mamas & the Papas' hit song "California Dreamin'" blasted from my 1964 white Pontiac Catalina convertible as I drove cross-country from Western Pennsylvania to Central California in the early summer of 1966. It was the perfect theme song for a 24-year-old newly minted Navy pilot who had just received his wings and was heading for his first fleet squadron assignment to fly the A-4 Skyhawk, the Navy's workhorse attack fighter.

For a young, single fighter pilot, meeting girls was a high priority—second only to flying! A few months after returning to the Naval Air Station at Lemoore, California, one of my roommates set me up on a blind date with a sorority sister of his fiancée. I was stoked! But after a lot of teasing and warnings from the guys that—and I'll say this more politely than *they* did—not all blind dates include *pretty* girls, I began having second thoughts.

Anxiety crept over me as I waited in the lobby of the sorority house to meet my blind date. And then a real "California dream" came walking down the staircase—very pretty and wearing a bright yellow dress. I was dumbstruck. I was smitten. I don't remember what we talked about, but we hit it off immediately. We talked like we had known each other for a long time. I quickly went from being smitten to being head-over-heels in love with this lovely coed named Karen Nelson.

Throughout 1966 and '67 The Supremes' great song, "You Can't Hurry Love," was a huge hit. But it was as if Karen and I never heard a word of it. We couldn't slow down. During the next five months, before I would be leaving for Vietnam, Karen and I were together every possible moment. The sometimes awkward "meeting the parents" was not a problem for us. Karen's folks lived nearby, and not only did we get along, but they also just sort of adopted me.

Fighter pilots need to be optimistic—as our work is extremely dangerous. Even though Karen and I never got "officially" engaged, we were both sure that we would get married in eight months, that's when I would return home at the end of my tour. Little did we know that the upcoming six months would bring the highest losses of the air war over North Vietnam.

VIETNAM

My first combat tour had been in August 1966, flying missions off the aircraft carrier *Oriskany*, near the coast of North Vietnam. Flying combat sorties was simultaneously challenging, over-the-top fun—and sometimes terrifying. That deployment was cut short when in October, a magnesium flare ignited a locker full of flares. The fire and smoke quickly killed 43 crew members, mostly pilots. It was a long and sad trip back home.

Now back on my next tour, on August 31st, 1967, the anti-aircraft artillery flack was thick, but the greatest threat was two surface-to-air (SAM) missiles, about the size of small telephone poles, which were heading directly at us. Missile one missed completely. Missile two flew between me and my flight lead. I maneuvered my plane wildly, trying to get away from that missile. I remember every detail of the next terrifying minutes. I can run it forward, backward, fast-motion, slow-motion, stop-action. I was upside down yanking hard on the stick when a huge explosion blew the tail off my plane. Forward motion stopped as though I had hit a brick wall. My multi-million-dollar fighter jet was inverted, shuddering and bucking like a rodeo bronco. Time seemed to slow down. Even though the aircraft was falling like a rock, the seconds seemed to pass like minutes.

Spinning through 4,000 feet, I ejected and parachuted into the center of a small village. I was captured immediately and taken to the Hanoi Hilton.

My first few months brought some of the worst treatment. At one point after an extreme torture session, I was in such physical and emotional pain that my mind couldn't think logically or remember much at all. Then a line came to me from my childhood memories. "The Lord is my shepherd." I regretted that I had not thought of it in years, yet it kept coming up—and it gave me comfort. Over the following few weeks, I remembered the entire psalm. And as it came back, my mind returned to normal.

Eventually the "in-processing" torture ended, POW life became more stable, and I had many hours and days in which to reflect on my life.

I had no idea what was happening with Karen, but I loved her deeply and thought of her constantly.

We guys had no idea how long we would be prisoners, but we all expected that *someday* we would return home. And I believed that Karen would be waiting for me. I did have one nagging concern—she had a lump in her breast shortly before we deployed. Fortunately, it was not cancerous, but that issue floated through my mind occasionally.

Most of us called our cells "rooms." We had roommates, not cellmates. That was our own bit of psychological warfare, which helped us keep a positive attitude. We held many kinds of competitions, both mental and physical. When the actual Olympics happened, we held our own Olympics. The record for push-ups was over 1,000, and for sit-ups over 4,000. Although we were skinny, many of us were in pretty good shape.

When I lived with a group of 20 men, it happened that only six of them were married. We came up with the idea that the married guys should provide the bachelors with a marriage counseling class. We argued that someday, should we get married, there was no need for us to make all the same mistakes that they had *already* made! The married gurus loved it. They would confer for hours and hours during the week, and on the appointed day the class would convene. The gurus would seat themselves as a panel at one end of the room, and we, the students, would sit at their feet. They taught us everything there is to know about women, from female anatomy to what makes them tick. (After several years of marriage, I realized that some of the "wise advice" from the gurus was actually bull!)

DREAMS & POEMS

Daydreaming about Karen was one of my favorite pastimes. That blind date and the memory of that beautiful girl in the yellow dress had a huge impact on me. Over time I composed several poems to describe my love for her.

Yellow Clad Dream

The night that we met, it rained, I recall
The Hi-Life, the movie, the oranges and all.
The places we'd been, the things we had seen
Paled in the mist round a yellow-clad dream.
Through the next few months, our love, how it grew
My world was aglow with, my darling, you.
Now times of duress and trouble and pain
My comfort comes from our love's sweet refrain.
You're strength when I'm weak, and joy when I'm sad
Courage against heartaches and problems I've had.
Your memory's with me, alone and afraid
Companion and refuge, never to fade.
Your love and your faith my guardian theme
Hope for the future, my yellow-clad dream.

In the prison cells I often reflected on our relationship; our short romance and what attracted me to feel this incredible love. Karen had a vivacious and outgoing personality. She was very comfortable with driving a conversation, yet she could adapt easily, becoming silent and listening intently. I had dated a lot of girls, some of whom were way too quiet, and some of whom couldn't shut up! Karen had a lot of inner confidence, and she was comfortable with herself. So, I found her personality and style to be a re-markable combination that was very attractive to me. During my years of imprisonment my memories of Karen brought joy to my heart and lifted my spirits…as I expressed in this poem from those dark dungeons far away.

Dreams of You

Now when I think of days gone by,
Memories that I hold dear,
Mount Diablo and sunny sky,
I thrilled to have you near.
That April day that scared us all,
How happy was the word,
Your booby made it through okay—
The story I have heard…
The night you told me you loved me,
You gave my heart its wings,
I made the long journey homeward,
You couldn't hear me sing!
The trip to Anchor Bay, the truck,
How well we knew the way,
The road, the wreck, the broken clutch,
Your company saved my day.
The day we sailed Oriskany,
The world to which I'm bound,
How glad to know you understood,
My world of speed and sound.
The little toy cars you sent me,
Spent your money to buy,
I've passed the days and months and years,
Always wondering "why?"
The breakfast coffee with a kiss,
Those things done just for me,
My words of thanks, inadequate,
How 'ere sincere they be.
Now when I think of days ahead,
My hopes, my dreams for two,

> The ones I think of most of all,
> Are those including you!

I had written several poems to Karen (including one in French, which I had learned at the "Hanoi Hilton University," and when I came home I had them framed. I gave them to her the night before our wedding, just six weeks after my release. (Truth be told, I had wanted to get married *immediately*, but Karen thought we should wait just a *little* while…so she could make sure I wasn't going to go—or be—crazy. I held it together and tried to act normal. She decided that I was normal—well, normal enough! We got married and then it was too late to change her mind.)

During my captivity I rearranged my life priorities. Previously I had wanted to fly off aircraft carriers for as long as I possibly could. But I realized that marrying Karen and having children was more important. I changed in other ways, too. Karen said that I was much more sensitive and understanding, more able to communicate my feelings, more thoughtful and more tolerant.

Karen was a genuine heroine in my eyes and those of my fellow POWs. As soon as we returned the word spread like wildfire: Karen had waited! The guys knew about Karen because I talked about her a lot during our years of imprisonment. We guys began planning, in elaborate detail, the wedding Karen and I would have when we were all released. The most elaborate ceremony was for a wedding in Hong Kong, complete with a rickshaw caravan. Our eventual wedding was, of course, nothing like any of our plans, but it was a great way to pass the time. The guys came to love her.

BATTLES AND TRANSITIONS

We spent the better part of 23 years in San Diego. I was stationed at Naval Air Station Miramar. I bounced between command of a couple of squadrons and the Air Wing staff. My last job in the Navy was as the Commanding Officer of the Naval Amphibious School on Coronado Island. Following that tour I decided that it was time for me to retire from the Navy.

I retired in January1986. Life continued to be great! We had two wonderful children, Jeff and Alyssa. I went into business for myself as a professional speaker, consultant, and trainer. Business began flourishing. And then, in

August 1992 Karen discovered a small lump in her right breast. It turned out to be cancer. The news hit us like a truck. The love of my life had cancer—and I was helpless (not something fighter pilots are used to feeling). Bravely she chose the most aggressive treatment she could find. A year later she was given a clean bill of health, and we began putting our lives back together. A year after that we discovered she had lung cancer. And then liver cancer. My Karen battled bravely but continued to deteriorate. In her last days she was in a deep coma. One day around noon I was reading aloud several scripture verses to which we had been clinging.

> The Lord is my shepherd, I shall not want,
> He makes me to lie down in green pastures,
> He leads me beside the still waters.
> He restores my soul and leads me into the paths
> of righteousness for His name's sake.
> Yea though I walk through the valley of the shadow of death,
> I will fear no evil.
> Your rod and Your staff they comfort me.
> You prepare a table before me in the presence of my enemies,
> You anoint my head with oil, my cup runs over.
> Surely goodness and mercy shall follow me
> all the days of my life;
> and I shall dwell in the house of the Lord forever.
> **Psalm 23**

Around three o'clock Karen quietly went to be with her Savior. Karen, the love of my life, my wife of 23 years, died after a four-year battle against cancer. Following Karen's death, I traveled a lot and kept myself very busy with my speaking and consulting business. I thought, "I'll get a little apartment somewhere. I'll make a pretty good bachelor. I'm on the road a lot and I have no intention to remarry. As a matter of fact, I can't even *imagine* being in love with another woman!"

That went on for about 10 months until…I went to church one Saturday evening. It was dark, and I found an open spot and sat down. When my eyes adjusted, I looked around and the person next to me happened to be Sandy.

Now, Sandy lived about a mile from where Karen and I used to live. She and Karen had met at a women's retreat, following which Sandy had come over to our house once to talk with Karen about something. I came home while she was there and briefly met her, no big deal. So, when I sat down in church next to her, I said hello and we chatted for a few minutes. I had met her husband and knew they were divorced. We had a nice, comfortable connection. I remember leaving there thinking, "That was interesting!"

It then took me about two months to get up the courage to call and invite her to go to out. I was messing with my kayak and just thought, why not; I'll invite her to go to the beach with me. This led to another date…which led to another date…and another…and another. We grew closer and closer very quickly. I loved her vivacious and outgoing personality. She was a confident, self-assured woman, who could hold her own in any situation or conversation. She was also very comfortable with herself and very comfortable to be around. We "clicked." We soon realized that we were in love. It was really quite amazing. I understood love *intellectually*, of course, and I knew that love really has an infinite quality. But *practically*, I could not imagine how I could love another woman. But, of course, in God's infinite wisdom the impossible is possible!

And within a few months we were married. That was 24 years ago, and our relationship has been fabulous! Sandy had two children of her own. Through our combined families we now have four of the most wonderful grandchildren. My life, what an amazing dream! God has blessed me with two wonderful women for a total of 48 years—and counting—of wedded bliss.

I have been blessed beyond anything I deserve, and anything I could have imagined.

LOVE LESSONS

POETRY

You don't have to *write* poetry to understand that love is like a poem: structured and flowing, delightful and engaging, deep and meaningful. And a life-long love affair is like an epic, heroic, narrative poem. Poems inspire us and remind us of life's glories.

OPTIMISM

Expecting the best—even in the midst of horror and over long periods of uncertainty—is a mindset that helps people accomplish the near-impossible. Optimism helped keep our POWs sane and positive day after day, month after month, and year after year. And optimism can keep loving couples together over separation, time, and distance.

FOLLOW YOUR HEART

Can a person have more than one "Love of your life"? Dave Carey (and two other POWs and four widows in this book who had very successful first marriages) prove that the answer is a resounding "Yes!" After losing his wife of 23 years, Dave had no intention of getting remarried. But he did keep an open mind—and an open heart—which connected again when he stumbled upon his second soulmate.

Dave & Karen

Dave & Sandy

1   LTJG David J. (Dave) Carey USN, A-4 Skyhawk, POW 31-AUG-67 – 14-MAR-73, Retired CAPT USN (0-6)

PROPAGANDA-THE BITCH BOX

Shortly after our capture, we saw how the communist party dominated life with non-stop propaganda. Every village and even the rice paddies had speakers blasting out the latest party line "news" several times a day and playing patriotic music to energize the workers. The POW camps were exposed to their English language propaganda outreach to US soldiers.

Following in the footsteps of Tokyo Rose, the infamous World War II radio host, Hanoi Hannah reported twice a day over what we dubbed the "Bitch Box."

Early morning. Hanoi Hanna gave an update on the war. She seemed to end every sentence about US bombing attacks with "bombing hospitals, dykes, and schools—killing old folks, women and children." (Of course, our Rules of Engagement prohibited that.) Her focus was to convince American soldiers to desert and abandon their country, their commitments, and their fellow POWs.

Bedtime. Hanoi Hanna again gave the latest twisted news about the V's victories. She always closed out with "GIs, why should you die 10,000 miles from home? Lay down your arms now and come over to the people's side." After a few months, we learned to flip the switch in our brain to shut it out.

In addition to Hanoi Hannah, most days after lunch there was a tape of some American anti-war activist. The first day Ken Fisher and I were in Hanoi, we heard Tom Hayden, then president of Students for a Democratic Society (SDS, a communist-oriented front group at the University of Michigan). He later became a congressman in California and married Jane Fonda.

During those years in Hanoi, we POWs saw firsthand that communist governments rely on propaganda, lies, and force to stay in power. They cannot survive policies based on truth; therefore, they seek to control every aspect of the culture. If you talk with those who have grown up under communist regimes, you will learn that the control of the media is foundational to their remaining in power.

12 | INDEPENDENTLY INTERDEPENDENT

THE STORY OF
Mo & Honey Baker

Friends have described their blended family as "The Brady Bunch." In some ways that's accurate: Mo[1] and Honey (aka Elmo and Marjorie) each had a son and a daughter from previous marriages. All the kids bonded quickly, grew up together, and now four generations enjoy each other's company.

But in other ways the "Brady Bunch" comparison is inaccurate: Both Mo's and Honey's lives were upended by the Vietnam War, and they both endured years of uncertainty, loneliness, and struggle. (And this was *before* they met.) And while their marriage hasn't been a sitcom, it *has* been a love story that has thrived for 48 seasons—er, years—and continues to this day.

Mo, now in his tenth decade of life, is active in Rotary and plays golf regularly. Honey plays golf occasionally and hangs out with her children.

How did two independent and strong-willed people forge a strong, happy, and long-term marriage?

"We're independently interdependent," says Honey.

"We respect and honor each other unequivocally," says Mo.

THEMES & PASSIONS

Honey's and Mo's lives share two themes and passions: the military lifestyle and flying.

Honey's father, Dwight Monteith, retired from the Air Force as a Major General. During his career he was stationed in many locations around the world, and the family moved frequently. Honey had a lifetime of military experience. At an early age she learned to adjust to change, make friends, and be social and confident. She flew often with her first husband, Vince Connolly, an Air Force pilot. They loved to fly together, and Honey quickly became adept at navigation.

Mo, on the other hand, grew up in Kennett, Missouri, a small farming community on the Mississippi River Upper Delta Region. He says, "I had a Tom Sawyer boyhood. My interest in flying began as a six-year-old lad. For Christmas that year my parents gave me a kit that had an impressively complex airplane dashboard with stickers of instruments as well a yoke with a steering wheel with real buttons to push for the imaginary radio. I had great fun lining up the dining room with straight-backed chairs and playing pilot. I coerced my family and neighborhood playmates to sit in my airliner while I piloted the plane, making mandatory position reports and narrating our adventures in the air.

"Thirty-six years later I met a beautiful MIA widow who quickly turned my life upside down!

Thirty-six years later I met a beautiful MIA widow who quickly turned my life upside down!

"Honey entered my life just seven weeks after I returned to America. I met Honey Connolly at a VFW lunch in Austin, Texas, which honored returned POWs and also the brave MIA wives who had no husband to return to them after the war.

"I was immediately impressed by Honey. She was poised, confident, and friendly. And good looking!" Mo smiles. "We soon discovered that her great aunt Jo was from my hometown, Kennett, Missouri. We then discovered that I knew many of her relatives, and she knew mine! And then we discovered that Honey and I had met casually many moons ago—when she was six, and I was 16 and a lifeguard at the municipal pool where Aunt Jo brought her one summer! All these connections added depth to my budding relationship with Honey."

She adds, "With Aunt Jo's stamp of approval of Mo, we began dating in earnest, and our lives changed forever as we bonded through our common interests and heritage."

AN INDEPENDENT MIA WIFE

Jumping back a few years, before Honey and Mo met…

In an instant, on November 4, 1965, Mrs. Honey Connolly became an independent "single" mom when her husband of four years was shot down and declared missing in action. This was a mere two months after he had begun conducting tactical reconnaissance missions over North Vietnam, piloting RF-101 jets.

Thus began Honey's life in the agonizing limbo of an MIA wife. She waited for seven-and-a-half years, until the Vietnam War ended, before she received confirmation that her husband, Vince, had been killed in action. She had kept a very low profile, not telling anyone that he was either MIA or a POW. During those lonely, difficult years Honey became both mother and father to her two children.

And she made good use of her time and resources. With the help of Jewel Lane, a well-known real estate broker in Austin, Texas, she purchased a building site in West Lake Hills with the intention of building a duplex in this prestigious location. There were problems along the way. The mortgage companies did not know how to handle a female applicant whose husband was MIA. With Lane's endorsement, they won the battle and were granted the building loan. Honey, her two children, and her mother settled into the duplex and prepared for the unknown date of repatriation of the POWs in Hanoi. Unfortunately, when that day came in 1973, her husband was not one of the survivors who returned. He was declared KIA. Her limbo was over.

A few weeks later Honey met POW Mo Baker. And 12 months after that, just before their wedding, Honey's independence became crystal clear when she edited her wedding vows. "I wasn't about to vow to *obey* my husband in some outdated manner! Mo and I knew from the beginning that we were co-equals."

I'M IN LOVE...WITH MY PLANE

Here is an unexpected confession from Top Gun pilot Colonel Elmo Baker: "Fighter pilot wives say their husbands are in love with their aircraft. They say she is his mistress. It is probably true. I fell in love with flying when I was 16, when riding in a Piper Cub at a local carnival. I was smitten, and I knew I was meant to fly jets.

"The very first time I flew an F-105 Thunderchief, during flight training, I think she (my plane) whispered to me, *'Mo, we will be great together. I am yours. I will do anything you tell me to do.'* I didn't share these private conversations with anyone. I think it was partly because they were precious to me but mostly because the brass would probably think I was crazy and bounce me out of the program! I was thrilled to be flying state-of-the-art fighter jets, and I was having the time of my life. I was doing what I believed Mo Baker was put on this earth to do."

For many years Mo owned a Cessna T-210. Honey once described flying as therapy for him.

She smiles, "So you can see what we wives had to put up with! My first husband clearly loved his plane, too, but I figured I could accept him having a mistress—as long as she was made of metal and weighed 50,000 pounds!"

During his ten years in the Air Defense Command, one of Mo's favorite flings was with a Convair F-106 Delta Dart, designed to intercept and destroy attacking Russian high-altitude bombers. One night, while on patrol above Washington, D.C., Mo practiced a "snap-up maneuver," which leads to what is known as a hammerhead. Leveling at an altitude of 45,000 feet, the pilot accelerates to 1.5 Mach (much faster than the speed of sound) and then pulls the plane into a vertical climb, racing up to 65,000 feet (where you can see the curvature of the earth, and the atmosphere is so thin that the sky is dark enough that you can see stars during the day), until the engine stalls. Then the plane tips and drops straight down in a powerless uncontrolled dive. As the plane descends, the pilot restarts the engine and pulls out of the dive. But Mo's aircraft was so sleek that in the vertical dive, it quickly went supersonic again. "It's quite a rush!" Mo exclaims. He was exhilarated—until he returned to base and the commander demanded,

"Why did you 'boom' the White House?" Earlier, around 3:00 a.m., upon being shaken awake by the sonic boom, President John Kennedy had called the Pentagon demanding to know if he was under attack! When the General on duty called him, quick-thinking Mo saved his skin—and career— by using military lingo and "mumbo-jumbo" to create a barely acceptable explanation. From that day forward aircraft training has been forbidden within a 30-mile radius around the White House!

MO IN VIETNAM

On his 61st combat mission over North Vietnam (many of which were attacking military and industrial targets near Hanoi), Mo's fighter-jet was hit by anti-aircraft fire. "My aircraft was now a high-powered, unguided missile streaking through the North Vietnamese sky at greater than 550 knots (633 miles per hour) in a three-degree nose-low attitude. I had no control over the fate of the aircraft. That was not a good place to be. It's time to ride the rails."

> **[Lee's coauthor note]**
> *You can see that Mo has a dry sense of humor and is a master of understatement.*

"I separated from the ejection seat, my main chute deployed, and I drifted slowly towards the earth below. Like Alice stepping through the looking glass, I stepped into another world. And, like Dorothy in Oz, I too would soon confirm that 'we were not in Kansas anymore.'" Mo had suffered a femur broken into three pieces. As he was dragged by his captors, one of them derived an evil pleasure from twisting his leg 180 degrees, pointing his foot backwards. Thus began "five-and-a-half years of imprisonment that makes the Wicked Witch of the West look like Shirley Temple!"

In his first interrogation, Mo was beaten into unconsciousness several times. He says, "I realized that I should not let these godless interrogators terrorize me. I thought, 'God is still in charge of my fate. Even if I die in this dismal room, I should not worry. It will be part of God's plan for me.' I relaxed. I smiled. I realized that this ordeal was part of a larger, more important plan that is being played out. From that moment on I wore that faith like armor. I was not afraid to die.

"The North Vietnamese could not understand it. But most POWs were very courageous and were hard to terrify into cooperation. In the end, the North Vietnamese found their approach to dominating the American prisoners through torture and deprivation to be counterproductive. They learned that Americans were extremely patriotic and valued their national honor far above their own personal safety and comfort. They discovered that the application of excruciating pain may force an American soldier to yield to the immediate demands of the torturer, but the next attempts to gain cooperation would be more and more difficult for them."

All the POWs had personal "mental projects" that were good for distracting them from pain and depression, relieving their boredom, and giving them something productive to do. One of the POWs, while in solitary for several months "wrote"—in his head—a one-thousand-word epic poem! While Mo was in solitary he started "writing" a three-volume cowboy novel. "The hero looked a great deal like me," Mo chuckles, "and he had a sidekick named Larry Carrigan—my cellmate for over three years. I didn't finish the trilogy, but I did recite the story to the guys.

"The Tap Code kept us all connected. As goes communication, so goes morale. It was the most important activity we did for each other. Our obligation was, man for man, to help the guy on the other side of the wall anytime he had a problem. One fellow tapped, 'I'm out of my mind with boredom; send details on WWII.' Lots of us jumped in and told him everything we knew about that war. After a few months we had expended all our collective knowledge to our bored brother. It was helping him—but he wanted more. So, we started making up stuff! A good story can go a long way to help keep a person sane."

FAMILY LIFE

"Upon returning home my first wife divorced me. It wasn't a big shock to me, which surprised her and the military psychiatrists. More than a year earlier she had written to me, indicating that we might be through. In the camp I had more than a year to adjust to this change. Many of the married POWs had the same doubts. I was thankful that during this time all of us were kept in rooms that held 50 or so men. The friendship and support of all the guys was invaluable to me.

"The hardest part for me was missing nearly six years of my children's lives. They were eight and ten years old when I'd left the country, and they were 14 and 16 when I returned. The adjustment was agonizing. I am so grateful that I met Honey so quickly after my return. I was overjoyed to find a military-seasoned wife who was so well suited to my lifestyle. And amazingly, Honey's kids were eight and ten, the same age mine had been when I had last seen them—so I got to experience them growing from youngsters to teenagers. I got to see them go to dance lessons, play Little League, and do all the growing-up that I had missed with my kids. For a very math-oriented person I was thrilled to teach the young ones the multiplication tables and fractions! I became an important part in their lives—I became the dad they needed. Honey and our four children were, are, and continue to be among my greatest blessings."

> **The hardest part for me was missing nearly six years of my children's lives.**

Honey adds, "Mo and I both believe that strong family values are crucial for children and for America. We never let my kids forget who their father was, and the sacrifice that he made for our country. Their dad's photos and his display of medals hang in our personal hall of honor to this day."

Mo says that the most important thing he learned about making a marriage and family work was to stop criticizing his wife and children. "In my mind I was *helping* them. But they often experienced it as me *criticizing* them. In the military we simply follow orders, and we don't take things personally. But a family ain't the military! For me this was a radical change in my mindset. Another thing I had to adjust to was how profoundly American culture had changed in the five and a half years I had been away. Kids had become much more independent and outspoken. The protests! The long hair! The braless look! I was quite bewildered at first."

He adds that right from the start he respected Honey, but he had to learn to respect her wants and needs and points of view and then adjust his own thinking and actions accordingly.

They lived in the Washington, D.C. area for several years and enjoyed everything the town had to offer—museums (especially the National Air and Space Museum at the Smithsonian), cultural events at the Kennedy Center, and social and business dining that often included "olive soup" (a colloquial term at the time for "a martini"). Honey notes, "A lot of serious and important government work was accomplished in these settings." Mo and Honey also enjoyed many vacation cruises together over the years.

While Mo doesn't really consider himself to be classically "romantic," over the years he has commissioned several pieces of custom jewelry for Honey. Her favorite is a finely crafted Celtic cross, which was his first jewelry gift, given on their fortieth anniversary. Mo has earned a lot of "Husband Points" for this kind of personal, meaningful, and creative gift!

Four years after his return from Vietnam, Mo retired from the Air Force, and he, Honey, and their children settled into a small ranch just outside Fort Worth, Texas. Even after his retirement from the Air Force, Mo continued flying missions—in fact, some very dangerous missions. In the mid-1990s he flew air surveillance in Colombia, helping locate the insurgents of the National Liberation Army and the Revolutionary Armed Forces of Colombia. Honey, shaking her head, said, "He likes the whistle of bullets flying by. At one point Mo had a bounty on him! Of course, I worried about him, but I'd learned that when Mo took on a mission or cause, he was unstoppable!"

The Baker Clan now consists of four children, eight grandchildren and seven great-grandchildren. Mo rarely talks about his time as a prisoner of war, but the children want to hear his stories, which he tells in a G- or PG-Rated manner.

LOVE LESSONS

INDEPENDENCE AND INTERDEPENDENCE

Every successful couple has to figure out their own approach to balancing independence and interdependence. Every person is unique, as we all have many personality traits, interests, and communication styles that must be taken into account.

RESPECT AND AFFECTION

Respect and affection are foundational. Respect gives each person support and confidence, and affection makes being together comfortable and joyful.

HUMOR

Humor is a relationship lubricant. This doesn't mean laughing all the time, but humor bonds us in the good times and helps us weather the tough times.

Mo & Honey Baker

1 Maj Elmo C. (Mo) Baker USAF, F-105 Thunderchief, POW 23-AUG-67 – 14-MAR-73, Retired Col (0-6)

MAN ON THE MOON

During the summer of 1969, when Americans were celebrating the landing of Apollo 11 on the moon, the POWs were suffering some of our worst treatment ever (mentioned earlier on page 93). As the torture swept through every camp, two of the five men in my cell were thrown into solitary for several months. But finally, when the torture and punishment stopped that fall, the fellows returned to entertain us with many amazing stories of resisting our enemy—often through cleverness and psychological games.

Intentionally, the V never gave us good news from home. But in February of 1970, Hanoi Hannah inadvertently gave us a lift during a morning "Bitch Box" broadcast in which she made an offhand comment. To paraphrase, "If Neil Armstrong were to go to the DMZ (Demilitarized Zone), the [bomb] craters would look very familiar to him!"

That statement was a subtle clue with an out-of-this-world insight! We knew that Armstrong, a former Navy fighter pilot, was an astronaut, and this could only mean that he had walked on the moon! The USA had beaten the Russians. This unintended disclosure of a history-making event electrified us.

Later that morning, the five of us from Cat House cell 4 (Son Tay camp) were walking across the compound to the wash house when Capt. Ken Fisher, our SRO, happened to look up and—lo and behold—there was a crescent moon. With a big smile, he pointed to it and said, "Gentlemen, our flag is on that moon." We all came to attention, looked up to face the moon, and saluted. The guards were baffled. We were bursting with pride and celebrating! The news of this accomplishment was a huge boost to POW morale at a time when we really needed a lift.

13 | A NAM-POW MIRACLE

THE STORIES OF
Bob[1] & Anita Barnett plus "Percy"[2] (Bob) & Suzanne Purcell—and then Bob & Suzanne

By Sweethearts Bob Barnett and Suzanne Purcell

Bob

As we were writing our story for this book, it occurred to me that I've had a long, happy life filled with blessings. Despite spending more than five years in Vietnam POW camps, I can truly say that I've also had a life filled with love and romance…with *two* amazing women. It all began a long time ago.

ONCE UPON A TIME…

Growing up in Los Angeles in the 1930s and 40s, Anita, my future wife, and I lived on the same street, but we didn't meet until she had graduated from high school and returned home after living in Mexico for a year. By 1949, I had returned home from three years in the Coast Guard and had been in college for a year when Anita returned. One day my younger brother Don said, "You gotta see Anita! Now!" I did and ogled her often as she walked by our house on the way to work. And I liked what I saw. She was a beautiful girl. I called her and we dated a few times, and we were hitting it off, but I realized that I was getting in too deep, too fast. I was only 22 years old, I was still in college, and I wasn't ready for marriage. So, I left town to visit my cousin and took a month off from Anita, thinking we would just drift apart. But Anita called my mother, asking why I hadn't called her. My mom chewed me out! So, after that I went peacefully. We dated for a year and a half; then we got married. It was the best decision I've ever made!

My parents were Canadian, and Anita's father was Canadian and her mother Mexican. Blending our cultures was surprisingly easy and lots of fun. When I proposed, Anita told her mother. Her mother was aghast. She said to Anita, "He is not Mexican!" Anita said, "My father is not Mexican!" Anita's mother countered with, "He's not Catholic!" Anita said, "My father isn't Catholic!" Finally, her mother said, "His name is Barnett!" Anita's mother was raised in a caste system in Mexico, and the Barnetts were considered the bottom of the barrel.

Anita was 20, and I was 23 and a junior at the University of Southern California when we married. I was a member of the Air Force ROTC with a slot to flying school when I graduated. Right after we came back from our honeymoon, I went off for six weeks of "summer camp." This set the stage for our military way of life together. I was incredibly lucky that Anita was an outstanding Air Force wife. She was confident and independent; she made friends easily, and she never complained when we were transferred to another base, which we did more than 20 times during my Air Force career.

Our daughter Lori was born while I was away on a remote tour in Iceland. She attended three different schools during her first-grade year. She was—and still is—as resilient and flexible as her mom was. Anita deserves the Best Mom of the Year award many times over. Before I left for Vietnam, I got them settled into a small apartment in Hawthorne, California, near both of our families, before what was supposed to be my "eight-month tour." They ended up living there until the war ended and I was freed—six years later!

Our biggest separation—by far—was the 1,989 days (five and a half years) I spent as a prisoner of war in Vietnam.

In the 24 years I was in the Air Force, Anita and I experienced constant moves and separations.

Our biggest separation—by far—was the 1,989 days (five and a half years) I spent as a prisoner of war in Vietnam.

VIETNAM

I evaded capture for three days after being shot down on October 3, 1967. I was listed as MIA for my first two and a half years. This left Anita to deal with a huge amount of uncertainty. Her list of worries shifted when my status was changed to POW. Was I being tortured? Was I malnourished? Was I lonely and afraid? Still, Anita didn't know specifically how I was doing. I didn't receive my first letter from her until September 8, 1970, three years later. The letter said that she didn't know whether I was alive or dead. A downer to say the least. We were allowed to send "approved" letters occasionally, letters of only six lines long. Not much, but Anita knew I was surviving and would hopefully return home someday.

Before the war I had not been very religious. And perhaps I am still not, at least in the classic sense. But I know for certain that God came into my life in the camps and sustained me. My daily prayers and the church services—which we were allowed to hold starting in 1970—gave me great comfort. Also, I have always and will always believe in our country. And we POWs believed in the mission we had in Vietnam.

After our treatment improved in late 1969 into 1970, we were housed in rooms of 40 to 60 men. We got organized and began conducting classes. Whoever had the most expertise and experience became the teacher. Because I had become fluent in Spanish during my exchange tour in Ecuador, I was the Spanish teacher. Keeping busy with various classes helped us pass the time.

BACK HOME

I cannot adequately express my joy at returning to the good old USA and to Anita. While I was away Anita became a magician: She worked several jobs and she saved nearly all my paychecks and deposited them in an interest-bearing account. This ensured that we were able to pay cash when we built our beautiful home in the foothills of Tucson. All of this *and* she was able to maintain her status as a world-class shopper. She made sure that our house was big enough to accommodate her shoe collection. I'm pretty sure she had more than 100 pairs of shoes, but I was never able to get an accurate count. I trusted her and let her shop without any criticism from me. That may be the *real* secret to our long and happy marriage!

I attended the University of Arizona and earned my master's degree in Latin American Studies. Upon graduation I remained at the university as the Professor of Aerospace Studies. I retired from the Air Force in 1977 and started an airplane business at the Tucson Airport—which I had dreamed about while serving time as a POW. I had taken out a mortgage on our house to get started, and it was a successful but risky business. Despite inflation over 16% and interest rates as high as 22%, we were successful, but it was very challenging! I developed a tremendous respect for business owners. I finally sold the business and made a profit. I often said, "I was liberated for the second time in my life!" Not surprisingly, Anita always supported me through those tough times.

Now that we were free of the business and had some money in the bank, Anita and I toured Europe for nearly six months. I once surprised her with two around-the-world airline tickets. We had a grand time, but when we arrived home after two months, an exhausted Anita gasped, "We don't have to *travel* again, do we?" I smiled, "No, dear, we've done it all!" So, we settled down to enjoy retirement and our grandchildren.

But soon I was back in the air.

TRANSITIONS

Two months later I had an unexpected opportunity to ferry a Learjet to Geneva, Switzerland. And then I received a lucrative job offer to captain the Learjet for a successful Swiss entrepreneur. I called Anita and said, "Guess *what*…?" My amazing wife hopped on a plane and joined me in Geneva. For over a year we got to jet around Europe and flew many Atlantic crossings to Canada and the US. When this job ended, I returned to Flight Safety International as an instructor for Learjet pilots.

Eventually I *did* retire, and Anita and I had a great life together. But then, just after Thanksgiving 2012, Anita was diagnosed with pancreatic cancer. She hadn't felt well for a short while, but this news and her rapidly deteriorating condition came as a complete shock to us all.

I have been blessed with the best family ever. When Anita was in hospice, my brother Don came to live with me. My sister-in-law, Carol, our daughter, Lori, and her husband, Tim, were always there for us. My granddaughter, Jordan, handled all the hospice details. Just a few weeks after learning of Anita's illness, we lost her. At 10:00 on Christmas Eve Anita left this world. She was very brave as she faced her destiny with dignity and courage.

Anita had been an avid bridge player and had many, many friends. A great number of people attended her funeral, including many of our NAM-POW friends. My life changed dramatically. Now I was alone in my big house in the foothills overlooking Tucson. I didn't want to live there anymore. I accepted that my life was going to be different, and I wanted to change things.

Many people advised me not to do anything for a year.

But I didn't listen, and I'm glad I didn't because a miracle happened that led to a new life that I never could have imagined!

> **But I didn't listen, and I'm glad I didn't because a miracle happened that led to a new life that I never could have imagined!**

And this takes us into my *second* love story.

THE WIDOWER MEETS THE WIDOW

Bob

Here's where the story gets interesting. We'll need to step back several decades, back to Vietnam.

My friend "Percy" (Bob) Purcell was a fellow Thud pilot and a Vietnam POW who had survived seven and a half years in the prisons—two years longer than me. Percy was one-of-a-kind. He had a wild side that got him into trouble occasionally, but as a pilot he was a consummate professional. Percy was a courageous POW. When one of his fellow POWs at the Zoo camp had been tortured and starved, Percy figured out a way to climb into the attic so that he could crawl over to his cell, push down the hanging light base, and drop him pieces of bread. He gave him some encouraging words and crawled back to his cell before the guards would discover him missing. Later, as the Senior Ranking Officer in Room 2 in the Hanoi Hilton, he was a creative and admired leader for the 40 men living elbow to elbow for two years.

When Percy returned home, he tried to make his troubled marriage work, but the couple soon separated and began a long divorce process. Like most of his fellow POWs, he was very good at bouncing back from adversity. And like most single pilots, Percy had a radar for nice looking ladies. His was apparently in search mode during his trip back to his hometown of Louisville—and while waiting for his flight, Suzanne caught his eye. I'll let her tell you about *her* first love story…which lasted 32 years…until Percy passed away, which opened the way for us to co-create *our* love story.

Suzanne

Fate brought us together in Chicago O'Hare airport. Percy and I were both bound for Louisville, where he was going to go to the Kentucky Derby. I was going to visit my family and also attend the Derby. Even though we were complete strangers, he confidently asked me if I would watch his bag while he ran an errand. (He had been nice enough to clear up a time change issue for me a little earlier.) So, I was happy to help him out with his bag. When he returned, we chatted easily and traded the short versions of our life stories. When I learned he had been a Vietnam POW, I couldn't believe how *normal* he seemed! After all, he had been captured way back in 1965 and had suffered terribly as a POW for seven and a half years.

On the plane we sat apart, but upon arrival Percy was waiting for me to disembark. He asked me out and handed me a long list of phone numbers where I could reach him. I was reluctant at first because I thought he was way too old for me. And he had an ex-wife and five children! But my family encouraged me to call him. We went out to dinner that week, and we connected immediately. We embarked on a long-distance romance, with me in Toronto and Percy in Omaha.

When he first returned from the war, Percy was the toast of Louisville, as he was the only POW from the city. He was a true American hero, but he remained humble and down-to-earth. He never bragged and he never used his status to attract attention or gain favors. He was very positive *every day*. He had a lot of charisma and a terrific sense of humor. Was he romantic? Let me just say that he was born on Valentine's Day.

The long-distance romance was lovely, but we soon realized that we wanted to be together. We became engaged in Louisville at Christmas 1976 and were married in Omaha in March 1977. This Canadian girl married a full colonel and didn't have any idea what that entailed. I had a lot to learn, but I dove in and thoroughly enjoyed our life in Omaha. We had a beautiful apartment in which we often entertained Air Force couples, and that helped me learn more about military life. Our next assignment was to Carswell AFB, near Fort Worth.

We were only at Carswell AFB for a very short time because Percy decided to retire in 1980. The Wing Commander threw a huge retirement party for Percy. We invited family, friends, and lots of ex-POW buddies to attend. It was almost like a POW reunion.

We decided to settle down in Fort Worth. Percy worked for American Airlines as a simulator instructor. His hobbies included working on antique VW bug convertibles. He would fix them up by turning them into gorgeous collector's items. Then he would reluctantly sell them.

Our son, Matthew, was born in June 1988. As I said earlier, Percy already had five children, but he was over-the-moon happy when Matthew was born. In fact, both of our families were thrilled for us. The three of us had a lot of rewarding adventures together. We traveled a lot, skied in Canada, fished in our little lake, did Little League and every youth sport possible, and played tennis. Percy played a lot of tennis with John Yuill, a beloved ex-POW buddy. We would spend every Christmas in Toronto with family. This was an almost sacred tradition, one that all three of us treasured.

We had a long and very happy marriage.

On the morning of December 31, 2005, when Percy was descending the stairs, his running shoe got caught on the carpet causing him to fall. He tumbled to the foot of the stairs and broke his neck. He became an "incomplete quadriplegic." Over the next four years Percy and I worked extremely hard to manage his very difficult recuperation. Unfortunately, he never recovered, and eventually passed away on December 6, 2009. My wonderful husband and American hero, Percy, was buried at Arlington National Cemetery in a beautiful and patriotic service on April 29, 2010.

[Greg's coauthor note]

Her friends called her Saint Suzanne because she had been so very dedi-cated to Percy's care.]

After a year went by, I decided that I needed to do something with my life, so I offered to volunteer at Fort Worth Country Day school, the school Matthew attended and where I had taught French for many years. I had lots of dear friends at the school, so it was a very comfortable environment for me. I soon got a part-time job at the school library. It felt so good to be back among friends.

Matthew graduated from Texas A&M in 2010. I had the support of my family, old friends, and a new group of widowed friends, but I had abso-lutely no great desire to date. I didn't think I could possibly find anyone that I would be interested in or be attracted to. I was wrong.

Bob

Our two paths were about to merge.

[Greg's coauthor note]

As you've probably noticed in the other stories in this book, timing is often divine.

My friend Bill Hosmer had been Percy's flight leader at Okinawa and was on the mission when Percy was shot down. He had stayed in touch with Percy and Suzanne over the years. Early in 2013 Bill and I decided to meet at an upcoming F-105 "Thud" reunion in October. Bill told me that Su-zanne was planning to attend the reunion too. I thought I'd like to be her "date" for the event. But I had two challenges: One, we hadn't even met yet, and two, it was eight months away.

It happened that two months later I attended a different reunion, for the 560th Freedom Flyers in San Antonio. And, luckily for me, Suzanne hap-pened to be there. That's when I saw her for the first time. I'm not exactly shy, so while sitting behind her on a bus from the hangar to the club for lunch, I tapped her on the shoulder and said, "You have a date to the Thud reunion." She said, "I do? Who is it?" I answered, "Me!" She laughed and said, "Yes."

At about that time, Lori had convinced me to buy an iPad. It would be an easy way to stay in touch with friends and family. It changed my life! It was one of the best purchases I've ever made because it became an important part of the key that would unlock the path to our NAM-POW miracle.

Three months after the 560th reunion, my brother Don and I went to Russia. I took my new iPad with me. Suzanne and I continued to email each other every single day. We had become modern day pen pals. The pen pals eventually began to discover that something magical was happening in these emails. We were falling in love.

In October I drove to Suzanne's home in Fort Worth. She was so beautiful and easy to talk to. We went out for lunch and then drove to the Gaylord Resort to attend the Thud reunion. We had a great time and really hit it off. When the reunion was over, we discussed whether or not we wanted to continue our relationship. And we agreed that we really liked being together. We returned to our respective homes and continued to talk and email every day. It was clear that our romance was growing quickly, and soon we acknowledged that we were in love and that we wanted to be together forever.

SOULMATES ON THE BRIDGE OF AVIGNON

Suzanne

When I was teaching French to elementary school children, I loved to introduce them to popular French children's songs. One of our favorites was *"Sur le Pont d'Avignon."* It's an action song about a dance performed on the Avignon Bridge—lots of fun for both adults and children. It was always my dream to visit this famous bridge one day, but I didn't think it would ever happen.

Now, back to the Christmas of 2013. Bob gave me a River Cruise through France for my/our Christmas gift. It was a romantic and thoughtful gift filled with opportunities to visit so many gorgeous cities. And to speak French!

The most special moment of the cruise happened when our boat docked in Avignon. Bob and I walked hand in hand to the Avignon Bridge. When we climbed to the top, Bob invited me to dance with him. We sang the song and danced to the delight of fellow tourists.

Bob

Suzanne and I have been together since January 2014. We haven't spent a single day apart…and we are still loving every moment together.

WE HAVE BEEN BLESSED BY THIS NAM-POW MIRACLE!

[Lee's coauthor note]

Sadly before the book was published, my friend and former cellmate Bob Barnett passed away. I (Lee) had visited Bob and Suzanne in Tucson just six weeks earlier and it was an absolute joy to be with them. Their smiles and positive energy made it clear that every day was a joy for them and those who were with them. Bob, may you RIP and our prayers go out to Suzanne.

LOVE LESSONS

TRUST
Without trust there cannot be love. And trust requires honesty, open-ness, a generous spirit, a positive mindset, a strong commitment—and patience…lots of patience!

FLEXIBILITY
Being open to the unexpected is a common thread in many great re-lationships. Bob and Anita, and Percy and Suzanne, were all flexible and accepting people. This helped them survive the hard times, and it greatly enhanced the good times.

FAITH
There are many shades of faith. Faith in God, faith in country, faith in yourself, faith in family, and faith in your soulmate. Everybody has their own combination of these kinds of faith, but regardless, people with strong faith create the strongest couples.

---

1 Maj Robert W. (Bob) Barnett USAF, F-105 Thunderchief, POW 3-OCT-67 – 14-Mar-73, Retired Col (0-6), RIP 4-SEPT-22

2 Capt Robert B. (Percy) Purcell USAF, F-105 Thunderchief, POW 27-JUL-65 – 12-FEB-73, Retired Col (0-6), RIP 12-JUN-09

Bob & Anita Barnett

Percy & Suzanne

Bob & Percy

Bob & Suzanne

THE SON TAY RAID

The night of November 21, 1970 will always be a night to remember for Vietnam POWs. I was resting in the arms of the POW's best friend—sleep. It was our escape from the harsh, crushing reality of the camp and from the pain of missing our families.

Suddenly we were awakened as the building shook from the explosions of a nearby air strike. Later we learned that it was a diversionary tactic for a raid on the Son Tay POW camp some 12 miles away.

Son Tay had housed 52 of us for the previous two years, but we had been moved to this new camp four months earlier. The move was a key step in the North Vietnamese strategy to improve their international image by housing us in a "showplace camp."

The US raid, conducted by an elite team of Green Berets and Air Force specialists was brilliantly executed—but the camp was empty. Many people in America called this raid a failure, but you could never convince the POWs of that. For you see, it turned out to be the greatest unifying factor that ever happened to the prisoners in North Vietnam.

As a result of this raid, the V moved us back to the Hanoi Hilton—to an area that had previously held hundreds of Vietnamese prisoners. With 335 of us together in one camp, we were for the first time locked in cells of 40 to 60 guys each. That may seem uncomfortably cramped, but to us it was more exciting than any Christmas one could imagine! We could talk freely, play games, conduct classes, and hold church services.

The Green Berets and all those supporting that courageous undertaking are our heroes. They came deep into enemy territory to get us, and they left us a gift that kept on giving.

To all the Raiders, we say a big thank you, or as we soon learned during our language lessons in those big rooms: "Merci Beaucoup," "Danke," and "Muchas Gracias."

14. | BESHERT*

THE STORY OF
Tom[1] & Yona McNish

Tom

For me, it all began in a prison cell. During the previous 18 months of torture and starvation, I had time and energy for only one thing: thoughts and dreams of mere survival. I had no energy left to even think about life after release. But, when things eased up a little in 1968, I began fantasizing about the "Ideal Woman for Tom McNish," the woman I would meet, marry, and live with happily ever after—once I got out of the Communist prisoner of war camp where I had taken up residence on September 4, 1966. As a young single man in that hellhole, that seemed like my only escape.

What started out as an idle fantasy became one of my lifelines for surviving as a POW. If you had told me then that I would have four and a half more years to create and perfect my Ideal Woman, I would have said you were crazy! My other lifelines were my great faith in my God and my country. I never doubted for a moment that my country would get us out. As for my faith in God getting us out? Well, believe me, my faith was tested many times and more than a little bit on many occasions. But, my faith always returned. Always.

My Ideal Woman fantasy was one of my strategies for keeping my sanity. This was a literal struggle, not a metaphorical struggle. Surviving physically was obviously a challenge. But the mental and emotional struggles

*Hebrew for Soulmate: "The one person whom an individual is divinely destined to marry."

were, in many ways, much harder. As you well know, many Vietnam vets suffered terribly from PTSD, depression, and other maladies after the war. I know it sounds crazy to say that we POWs were lucky, but in some ways it's true. While we endured many years of harrowing treatment, we also spent years locked up with teammates who had endured worse conditions, and we had time to adjust and decompress with them. Through that unique experience we learned profound lessons in resilience, camaraderie, and faith. We emerged stronger and more mature than when we entered. This contributed to our very low incidence of PTSD after returning home. The foot soldiers didn't have these benefits.

How did I survive with my sanity intact? As I said, God, country, and Yona. Except that, at the time, I didn't yet know her name. But I was certain that I would recognize her when I met her, because I had a carefully constructed picture of her.

She would be Christian—because I saw how religious differences were a key element in destroying the closeness my parents once had. She would be tall, statuesque like a model. She would be a striking brunette. She would be an optimist, to match my upbeat personality. She would be very family-oriented, but never married. But—and this is important—I would *not* meet her immediately upon my return to the States. Why? Because my wild and carefree bachelorhood had been stolen from me! When I was shot down and captured, I was a hotshot 24-year-old single fighter pilot. In seconds I went from being on top of the world, and in near total control of my life, to being a powerless prisoner with control over nothing—except my mind. My plan was to date, but nothing serious for at least a year, so I wouldn't have any significant commitments before I started looking for My Ideal Woman.

What was the life of a Vietnam POW like? For the first three years of my prison existence, my life consisted of endless hours of boredom. Boredom punctuated by hours of being terrorized by interrogation, beatings, and torture. All too frequently, those hours turned into days.

This is supposed to be a *love* story, not a *war* story, right? So, skipping over 2,373 days of captivity…I finally—*thank God!*—landed on American soil at

Maxwell Air Force Base in Montgomery, Alabama. Stepping to the microphone I said a few practiced lines thanking my country and the welcoming crowd, but then my subconscious mind took over.

I spontaneously added, "I'm a 30-year-old bachelor with a lot of living to catch up on!"

Amid the applause I didn't hear a beautiful woman on the roof observation deck of the base ops building yell, "Right on, baby!"

I spontaneously added, "I'm a 30-year-old bachelor with a lot of living to catch up on!"

I then turned and dashed to the car where my dear mom waited for me. She had waited for six and a half years to once again see her son. She had defied death from a fatal disease (one that was to take her life just a year later). I was finally home!

Yona

For me, it all began in a beauty salon in 1965, one year before Tom got captured. But of course, I didn't know him then. It was at the Style Art Salon that I met my soon-to-be best friend, Jerry Sisson. She later became my only connection to the military and the Vietnam War when she married a young Air Force pilot, Michael McCuistion.

Life was marvelous in Montgomery, Alabama! Jerry and I developed a close bond, we were both happily married, and both had young children.

But then Michael was called to Vietnam. When he was shot down in May 1967, Jerry and I became closer. When he was listed as Missing in Action, Jerry's life became nerve-wracking and dark. She didn't receive any letters from him, so his fate was completely unknown for nearly three years. Jerry and I bonded even *more*. She received no information about her husband's status from the government—just like the thousands of other POW/MIA wives. Most of them lived in a horrible twilight zone that stretched on for years.

During that time, my husband Morris was diagnosed with cancer, so then I was on my own frightening emotional roller coaster. Morris battled that horrible disease for five months before we lost him, and I quickly experienced the dark side of life—much like a POW/MIA wife.

Then one day, out of the blue—more than two years after Michael had been declared missing in action—a letter from him arrived in Jerry's mailbox. *He was alive!*

Jerry had become active in the POW/MIA movement, which was started by military wives. She introduced me to the POW/MIA bracelet program when it began in 1970, which was soon after my husband died. I proudly wore a bracelet bearing the name of Michael McCuistion. I also sold lots of bracelets; school children would stop at my house to buy the silver bands. I became known to the kids as "the bracelet lady." The POW/MIA movement snowballed and eventually caught the attention of President Nixon. Our government began to pressure the communists about POW/MIA accounting and treatment. This—in addition to the death of the communist leader Ho Chi Minh in 1969—led to major changes in the way America dealt with North Vietnam, which led to improved (but still arduous) conditions for our POWs. Jerry and her fellow MIA wives lived for years with uncertainty and fear. But I'm only a footnote in that amazing story.

Jerry had to endure over three more years of loneliness until March 4, 1973, when she and I each sat in our respective living rooms, in front of our TVs, with our telephones in one hand and tissues in the other, watching our TV screens to see our brave former POWs deplane at Clark Air Base in the Philippines. I saw Michael and screamed with joy into the phone along with my best friend. We were both ecstatic! Later, alone, I wept for me.

Three days later, my daughters (then four and seven) and I joined Jerry to greet Michael and four other former POWs when they flew into Maxwell Air Force Base. (This was after I had to race to Jerry's house and physically pull her out of the bathtub. She was almost catatonic with anxiety and excitement.)

Our servicemen exited the plane one by one, and they each said a few words to the excited and loving crowd. All I really cared about was seeing Michael's return, but I listened politely to the nice little speeches. Then I heard one of the POWs declare, after completing his prepared speech, *"I'm a 30-year-old bachelor with a lot of living to catch up on!"*

At that moment, something just came over me and I yelled, "Right on, baby!"

Amid the hubbub Tom didn't hear me. But the next day, when Michael introduced Jerry to him, the first thing she said to Tom after "Welcome home" was "Have I got a girl for you!" And she gave him my phone number. Tom later thought, "I'm back in America for only one day and already I'm set up for a date! Hot-damn! Here comes the bachelor life!" However…

…We were *inseparable* after that first date! That was March 15th, only eight days after his feet touched American soil. Then five weeks later he said those three magical words—"I love you!"—on a long-distance phone call from his home in Franklin, North Carolina to mine in Montgomery, Alabama.

And five weeks after that he took me to dinner… at the White House!

And five weeks after that he took me to dinner…at the White House!

The Nixons hosted a formal dinner to honor our former POWs. It was a dazzling night of celebrities (including Sammy Davis Jr., Bob Hope, John Wayne, and Jimmy Stewart), and VIPs (including Henry Kissinger and many military brass), all honoring our returnees. Each fellow could bring a guest. Tom's mom was too ill to attend, so he brought me, his new love.

I had thought that the highlight of the White House event was Irving Berlin closing the evening by leading all of the assembly in singing his beloved song "God Bless America." But little did I know…

Around midnight President Nixon and his wife, Pat, excused themselves for the night but invited everyone to stay as long as they liked and gave us free rein to wander the White House. He said, "The band will keep playing, and the bartenders will keep pouring until the last one of you leaves." Tom was blown away! A few weeks earlier he was in Vietnam, in a stinking prisoner of war camp; and now he was in America, wandering the White House halls! But the best part? We were there together!

So anyway, it was two in the morning. We left the party in the East Room to wander through the White House. We were alone by the fireplace in the Green Room, and Tom said—

"I only plan to say this once in my life…Will you marry me?"

My first answer was, "Are you sure?"

I said that because I didn't know if Tom was really ready for an instant family. But then I *did* say yes!

It was a spontaneous proposal, but it just felt right. Tom wasn't nervous, because he knew that we were meant for each other. But it was a huge change of plans for him. He had to let go of his fantasy bachelorhood!

Well as they say, "No battle plan survives the first engagement." Okay, to recap, the specs for his wife that he had created while a POW for over six and a half years of dreaming, fantasizing, and planning: She would be Christian, model-tall, a striking brunette, an optimist, never-been-married, no kids, treasured family, and he would make no commitment with any woman, no matter how perfect, until at least one year after his return.

Then, in less than a month after his release, Tom's Ideal Woman turns out to be me...five feet, two and a half inches tall...blonde...Jewish...a self-described realist (*not* an optimist)...previously married...and not only family-oriented, but already had two daughters!

In a very short time, we found that despite our differences, we *totally* shared key values. We both treasure family above all, we love our country, and we deeply believe in right versus wrong as defined by Judeo-Christian values.

We are living proof that love can transcend differences, as long as you respect those differences, cherish your similarities, and practice what you preach.

Tom has come to love the Hebrew word *Beshert*, which we use to explain "us."

Beshert means "soulmate" or "the one person whom an individual is divinely destined to marry."

A KALEIDOSCOPIC LOOK AT ONE AMAZINGLY HAPPY MARRIAGE OF 48 YEARS...

Three months after the POWs returned home Tom and Yona attended a huge celebration at the Cotton Bowl during which Tony Orlando and Dawn sang their hit song "Tie a Yellow Ribbon Round the Ole Oak Tree."

After the show Tom took Yona by the hand and led her onto the stage where he called out, "Mr. Orlando! Mr. Orlando!" He held up Yona's hand to display the new engagement ring. "Because of your song this came in a box tied with a yellow ribbon!" A friendship was born. They've stayed in touch for more than five decades, and Tony still refers to them as "The Honeymooners."

Tom became a medical doctor specializing in Family Practice and Aerospace Medicine. He combined his love of flying with his medical calling when he became an Air Force flight surgeon. He then had the best of both worlds, being a combat-ready A-10 pilot and a flight surgeon/MD. During his training he graduated first in his flying class and earned the Top Gun Trophy.

Yona smiles, "Tom was blissfully chasing the windswept clouds. That man loved to fly!"

Tom served in many positions, including Chief of Flight Medicine for the Air Force, and then Command Surgeon of the USAF Reserve, working in the Pentagon. He retired in 1994.

Along the way Tom and Yona had a son, and together with their two daughters (whom Tom had adopted as soon as legally possible) the McNish family were military nomads, living in Georgia, New Mexico, Arizona, South Carolina, Virginia, and Texas. After Tom's retirement, they settled in San Antonio where they spend a lot of time doting on their three children and 11 grandchildren…and their six great-grandchildren!

"We have lived a wonderful life together and pray it continues throughout eternity because after all," Yona says, "it was just meant to be."

"Beshert!" adds Tom.

Two themes run throughout Tom and Yona's marriage. The first—no surprise—is *flying*.

For Tom's first birthday after they met (just 11 days after he told her "I love you") Yona gave him a plaque with pilot's wings and the famous poem "High Flight."

High Flight

By John Gillespie Magee, Jr., in 1941
Pilot Officer, Royal Canadian Air Force

Oh! I have slipped the surly bonds of Earth
And danced the skies on laughter-silvered wings;
Sunward I've climbed, and joined the tumbling mirth
Of sun-split clouds—and done a hundred things
You have not dreamed of—wheeled and soared and swung
High in the sunlit silence. Hov'ring there,
I've chased the shouting wind along, and flung
My eager craft through footless halls of air…
Up, up the long, delirious burning blue
I've topped the wind-swept heights with easy grace
Where never lark, nor ever eagle flew—
And, while with silent, lifting mind I've trod
The high untrespassed sanctity of space,
Put out my hand, and touched the face of God.

That plaque has been hanging in their home for over 48 years.

Tom was crazy about flying since he was 12. He still collects figurines and artwork of eagles. ("A man can't have too many eagles.") Tom and Yona both love the book *Jonathan Livingston Seagull*. They believe their marriage fulfills a line from that book:

"So this is heaven."

A second theme in Tom's and Yona's life together is the value of *time*. For Yona's birthday one year, Tom gave her a bottle with a watch inside. On the enclosed card, he included the lyrics to Jim Croce's song "Time in a Bottle."

They believe that it's important "to save every day 'til eternity passes away, just to spend them with you."

For another birthday he gave her a custom-made grandfather clock. It was special because it was made from a walnut tree that had fallen

> **They believe that it's important "to save every day 'til eternity passes away, just to spend them with you."**

on the farm where he was raised in North Carolina. And it was especially meaningful because it was designed after a grandfather clock made from that same tree, that Tom's uncle owned, and which Yona loved. But wait—there's more. Tom placed a plaque on the clock that reads…

"All time is ours."

LOVE LESSONS

SOULMATES

Early in their relationships many successful couples experience "coincidences" that they later interpret as fate, or signs that they are "soulmates." The concept of soulmates (or *Beshert*) is not modern or radical.

FOCUS ON SIMILARITIES

Devotion to different religions does not preclude a couple from working together in harmony. You can choose to focus on the *differences*, which leads to conflict, or on the *similarities*, which leads to connection and closeness.

FLEXIBILITY

Your idea, image, belief, description of "The perfect mate" may be 100% wrong! (So, keep an open mind!) Tom McNish found that the perfect woman with whom to spend his life—and eternity—was almost the opposite of the one he created in his mind while in prison.

Tom & Yona McNish

1 1st Lt Tomas M. (Tom) McNish USAF, F-105 Thunderchief, POW 4-SEPT-66 – 4-MAR-73, Retired Col (06)

THE HANOI UNIVERSITY

Hanoi University began to emerge in the cells in late 1970. We had no books or learning materials, yet we studied physics, calculus, and poetry...engineering, history, and geography...French, Spanish, German, and Russian... public speaking, music theory, and ballroom dancing...Shakespeare, chess, and piano (with a keyboard drawn on toilet paper).

Here's the backstory...

Two days after the Son Tay Raid, we all returned to the Hanoi Hilton and were herded into an area where Vietnamese prisoners had been held earlier. We were packed elbow to elbow in rooms holding 40 to 60 men. Most people would find that environment claustrophobic, but we were ecstatic! We could talk without fear of punishment, we could exercise, play games, and joke around. But the most amazing thing was that we had structured educational programs. In Room Three we had classes every day, with three hours in the morning and two in the afternoon. We were in small groups, learning subjects like French, Spanish, German, Russian, and math. We would have classes for eight weeks, take a two-week break, and start again.

We had no books; we just taught from memory. For example, Naval Academy math major Denver Key taught differential calculus using a broken chunk of roof tile as chalk to work problems on the concrete floor. I taught beginning French. It helped that I was studying intermediate French three days a week and speaking it with Paul Galanti for five minutes every day. We had a lot of knowledge, many talents and interests, and some of the guys were extremely creative. In my cell Bill Butler recruited and conducted a choir that amazed and entertained us. They even performed the musical "South Pacific."

Every room had a chaplain, we held weekly church services, and we were inspired with amazing homilies delivered by grizzly old fighter pilots. All these mental activities not only kept us busy, but they helped us get mentally and emotionally ready to return home when the war ended.

15 | THE HEROES' WIFE

THE STORY OF
Dora & Jimmie Griffin & Jim Bell

I have been fortunate to have been loved by two men who made great sacrifices for their country. My story has been written, really, by three people: By myself, by my first husband, Jimmie Griffin[1]—through his letters—and by Jim Bell,[2] a POW who came home to find that during his seven-year absence he had lost the most important thing of all—his family—as his wife had divorced him during his captivity.

I waited for my first husband, James—Jimmie—for more than five years without knowing his fate. The Navy listed him in a POW/MIA status, but it wasn't until our POWs were returned in 1973 that I learned he had died two days after his capture in 1967.

I met my second husband, *another* James—Jim—soon after his return home from Vietnam. It's a little complicated but…let's start at the beginning.

THE ROMANTIC NAVY PILOT

I first met my future husband at my sixth birthday party…although I don't remember his being there. But I most *definitely* remember meeting this handsome man many years later on the steps of my grandmother's little country church in the community of Forked Deer, Tennessee. He was so different from the local boys I had dated. I later realized that was because he had gained some polish during his first year as a midshipman (at the US Naval Academy), and he no longer had a Tennessee drawl. A week after he graduated from Annapolis, we were married in that same country church.

How good a pilot was Jimmie? Once when he was landing aboard an aircraft carrier, the nose-wheel collapsed. I was notified through a garbled message that the pilot had been injured. I was soon relieved—and proud—when the Air Wing called me and explained that Jimmie had not only walked away with no injury, but he had handled it so smoothly that his navigator sitting in the back seat didn't even know anything unusual had happened!

Jimmie's first deployment to Vietnam was aboard the *USS Kitty Hawk* to fly his RA-5 Vigilante fighter jet. It was 1965 and our little family was growing, with a young son, Jamey, and a toddler daughter, Glyn Carol.

My dashing pilot was *so* romantic! Before and during the war, whenever he was away on maneuvers or a deployment, he would write to me nearly every day. Here's a sample of the hundreds of letters I have from him:

> Dear Dora,
>
> I guess when they say that love is boundless, it means just that. And I can't think of a sweeter way to face the life ahead. With the kids we have, and all that God has given us, we must be the most fortunate two people in the world. Give a kiss to the kids for me.
>
> …I get some fine dreams, just thinking back over some mighty fond memories of the sweet times we have had together. Maybe that's what makes the time go fast. The multitude of sweet memories is so great I can't possibly recall them all. Here's to the day when we can bank up a whole year's supply in just a short time together.
>
> *Sweet dreams, sweetheart,*
> *I love you, Jimmie*

And when he was too busy to write a "real" letter, he often sent something fun and creative like this:

My Darling,

I
L
O
I L O V E Y O U
E
Y
O
U

Always, Jim

100+ COMBAT MISSIONS

In one of his first letters during the war he mentioned that one of his fellow Vigilante pilots had been shot down. His name was Jim Bell (who emerges as a hero later in this story).

I could never have imagined what Fate had in store for us!

And so, as you can imagine, about two years later, during his second tour in Vietnam, when I received no letters at all after my Jimmie was shot down over North Vietnam, it was quite a jolt that never stopped hurting.

When the house was quiet, I would go into the little study and practice a ritual I had created for myself. I had two huge boxes of letters from Jimmie (I'd saved every one). Each evening I read one letter from him, which he had written almost every day on his two deployments to Southeast Asia. He had written me often every time we had been apart, beginning during the days of courtship when I was in college and he was at the US Naval Academy. The letters offered me comfort and hope, and there were enough letters to get me through almost two years if I read only one each night.

Jimmie, being utterly fearless and a true patriot, served two deployments to Vietnam. Early during his second deployment he completed his one-hundredth combat mission over North Vietnam. This is a significant military milestone! Jimmie had been flying a low-level reconnaissance mission when, in May 1967, his luck ran out, and his jet was shot down. (It happened to be Ho Chi Minh's birthday.) Radio Hanoi broadcast a statement saying that he had been captured. The broadcast, heard around the world, included Jimmie's voice. So at least I knew he was alive. But I also knew that Jimmie would never voluntarily cooperate with the communists or make any kind of statement—unless he had been tortured. I received no news from the Navy, and no direct information about Jimmie's fate, for five years.

A few years after his shoot-down an anti-war leader informed me that she had received word from the North Vietnam government that Jimmie had died shortly after his capture. I didn't know what to believe, but I hung onto the belief that my husband was still alive as a POW.

In 1970, three years after Jimmie's plane went down, the National League of POW/MIA Families was active nationwide, and I decided it was time for me to be active, too. I solicited letters to the North Vietnam government from local folks and from people across the state of Georgia, demanding a full accounting of the POWs, and humane treatment of them. I opened up for TV interviews, and after several months I became comfortable in that setting. I had found my niche! I eventually cohosted a local afternoon talk show.

Early in 1973, when the Paris peace accords were signed, I received a telegram from the Navy stating that the official documents listing all prisoners of war in North Vietnam did not include Jimmie's name. Even then I kept hoping against hope…but finally my casualty officer came by and confirmed my worst fears. As the returned prisoners were debriefed, they said that Jimmie's name was passed through the prison network, but no one had ever seen him.

ENTER THE SECOND JAMES…

Before the war Jimmie was a friend of fellow pilot Jim Bell, from when they were stationed at the Naval Air Station in Sanford, Florida. Jim had been shot down in 1965, two years before my Jimmie. Jim survived almost eight years in the POW camps. And then he survived the heartbreak of having his wife divorce him during his time in captivity. I hadn't had any contact with Jim until one night, three months after he and all our POWs returned home, when the phone rang. I answered and a hesitant, unfamiliar male voice on the phone put me on guard, and my suspicious nature immediately kicked in. (My phone number had been unlisted since I began working as a television host, because I got crank calls from time to time.)

"*Who is this?*" I almost bellowed into the phone. The quiet voice tells me that he's looking for Dora Griffin, and that he is Jim Bell, formerly of Heavy Attack Squadron One. My throat constricted as I realized that, for the first time I am speaking to one of the returning POWs who knew my husband! He told me that he was passing through town and had stopped to meet some friends at the Officers Club, and he asked me to join them there. He seemed very shy, and immediately my suspicions transformed into compassion.

As the group gathered there at the club, Jim told a story with which he had entertained his fellow POWs as they were shedding their prison garb and dressing one-size-fits-all clothes to board the Air Force planes waiting to bring them back to America.

He seemed so quiet and shy, but as he confidently and effectively told the story, I think I fell in love with him right then, although I didn't realize it at that time.

From that evening our friendship grew. And that's just what it was, a friendship. Seeing how hurt he was over losing his family, I wanted to reassure him that his wife had simply rejected her *situation*, not *him*. She and I had been in the same shoes, and I knew how hard it was to cope. I was not expecting to find another man to replace Jimmie Griffin, with whom I'd had a great marriage. But I did like having a friend, and I think Jim needed a friend at that point too. Looking back, I suppose we were both pretty needy.

One turning point was the first time we danced together. We were at a supper club that had live music. When the band began playing, we each looked helplessly at one another thinking, "I'm not sure I remember how to dance!" (I realized that the last time I had danced was eight years before, in 1965, with Jimmie.) But when the music became spirited, I urged Jim onto the dance floor, insisting, "People don't really dance like they used to. I think we can just do our own thing." And to the tune of "Bad, Bad Leroy Brown" all his shyness vanished, and he quickly came up with some moves that put him at ease. It became his favorite song.

He seemed so quiet and shy, but as he confidently and effectively told the story, I think I fell in love with him right then, although I didn't realize it at that time.

185

Jim loved to tell stories, and many of them were very, very funny. I sometimes thought he should have been a comedian. He loved having an audience, and he had a talent for tailoring his stories to fit each audience. But when we were alone, he didn't try to be funny. We enjoyed and were comfortable with quiet times together. In fact, his friends would never believe it, but we often read poetry or certain books aloud to one another.

Over the years I spent a lot of time waiting in hospitals for Jim. He had several surgeries, but the scariest time was when he spent seven weeks in a hospital, most of it in the ICU, following a scuba diving accident. But he was tough. And, when he finally was able to talk again, I watched in amazement as he retold a joke that a friend had sent to him. When he changed the joke to fit two different audiences, I knew he was going to be okay!

WAR STORIES

Jim was a Naval Academy graduate ('54) who had flown fighter attack before moving to the same reconnaissance squadron that Jimmie was in. Jim fell victim to anti-aircraft fire on a low-level mission north of Haiphong. He explained, "I made it to the sea before ejecting, but after 30 minutes in the water, my crewman and I were picked-up by local fishermen in sampans. I was tied to the mast. At one point I recalled the movie I had watched in the wardroom just the night before—*Two Years Before the Mast*—and I broke into a laugh. It was my last laugh for a long, long time.

"During the subsequent 81 months of detention in North Vietnam, I never doubted for a minute that the day would come when I would return to the land of the free. Nor did I ever lose faith in myself and my abilities to withstand the physical and mental rigors of prison life."

But he was pushed to the edge during the Hanoi March, in which 50 POWs were marched through the streets of Hanoi while thousands of citizens had been whipped into a frenzy, and they became a mob that pummeled them, spat on them, and threw rocks at them. He and Ralph Gaither [whose story is told elsewhere in this book] were chained together and were in the last row of Americans in the "parade." Jim never shared many details of his years of imprisonment; in fact, he tended to make light of it. He related that during the march, as one woman beat him with her shoe, she screamed,

"Take that you millionaire son of a bitch!" Then he would say, "No one had ever called me a millionaire before!"

[Dora says it wasn't until recently that she read about all the horrifying details in the powerful book *The Hanoi March: Light into Darkness*, by Gary Foster.]

Over the years Jim and I traveled to about 30 countries. We visited North Vietnam, and he showed me Hỏa Lò (the "Hanoi Hilton") and several other nearby prison locations. Jim teared up during the visit, and I was nauseous and had to flee the building, coming face-to-face with suffering that both my Jims had experienced.

BLESSED

I don't know what I did to deserve amazing marriages to two war heroes—two pilots who were loving, generous, honorable, and open-hearted—but I am grateful for every minute of my lives with them. With Jimmie Griffin I got to experience young love, infatuation, and a young handsome graduate of the US Naval Academy, who wrote hundreds of loving letters to me over the years. And with Jim Bell I got to experience mature love and a deep, long-term connection with a decorated war hero; we bonded over Vietnam-related heartache, and we created a marriage based on devotion, affection, and shared values.

When Jim returned home, we had some tough times in the early years, when he was adjusting to an America that had changed drastically during his seven-year incarceration. But he adjusted, we made the best of everything, and we enjoyed a wonderfully happy marriage of 40 years and four weeks!

How Lucky I Am
(Written by Dora during the Covid pandemic)

Here I sit, tempted to feel a little lonesome as I "shelter in place," with no other family members in my household, but I remind myself that when Jim was in solitary confinement in Hanoi for two years, he didn't have…

Television for entertainment and news of the outside world…

A computer to connect him with family and friends on email and Twitter and YouTube …

A telephone for talking and texting to stay in contact with loved ones…

A freezer with enough meals to last awhile…

Food delivery from stores and restaurants and neighbors…

Mail delivery to bring him dozens of discount coupons from Talbots and hundreds of appeals for donations from St. Jude and animal shelters and the Wildlife Federation and political campaigns etc. etc. etc…

Spring flowers blooming outside his window…

A supply of his "favorite beverages" on hand…

A comfy bed to sleep in, warm blankets when needed, and heat or air conditioning as desired…

A shelf full of books to read, or a Kindle app to supply them…

The freedom to walk outside in the yard, or to feel a few drops of rain or sunshine on his face, or to see the stars at night…

Yes, when I count my blessings today, I realize HOW VERY LUCKY I AM.

LOVE LESSONS

GRATITUDE

People who remain grateful for what they have—regardless of their circumstances—are the happiest people in the world.

DEVOTION

People who are deeply in love remain devoted to each other, to their marriage vows, and they communicate their devotion on a regular basis through their gestures, gifts, activities, letters, and conversations.

SHARED VALUES

Strong couples share solid values that are at the core of their beings. These shared values can transcend different religions, different upbringings, and different personalities.

Jimmie & Dora Griffin

Jim & Dora Bell

1   LCDR James L (Jimmie) Griffin USN, RA-5 Vigilante, KIA 19-JUN-67
2   LCDR Jim James F. (Jim) Bell USN, RA-5 Vigilante, POW 16-OCT-65 – 12-FEB-73, Retired CAPT USN (0-6), RIP 30-SEPT-14

THE RELEASE PROCESS

The massive Christmas bombing of 1972 brought a quick end to the war. On January 21, 1973, we assembled in the prison yards, where the Rabbit read the release protocol from the Peace Agreement. We would be released over the next 60 days, with the first group departing Hanoi on February 12, 1973.

Air Force C-141s (which we dubbed the Hanoi Taxis) were there to take us directly to Clark Air Base, in the Philippines. Celebrations began the instant the airplane broke ground, and there were more cheers when the pilot announced: "We are now feet wet!" which meant we were over international waters. During that flight, we smoked cigars, hugged the nurses, and sat in the cockpit to see the skies. We were free at last.

When we landed, to our amazement there was a huge crowd of military families and personnel cheering wildly as we stepped off the aircraft. We were bussed to the base hospital where we changed into hospital outfits and headed to the cafeteria. We ate steak and eggs (one friend ate two dozen eggs) and then heaps of ice cream. During the next 48 hours we called home, had a physical, got a haircut and a new uniform.

In the months prior to our release, medical experts concluded that, due to expected psychological problems, we should be isolated for at least two weeks of treatment and observation. Thankfully, Secretary Laird directed a flexible approach; the decision would be based on the state of each POW. And because of his wonderful wisdom, we all climbed aboard those Hanoi Taxis and headed home in less than three days.

The American public welcomed us with open arms and parades and an outpouring of support. It was like waves of love coming at us from all directions. It certainly helped us in our adjustment back to the real world. Sadly, this was not the case for many who fought in that war.

16 | WON'T YOU COME HOME, BILL BAILEY?

THE STORY OF
Bill & Suzy Bailey

Couples delight in reminiscing over how they met and fell in love. It is fascinating and fun to trace the sequence of events that led each of them to the place that ultimately became their destiny. The events seem random and disjointed at first. For Bill[1] and Suzy Bailey many, many threads in their lives had to be woven together in just a certain way to bring about their meeting. Their falling in love was unexpected—yet meant to be.

Bill jokes that when he was 21 he was out of money, ideas, and girlfriends. He didn't know what to do, so he joined the Navy to fly jets. Suzy adds that when she was the same age (six years after Bill's decision to join the Navy), she was in a foreign country, in need of a better paying job, and out of ideas—she didn't know what to do, but she'd always had wanderlust, so she joined Pan Am Airways and enjoyed a lifestyle of exciting travel.

During the mid-1960s Bill was a Naval flight officer in San Diego and having the time of his life. During this same time Suzy was in Addis Ababa, Ethiopia, taking correspondence courses for high school and having the time of *her* life. Bill's and Suzy's childhoods were remarkably different. Bill was raised on a small, third-generation family farm in an isolated, rural area near Kosciusko, Mississippi. Suzy thinks that one of the reasons Bill survived so well as a POW was that he had such a wholesome childhood. His parents were hard working and loving people. They possessed the attributes of devotion, caring, resilience, patriotism, and love. This, and Bill's belief in his country and fellow man, sustained him during five years and eight months as a POW.

Suzy was born in Oklahoma in 1948. When she was two years old, her family moved to Germany where her father worked for Radio Free Europe and later was recruited as a foreign service officer for the US State Department. The family enjoyed eight years in Germany, four years in South Africa, and Suzy's high school years in Ethiopia. (That is a long, long way from rural Mississippi!)

The three years in Ethiopia were some of the happiest years of her life. She enjoyed the culture of racial equality and political and socio-economic diversity. The teenagers were of multiple nationalities, and they enjoyed weekly dance parties. The most treasured of her adventures were those she had accompanying an English Catholic nun, Sister Gabriel. Although officially retired and in her seventies, the elderly woman trekked 19 miles round trip twice a week to remote villages to care for the sick and those suffering from Hansen's disease (leprosy).

In June of 1966 Suzy returned to the US for college. At that time Bill was flying his first combat cruise in Southeast Asia and was shot down one year later, during his second cruise, as Suzy was beginning her second year of college.

Three years earlier, in 1963, Bill enlisted in the United States Navy. Two years later he joined Fighter Squadron 143 (the world famous "Pukin' Dogs") and flew the powerful F-4 Phantom jets. He flew 178 successful missions over Southeast Asia.

And then came mission number 179…when his F-4 was hit by enemy anti-aircraft fire. With warning lights flashing, Bill and his fellow crewman continued their mission, diving from an altitude of ten thousand feet at a 45-degree angle. As they rose back into the sky, the hydraulic system failed, and they lost control of the aircraft. Speeding along at about six hundred miles per hour in violent contortions, he experienced nine or ten Gs. Bill blacked out, and when he regained consciousness, the Phantom was nearing the ground in a flat spin. He ejected safely, landed unharmed…and was immediately surrounded by more than a dozen angry Vietnamese villagers armed with guns and sticks. He was taken to the infamous Hanoi Hilton, "Where the real fun began."

Bill's first three days and nights at the Hanoi Hilton were a non-stop series of threats, interrogations, and tortures. He was deprived of sleep and was fed very little food. He was placed in leg irons, and his hands were bound together behind his back. On day three the guard pulled his bound hands up behind his back over his head. The guard then put his foot on Bill's back and pulled as hard as he could, bending Bill's body into a ball, and almost dislocating his shoulders. The North Vietnamese wanted answers and intelligence, and Bill was determined to tell them nothing but his name, rank, and serial number. But the pain of the "pretzel" finally became unbearable. His captors demanded that he write military intelligence for them. He tried to write something just to get them off his back, but his hands were too numb from the many days of bondage. He finally told them the names of targets he had bombed over the past two weeks. After all, there is nothing as worthless as yesterday's news.

He felt wretched that he had given them any information at all. But he was secretly proud that all this information was completely useless to the enemy. Yes, the ropes had left painful scars, "but the real scar was my failure to uphold my sense of duty as a United States Naval officer. I was miserable. It wasn't until a year later that I learned that every one of the POWs—*every one* of them—had the same experience. One of my greatest lessons was realizing that the real measure of resistance to the torture and attempts to exploit the POWs was, first, the ability to minimize the information you gave up and, second, the ability to 'bounce back' and continue to struggle to resist the next attempt to exploit you for propaganda."

Bill recalls one of his happiest days as a POW: "After being in solitary confinement for six months I was moved into a cell with two other guys. I think it saved my sanity. You see, I was actually getting comfortable being alone—which is not really a healthy thing. I think I talked non-stop to those guys for three days straight!"

Bill notes that humor was a survival skill that kept the morale up among the men. "One day the fellow in the cell next door tapped that he was going to make a guard say the phrase, 'What's up, Doc?' from the Bugs Bunny cartoon. The anticipation was wonderful. Days later, after Bill's neighbor returned from his monthly 'quiz session,' he reported that he had told his interrogator that the food was bad. When he asked what was wrong with the food, the POW answered, 'There's not enough UPDOC in it.' And the interrogator replied—you guessed it—'What's up doc?'"

While Bill was a guest at the Hanoi Hilton, Suzy returned to Germany after college to pursue a post-graduate degree in anthropology. One afternoon while strolling in downtown Frankfurt, she passed the Pan Am building. She had never considered being a stewardess but, as she stared up at the building, she thought it might be a fun and exciting job, and it would give her time to decide if she really wanted to pursue more schooling. Lucky was the day she decided to take that stroll! This was one of those seren-dipitous and circuitous threads that eventually led to her meeting Bill. She walked in, applied, and walked out with a ticket to Berlin for an interview the next day. As luck would have it, that was the last day Pan Am was in-terviewing for the year.

Suzy

Early in 1972 I noticed that many of the other stewardesses wore a metal bracelet with a name on it. They explained that it was to raise the aware-ness of the American public that we still had POWs and MIAs in Vietnam. I wanted to support this cause so I mailed-in my $2.50 and received a bracelet.

My bracelet read:

Lt. James Bailey
6-28-67

(Years later I teased Bill by introduc-ing him as "My mail-order groom"!)

I was shocked to learn that he had already been a prisoner of war for more than *four* years. The letter that accompanied the bracelet said that I could write to the family c/o VIVA (Voices In Vital America). I received a form letter from his mother that contained a brief bio. She added that he goes by Bill and that her granddaughter's name is Suzanne too!

I wore the bracelet proudly and prayed for Lieutenant James Bailey every night.

Early in 1973 I was based in London and my parents sent me a clipping from *Stars and Stripes* (a newspaper for Americans living abroad) that included a list of POWs who were soon to be released. My mother had circled "James W. Bailey," and she wrote in the margin, "Is this *your* POW?" I was ecstatic! It's funny how I'd always thought of him as *my* POW. What are the chances that he would soon actually become "*my* POW"?

The man I'd been praying for was freed on February 18, 1973! I quickly sent a Western Union telegram to him that read:

> WELCOME HOME! IF YOU ARE EVER IN LONDON,
> MY ROOMMATE AND I WILL SHOW YOU AROUND.

Bill

Upon my return to America, I was flooded with more than *3,000 letters* from people wearing my bracelet. I was overcome with emotion for their love and support! Because of the incredible volume of letters, I had to resort to sending a form letter to everyone. Well, everyone except for a few of the single girls who wrote to me!

Suzy and I exchanged a few letters—between London, England and Kosciusko, Mississippi—for four months. Then I headed for Europe for a summer of R&R. And, of course, I arranged to meet her.

Suzy

First, let me say that I hadn't planned to fall in love at this time of my life. I was enjoying the freewheeling life of an international stewardess for Pan Am Airways!

The process of our actual meeting was a comedy of errors and lucky coincidences that were worthy of a sitcom! The final act of that story had both of us converging on my flat—Bill from Prestwick, Scotland and me from New York City. Bill had arrived on time in the morning, and my roommate let him in. Meanwhile I had "the most frustrating series of flights in my life," with maddening weather delays and cancellations. I finally arrived (in a very disheveled state) late that afternoon. I was so excited to finally meet this amazing man. I just *knew* that we were going to be great friends.

I tentatively entered the apartment, and Bill ran flying from the living room! This six foot-four man picked me up and twirled me around in circles! I was literally swept off my feet! I was charmed by his confidence, spontaneity, and utter joy.

My roommate took me aside and cried, "*That* is the man you are going to marry!" I shushed her, "Shhhhh! Don't say that! We'll be friends, that's all."

> My roommate took me aside and cried, "*That* is the man you are going to marry!" I shushed her, "Shhhhh! Don't say that! We'll be friends, that's all."

Bill

That spontaneous reaction was one of the best things in my life that I did right! Was it fate? Kismet? Was I blessed? I don't know. Whatever. Love at first sight? I didn't really think I believed in such a thing. But when it happens—well, you know it!

Suzy

I had vowed that I would just be Bill's friend, and I had no plans to fall in love. Well, *that* resolve lasted all of 20 minutes! I now believe that Bill was the man I was meant to be with. My feelings turned me into a mindless blob of complete infatuation! Seriously though, when a man is so kind and good and wears his personality on his sleeve, it is easy to see what kind of person he is. I'd never met anyone so unpretentious and natural and humble and intelligent. I felt like the luckiest girl in the world!

And I still feel that way 47 years later. Honestly, I don't think "love at first sight" is necessary—or even desirable—but that's how it worked for us. Blind love took over, and we simply knew we were meant for each other. I will admit that Bill had one little quirk from his years as a prisoner. I had made up the couch for him that first night in our flat—but he moved the pillow and sheets to the floor. Four months back in civilization and he wasn't yet comfortable sleeping in a bed. He preferred sleeping on the floor.

* * * *

After a few days together Bill continued traveling through Europe, and Suzy continued stewardessing. Two weeks later he called her from the Italian Alps and asked if she had any time off. Suzy told him she had a week off starting the very next day. (More serendipity!) He asked her to meet him in Paris the next day. Suzy says, "I just knew he was going to ask me to marry him—so I packed my birth certificate! Well, he *did* propose, and of course I said, 'Yes!'" Later that day, she said, "Let's get married right here, right now in Paris!" Bill, being the sensible person that he is, said that he couldn't deny his mother the joy of seeing him get married. That endeared him to Suzy all the more.

Although from vastly different environments they shared a strong belief in the same core values of family, honesty, hard work, and a desire to help those suffering from institutional racism, poverty, poor health, and other problems.

Their individual lives are both different and similar, as are those of most couples. Suzy prefers romantic films, Bill action epics. Both love to read, and they always have multiple books in progress. Suzy finds it hard to get interested in sports, yet when their children played a sport, she never missed a practice or game and was their biggest fan. Without weekly golf after retirement, "Bill would be climbing the walls!"

In 1974 Bill bought an acrobatic two-seater Citabria plane. He and Suzy enjoyed countless hours of adventures. Suzy learned the basics—taking off, flying, and landing the plane—while Bill, no surprise, learned advanced aerobatics!

The Baileys soon moved to Oxford, Mississippi where Bill completed his undergraduate degree, and Suzy obtained her master's degree in Communicative Disorders. This was followed by Bill's assignments to the Naval War College, jobs in the Pentagon, and a final tour as the Executive Officer of Naval ROTC at the University of North Carolina, Chapel Hill. After he retired from the Navy, Bill worked as a teacher and administrator in the Anderson, South Carolina public high school systems. Suzy worked part-time in clinics, schools, and home health systems until her retirement the same year.

Suzy

As with every couple, we learned through some difficult and trying times how to overlook our differences and concentrate on our similarities and shared interests. We realized early on that while we were alike in so many areas, we were also very different. Respecting and honoring our differences and finding mutual solutions was our goal. Fortunately, the overlapping areas for us were plentiful, with our love for each other being the main one. We knew the soul of one another and trusted its goodness and progress, and we respected each other's differences.

I playfully call Bill "Left Brain" because he is so logical and structured. And, as you might guess, he refers to me as "Right Brain" because I am more intuitive and flexible.

Our children have been our greatest joy! James, Anne, and John are the most remarkable individuals. They are immense fun to be around and have given us the most amazing grandchildren—and grand dogs!

I'm sure many married couples can relate to this, that through the years, we have grown more alike and share most of the same opinions. We love being together more than ever. I respect Bill so much and am constantly amazed by his resilience and strength. Amazingly, he harbors no ill will for his Vietnamese captors, and many times he has taught me through his actions about the true meaning of forgiveness.

Bill

When I first met Suzy in London, I felt intoxicated with her beauty, love of life, and ability to make every day special. She was—and still is—my ideal wife and confidante. Suzy's dedication to our marriage and to our children's welfare, especially under the stress of my extensive absences due to my Naval career, is a point of pride for me. I simply cannot thank her enough for all she's done.

One of the things I love most about Suzy is her singing. She sings in the car, at home, to the children. It brings me incredible joy.

LOVE LESSONS

VALUES IN COMMON

What is the secret to staying married—*happily* married—for 47 years? Suzy and Bill agree that the very first step is to find someone who is "a great fit values-wise."

BE RESPECTFUL

And the secret for keeping love alive? They agree: "Be respectful, giving and forgiving, loving, and attentive. Be unique individuals yet joyfully interdependent."

WALK THE TALK

Couples who live happily ever after practice what they preach. Bill and Suzy are ever mindful of this Bible passage that was part of their wedding vows:

> "Love is patient and kind;
> love does not envy or boast;
> it is not arrogant or rude.
> It does not insist on its own way;
> it is not irritable or resentful;
> it does not rejoice in wrongdoing,
> but rejoices with the truth.
> Love bears all things,
> believes all things,
> hopes all things,
> endures all things.
> Love never ends."
>
> (1 Corinthians 13:4-8)

Bill & Suzy Bailey

1   LTJG James W. (Bill) Bailey USN, F-4B Phantom, POW 28-JUN-67 – 18-FEB-73, Retired
CDR USN (0-5)

THE WHITE HOUSE GALA

All POWs from North Vietnam were released between the February 12 and the March 31, 1973. Our dreams had come true! We were finally back home and with our families. In April we received an invitation from President Richard Nixon and First Lady Pat to a welcome home celebration at the White House on May 24. Every returnee was invited and allowed to bring one guest. With more than 1,330 attendees, that event is still the largest dinner ever hosted by the White House!

In the afternoon, the returned POWs attended a private presentation by the president held at the State Department auditorium. Each POW walked across the stage and shook hands with the president. During that same time, the wives and female guests were hosted at a tea by Mrs. Nixon in the White House.

Some of the single guys like me (Lee) brought their moms, and many brought their new girlfriends. Several of those couples were married within weeks or months. As you read earlier in this book, one fellow proposed to the newly met "love of his life" in the Green Room at two in the morning.

We gathered at the White House for tours and cocktails and then headed to the seating area under a tent on the South Lawn. VIPs sat at each table. The list included John Wayne, Jimmy Stewart, Sammy Davis, Jr., Martha Raye, Phyllis Diller, Roy Acuff, Joey Heatherton, and Les Brown and His Band of Renown. Each came on stage to perform or express their joy at our return. It was a wonderful evening and it closed out with Irving Berlin leading us in his famous song, "God Bless America."

17 | BACH, MOZART & UNCHAINED MELODY

THE STORY OF
Don & Cheryl Heiliger

Don[1] and Cheryl Heiliger's 43-year marriage was a fairy tale. They held hands nearly all the time. Their adventures took them from Washington, D.C. to Chile, Uruguay, and Israel, where Don was a "spy," and Cheryl played the organ in local Lutheran churches. They attended or hosted elegant diplomatic events and attended symphonies and operas. They were both musically talented and had a knack for learning languages. Their family adventures with their own three young princes took them from the intensity of Washington, D.C. and Israel to the rural calmness of 40 acres outside Madison, Wisconsin.

Growing up, their families knew each other and had attended Our Saviour's Lutheran Church in Madison, and they first met when Don was 17 and Cheryl was five. When they met for the second time, that 12-year difference was a negligible gap. They fell in love in June, and they were married five months later in December.

But a lot had happened in the 19 years between those two meetings—a whole lot. Before the love story came the horror story.

Are you familiar with Psalm 23:4?

> "Yea, though I walk through the valley of the shadow of death,
> I will fear no evil:
> for thou art with me;
> thy rod and thy staff they comfort me."

Don spent 2,106 days—that's five years and nine months—in North Vietnam POW camps. Surely a valley of the shadow of death if there ever was one.

> **[Greg's coauthor note]**
>
> *It is important to note that fairy tales are not simply lovey-dovey happy stories. They include good and evil, dragons and knights, and damsels and heroes undertaking life-threatening quests before returning home triumphant. In my 40-some years as a relationship coach and author... after interviewing thousands of couples...and writing 17 books on loving relationships...I have never met a couple who actually* lived *a fairy tale life, but this one is close!*

THE FLYING PRINCE AND THE DRAGONS HE FOUGHT

> **[Lee's coauthor note]**
>
> *Don's quotations are taken from an oral history he recorded for the Wisconsin Veterans Museum in 1999. He passed away in 2016. Cheryl filled us in on the rest of the story.*

Once upon a time a hotshot Air Force fighter pilot, Captain Donald R. Heiliger, had flown 43 successful missions over North Vietnam. And then came mission number 44. He was flying the first nighttime radar, low-level mission against one of North Vietnam's most valuable and heavily defended railroad yards. Even under the best of conditions this mission would have been extremely difficult and dangerous. However, Captain Heiliger flew in the dead of night and in a single unescorted aircraft. After flying through the tenuous buffer zone between China and North Vietnam, and nearing his target, Don's F-105 Thunderchief fighter-bomber was blown out of the sky by enemy fire.

He parachuted into a tree on a moonless, dark night. "My plan was pretty simple. I was going to walk about 70 miles to the coast. But local villagers found me the next day. They took everything except my underwear and boots, but they turned out to be friendly people. In fact, I was beginning to think that this wasn't so bad. Back at the base we'd been thinking that the war would be over in six or seven weeks, and I thought I might as well spend it here. It wasn't a bad little village. But then a uniformed communist official arrived. He whipped up the people, and their hatred was palpable.

206

I was held at gunpoint inside a hut for about 40 minutes, and I thought I was going to die. After the first few seconds I was convinced that it was my time to go. But once I accepted my probable fate, I wasn't afraid anymore. I have a fairly strong Lutheran faith, and I said prayers over and over again. The one thing I *was* mad about was that no one would ever know where I was or what my fate was."

During Don's years as a POW, he was interrogated, tortured, and sent to solitary confinement many times. But his faith, his commitment to the military Code of Conduct, and the companionship of his fellow airmen sustained him. "Our secret Tap Code was our lifeline, allowing us to communicate with each other right under our captors' noses! We could tap almost as fast as I'm talking right now.

"Our last two years of captivity were quite a bit better than our first several years. The torture eased up, and instead of cramped, dark two- or three-man cells, we were kept in 40- to 50-man rooms. We were joyful just to be able to simply talk with each other! We exercised, played games, held competitions and church services, put on plays, and taught each other pretty much everything we knew. We had language classes, math and literature classes, Bible classes, and even dance classes! Some of the guys taught skiing and golf—without any equipment! We turned the Hanoi *Hilton* into the Hanoi *University*. We wrote textbooks, poetry, and our version of the Bible—all on toilet paper." (Don points out that this was a far cry from the soft, smooth toilet paper we're used to in America!)

"A couple of English majors taught us Shakespeare, and it was amazing, upon our return, to see how accurate they were, reciting those plays from memory!

"I swear, this is why Cheryl married me! She was an English major and was teaching school, and I could recite poetry for nearly six hours without repeating myself!"

Cheryl smiles, "Well, that's not the *only* reason I married him! But I *did* marvel at his ability to recite poetry for hours!"

"I swear, this is why Cheryl married me! She was an English major and was teaching school, and I could recite poetry for nearly six hours without repeating myself!"

Don had been in the Air Force for seven years before he realized his dream of becoming a fighter pilot. "I was 28 years old, when most of the other guys were in their early twenties. I had to prove myself to both the brass *and* the younger guys. But I knew that I had the grit, the fast reflexes, and the physical and mental toughness required for one of the most intense and dangerous jobs in the world."

SKETCHES OF THE MAN

"Don was one competitive son-of-a-gun," Cheryl explains. "He finished first in his navigator's class. He failed his first aptitude test to become a pilot—but he didn't give up, and he finished first in his pilot training.

"My limited experience with the Vietnam War was the polar opposite of Don's. Near the end of the war I was in college at the liberal University of Wisconsin, and the closest I came to anything Vietnam-related was walking through tear gas on my way to choir practice." (The tear gas was from clashes between anti-war demonstrators and police.)

"Don was truly an officer and a gentleman. One small example is that, on our wedding day, he wrote a thank you letter to Ross Perot—who had supported our POWs enthusiastically and generously for years—and included our wedding program!"

Cheryl is the only wife in this book who was not really a "military wife." Even though Don did work for the Air Force, Cheryl knew him only in his role as a military attaché. Their lifestyle was quite elegant, as Don continually met with heads of state and other high ranking government officials. "Wherever Don was stationed we lived in a large, elegant house. We hosted many business and social events there."

When they settled back in America, Don served as Chief of the International Affairs Division in the Pentagon. "Don never got tired of making humorous comments about the double entendre of the phrase international *affairs*!

"Don was adept at tailoring his demeanor and actions to suit any situation. He could be professionally quite serious and measured, and he could also be outrageously funny and energetic. I once had a caricature made of him in which he's depicted as a whirling dervish, and he's surrounded by all kinds of funny things. Don was a master at one-liners. He could have people rolling on the floor with laughter!

"In many ways Don didn't stick to cultural norms. Not only did he write a lot, he did all of his own typing—at a time when nearly all professional men had a secretary. He was so fast and accurate—and generous—that he typed all my term papers when I was in graduate school. Me? I *hand write* everything! His love letters to me were all typed, mine to him were handwritten. Don was also an early adopter of personal computers when they first came out. And he could be obsessively energetic about some of his house projects. One year he planted 3,000 canna lilies on our property! The man was a demon with a Rototiller!"

FREEDOM

When the POWs first returned to America, the military and medical experts handled them with kid gloves, as they were understandably concerned about potential mental and emotional problems as well as their definite physical ailments. Don's story shows the stability of this group.

"The first thing when we landed at Clark Air Base in the Philippines [was] they took me into a room with three shrinks and a couple of doctors. They said they had some really bad news for me. 'Your wife got a divorce in Juarez, Mexico while you were gone.' I burst out laughing. They must have thought I was crazy! The backstory is that we'd been having marital problems even before I left for Vietnam. Also, I'd received a letter a year earlier in which she indicated her intentions. The doctors were prepared for me to have a big breakdown. I'm sure they were disappointed!"

Don was disappointed but not surprised to hear about the divorce. But it was jarring to discover that years earlier she had told their three children that their father was dead. But Don felt no bitterness. "What would be the point?" He and his first three children eventually grew close, with his role pretty much that of a favorite uncle.

Moving on to Don's homecoming in Madison, Wisconsin…at his first Sunday service at Our Saviour's Lutheran Church he was delighted to see that the organist was the grown-up Cheryl Kay Edwards. "I didn't really know her, but having sung in the choir there, I learned to love classical music—and

I loved Cheryl's playing. So I went up to her and said, 'I'll be back in three weeks. Would you play an all-Bach program?' And sure enough, when I returned, she played all Bach! I smiled and said, 'Thanks! I owe you dinner.'"

That's when the happy part of the fairy tale began.

CHERYL'S FOND MEMORIES

"Our first trip together was to the massive Dallas Salutes celebration. The ticker-tape parade and the celebration at the Cotton Bowl were huge, meaningful, and inspirational. It was an incredible experience for a Wisconsin girl!"

> ### [Lee's coauthor note]
> *This is the same Cotton Bowl event where Carole Hanson met Jim Hickerson (Chapter 6), and where Tom and Yona met Tony Orlando (Chapter 4).*

Cheryl smiles as she reminisces. "Don and I connected on so many levels. We really were meant to be together. We both loved music—symphonies and operas, and contemporary bands, too. I played organ, he played piano. When Don came to pick me up for our first date, I was practicing Mozart's Fantasia in D Minor on a grand piano" (which still sits in the music room of their home in McFarland, Wisconsin). "Don exclaimed, 'I *love* Mozart!' I was surprised and impressed that a 36-year-old fighter pilot was *that* familiar with the composer! And then I was *really* blown away when he sat down and played 'Unchained Melody.' He was talented—*and* romantic!

"Before the war Don sang and played piano at our church. During the war he taught music appreciation to the other POWs. They didn't have instruments, but he got the guys to sing. He taught music history—the 'Three Bs': Bach, Beethoven, and Brahms—plus, of course—Mozart. One of his fellow POWs—Ken Cordier, an engineer with beautiful printing, who later was Don's best man at our wedding—transcribed his entire 20-hour course—several times—and the toilet paper 'books' were passed around to the other rooms. Later, their captors discovered the guys' books and confiscated them all. But upon their release another POW, Joe Crecca, had snuck out of the camps one copy of Don's course! Don was flabbergasted and honored. He later had copies made—'With errors and all,' he liked to say—and many people have enjoyed them. I still have his original copy in a treasured lockbox.

"We wanted children of our own, and within seven years we had three boys: Donald, Jr., and then the twins, Daniel and David. Their lives, and ours, were filled with music and sports—baseball, soccer, football, and especially tennis. We had a tennis court out back, and the friendly competitions were constantly ongoing! During that time all our parents were alive and living near us, and so was my grandmother. We and our boys were blessed to be able to experience and enjoy three generations of our families. Don and I referred to their childhood and teenage periods as the Camelot Years. It really was fairytale-like.

"Over the years Don's three children and our three boys became friends. They are now busy and productive and happy. The two sets of children continue to have a friendly rivalry over the Ohio State Buckeyes versus the Wisconsin Badgers. They are all prospering, and they are also busy with service and non-profit organizations.

"Don's three children gave us five grandchildren, and our three boys gave us three. We've long enjoyed family get-togethers over holidays, vacations, birthdays, and weddings."

Thinking about their personal relationship, Cheryl says, "Don could be mercurial.

One of his POW buddies advised me: 'Don can get angry in an instant. But be patient and give him 30 minutes, and he'll be over it.'

"One of his POW buddies advised me: 'Don can get angry in an instant. But be patient and give him 30 minutes, and he'll be over it.'

This was the best advice I've ever received! It really helped me deal with our first relationship hurdle: his temper. I guess what I did was to accept Don at face value. I didn't think of him as previously married, and I didn't define him as a Vietnam POW. I believe that thinking this way—accepting people at face value—is a powerful mindset…for everyone in a close relationship.

"My advice to younger couples? To make a marriage work in the long run you really need to *like* each other. Love is obviously important, too. But *like* is different. Truly *liking* who your partner is—at his or her core—can sustain you through anything. Another factor for most couples is having common interests and beliefs. Your shared experiences and your faith can also sustain you through anything.

"Don and I loved to dance. Also, we were both bookaholics and even liked many of the same books. One year we read the entire Bible—we took turns reading aloud one portion per day. When flying together, we held hands during every landing.

"Don was a vibrant, active man throughout our lives together. In the last few years of his life he struggled with diabetes. At one point he had an aortic valve replacement. When the end came, he died with dignity, with me by his side."

Cheryl pauses and smiles wistfully. "Don and I loved playing piano duets together. We performed at embassies, dinners, and special events in several countries. We introduced Scott Joplin's music to many people: They loved 'The Entertainer.' They also loved Gershwin! Our personal, special song was 'The First Time Ever I Saw Your Face.'

"Back home we played the hymn 'The Holy City' in church every Palm Sunday. We did this right up until the time Don died."

Cheryl and their son Dan continue this tradition to this day.

LOVE LESSONS

FRIENDS AND LOVERS

You can be friends without being lovers. And you can be lovers without being friends. But when you combine the two you have what it takes to create and maintain a partnership that can stay alive and vibrant for a lifetime.

HOME AND FAMILY

A safe, cozy, and welcoming home is a nest where a family can grow, connect, and thrive. It takes love, dedication, and patience to set the stage for the nurturing of many well-adjusted, happy, and productive people.

FAITH AND FUN

Faith and fun can come together in many ways. From the very beginning Don and Cheryl connected and communicated though music. They literally created "a joyful noise" at home, church, and work that bonded and inspired themselves and everyone around them.

Don & Cheryl Heiliger

1   Maj Donald L. (Don) Heiliger USAF, F-105 Thunderchief, POW 15-MAY-67 – 18-FEB-73, Retired Col (0-6), RIP 23-MAR-16

H. ROSS PEROT–OUR GREAT SUPPORTER & FRIEND

H. Ross Perot, US Naval Academy graduate (1953) and a wealthy businessman in Dallas, became the key supporter of the POW/MIA effort by the wives and families. His initiatives to fly the wives to Hanoi and embarrass the communists were obviously going to be turned back. But he knew it would attract the world press—and it did, serving the cause by putting our captors in a negative light in front of the world.

He also provided chartered aircraft and covered expenses to fly POW/MIA wives and families to the Paris Peace Talks and other key locations. There they confronted our communist captors about their treatment of POWs, and their failure to identify all of the POWs, KIAs and MIAs of which they were aware.

When we came home Mr. Perot wrote a check for $250,000 to bring the Son Tay Raiders and the Son Tay POWs and their wives/dates to San Francisco for a ticker-tape parade and a gala dinner. Actors John Wayne, Clint Eastwood and several others attended. We were entertained by songs from the Andrews Sisters and by a 35-minute standup comedy routine by Red Skelton. It was an amazing reunion and a great welcome home.

Then, shortly after the White House Gala, Ross Perot, W. W. Clements, and about 20 other Dallas business leaders organized a two-day celebration called Dallas Salutes. There was a ticker-tape parade, a large dinner dance, and a celebration concert in the Cotton Bowl attended by more than 30,000 people. And, as you will see elsewhere in this book, one of the key entertainers in that event was Tony Orlando and Dawn singing their number one hit, "Tie a Yellow Ribbon Round the Ole Oak Tree."

Mr. Perot continued to support the POWs in many ways until he passed 47 years after our return. His son Ross Jr. remains a devoted friend and supporter of our NAM-POW Association.

18 | 3,241,440 MINUTES

THE STORY OF
Dick "The Beak" & Alice Stratton

"I'M NOT LETTING YOU GET AWAY!"

Born and raised in Quincy, Massachusetts, Dick "The Beak" Stratton[1] bore the traditional New England traits of independence and privacy and the Irish traits of pride and family loyalty. He was all Navy—a man's man. He was known for his sense of humor. He could be delightful or earthy depending upon the circumstances, and with some of his fellow fliers he was a hail fellow and loyal companion with a taste for ribaldry and Irish whiskey. And like most single fighter/attack pilots, he loved to be around the ladies. He had no idea that the one who would catch his attention and be his teammate for life had recently arrived in town.

Alice had grown up in a solid family in a rural area near Detroit. She earned a master's degree in clinical social work from Michigan and was very committed to her goals. "My dream was to practice my profession, do a bit of traveling, marry, and raise a family while expanding my professional credentials. With my graduate degree and my counseling license in hand, I joined two of my friends in the same vocation. We decided that working in a big city would enhance our professional experience. There were plenty of jobs available in San Francisco, so we headed west." And although Alice was somewhat reserved and practical, she also had the inner confidence and strength to take on challenges.

The girls were having a tough time meeting "the right kind of young men," so they attended a blind date party. And guess what? Alice met this aggressive "up front" fellow who was the kind that she had always been attracted to. Bingo! It was love at first sight. They both knew right away that they had met someone special. They fell in love fast, and four months later when Dick was training in Southern California, they met on Manhattan Beach near Los Angeles and Dick proposed. They weren't planning to rush the wedding. Then, when Dick received an assignment for a ten-month cruise which was to leave in a couple of months, he assumed they would get married when he returned.

But Alice was having none of it. "I'm not letting you get away!" And so, within a few weeks they were married.

Dick smiles, "You would have needed a jeweler's magnifying glass to see the diamond in her engagement ring!"

FAMILY TIES

What followed were five happy and bustling years. They had adopted Pat in 1962, Mike in 1964, and then their natural son Charlie arrived in 1965. Dick loved Alice with a love and affection that bordered on worship. She was his counterpoint: bright, witty, attractive, and sometimes shy, yet very strong. She could handle Dick deftly, love him deliberately, confront him when there was an issue, and bend under his maleness when she chose to. Their matchup was truly one-of-a-kind. And there was a bond between them that could not be broken and which few outsiders understood. They both shared an extraordinary commitment to each other and their family. This would carry them through six years of separation and hell, and through almost 50 years of earthly heaven since his release for a total of 64 years of marriage.

"Dick was not—and still is not—a quiet man," Alice smiled at the understatement, "and sometimes his bluster and intimidating manners reached outrageous limits. But he was different with me than with other people. We have always had an easy, comfortable relationship. Dick has always been warm and accepting."

"It's true, I'm not all that demonstrative with Alice. 'You *know* I love you, honey! Why do I have to *tell* you?'"

"You see? But he's really got a soft spot for me!"

As Alice had found in her husband an ideal mate, she also discovered a doting father. "Dick spent a tremendous amount of time with the boys in the four years before he went to Vietnam. He was very patient, fun, and empathic with them."

At that time the Vietnam War was gaining momentum, and Dick decided that he needed to help in the US efforts there. "It was a war that I did not have to go to—but this was *my* war!"

Dick came from a long line of military men. His father's wars were in the Navy (WWI) and Massachusetts State Guard (WWII). His brother's war was Korea. Alice understood this mindset. Like many people of their era, several members of her family had served in wartime too. She supported his decision wholeheartedly.

WELCOME TO HELL

On the morning of January 5, 1967, as Dick was confidently screaming toward North Vietnam in his A-4 Skyhawk, he was not thinking of Alice. But 20 minutes later she would save his life.

While attacking the enemy, Dick's plane blew up, and plummeted out of the sky. When his plane exploded near the ground, and he was about to eject, several things flashed through his mind. His first thoughts went immediately to the torture some of his friends were experiencing at the hands of the communists. And he considered going down with his plane.

But then he remembered the last words that Alice had said to him as he had left her at Lemoore Naval Air Station in California for his Vietnam tour of duty: "Don't you *dare* die and leave me with three little kids!"

But then he remembered the last words that Alice had said to him as he had left her at Lemoore Naval Air Station in California for his Vietnam tour of duty: "Don't you dare die and leave me with three little kids!"

Dick gritted his teeth and ejected. (Alice later said, "Dick *knew* what was waiting for him on the ground, but rather than face my wrath through all of eternity, he decided to eject!")

[Lee's coauthor note]

A clarification of how "Dick's plane blew up." It was not enemy fire that destroyed Dick's A-4 Skyhawk. Yes, they were shooting at him. But he was blown up by the old and sometimes unreliable weapons he was firing at the enemy. How could that happen?

It was common for his unit to carry rockets that were developed about 20 years earlier, toward the end of WWII. When a defective rocket failed to fully deploy in front of his aircraft, it was sucked into the air intake of his jet engine. The compressor blades disintegrated, blowing up the engine and thus cutting the tail off the aircraft. An aircraft without an engine or tail is like an unguided missile headed for a collision with Mother Earth. Instantly, he knew that this mission was over. With seconds to spare, he pulled the ejection handle to save his life by parachuting into enemy territory.

After arriving in the POW camp Dick was tortured extensively. Like all the other POWs he soon learned that they could inflict so much pain that you would do things that you thought for sure that you would *never* do. Things like sign a confession of guilt or share information that might help the enemy. The torturers were quite good at making men suffer horrifically. They were also quite good at stopping just short of killing them—a grotesque practice. And likewise, the POWs were good at giving them "something" that was really "nothing."

Dick began to analyze himself and the situation, and he came up with a plan to publicly raise doubt about the communists' treatment of the POWs. He would give them what they wanted, but in a way that would backfire on them. He knew that it could backfire on himself also. Yes, it was an incredibly creative and courageous plan that *might* work, but to do it he had to go against his own commitments and give in to the enemy and "give them what they wanted." It was very risky from all angles, but he decided to take that path anyway.

Sure enough, his public confession and bowing performance were published in the media worldwide. He made it so bizarre that people immediately concluded it was the results of an enemy brainwashing. Dick Stratton became world famous. This caught the attention of the US Defense Department and was seen as evidence that POWs were being mistreated. It did raise some eyebrows, both in the camps and back home. However, it was 1967, too early in the war for the administration or the wives to jump on it and launch a big movement to confront the communists. Little did anyone know that the rest of the story would someday be told when The Beak got an opportunity to plot *another* step. Two years later his story would unfold and be like gasoline on the smoldering torch that would soon spread a worldwide burn on the North Vietnamese.

ALICE IN WONDERLAND

While Dick was facing life and death battles in the prisons, Alice was struggling to raise three young boys while working part time as a counselor. When she saw a magazine with his bowing press conference pictures and the articles on his confession, it was the day before their eighth wedding anniversary. She was crushed with overwhelming emotions.

Then as you will learn later, out of a desire to help her husband and not sit idle, Alice became very involved in the National League of POW/MIA Families. She was an attentive listener and soon was motivated to overcome her intense fear of speaking in public. A local Toastmasters Club helped Alice and several POW/MIA wives become more comfortable speaking in front of a group. She was not a particularly polished speaker, but her message was clear and poignant. "I knew if I let myself express my emotions I wouldn't be able to continue."

TRICKING THE V

Two years later, in 1969, Alice would finally receive confirmation that Dick was alive. The backstory is worthy of its own book, but we'll give you a thumbnail version here. The communists had nicknamed the hero of that story "The Incredibly Stupid One," but that turned into a blessing.

At 20, the youngest and lowest-ranking POW, Seaman Apprentice Doug Hegdahl was *not* stupid. He was, however, a simple farm boy from Clark, South Dakota. It being 1966, and Doug being patriotic, he volunteered for the US Navy. While on a cruise in the Tonkin Gulf he was exploring on deck at 3:30 a.m. when during a turn, their naval artillery suddenly cut loose. The turn plus the concussions tossed Doug overboard—without anything in his pockets. When the communists caught him, they quickly concluded that he was too young to have any worthwhile intel. Doug decided to play dumb. That decision turned out brilliantly for himself and his fellow POWs.

In the camps the communists let their guard down because they felt "The Incredibly Stupid One" knew nothing and was no danger to them. At times, they let him wander through the camp unattended (which gave him many opportunities to communicate covertly with other POWs), and the jailers talked freely around him (allowing him to collect valuable information). After two years, he was chosen by the V to be one of three POWs to be released—not out of kindness, but as a publicity ploy.

He didn't want to go, as it went against the prisoners' camp policy and the Code of Conduct. But his senior leader and former cellmate (the hero of *this* story), Dick Stratton, ordered him to return home and share the story of how the POWs were being treated. Former cellmate Captain Joe Crecca had helped the supposed simpleton memorize the names of more than 250 POWs. Not only that, but he also memorized their rank, Social Security number, and an identifying trait, such as a child's name or pet's name, for confirmation. (He memorized them by singing all this information to the tune of "Old McDonald Had a Farm.") When he returned to America, Hegdahl received massive publicity. More importantly he privately debriefed and shared the POW story with DOD officials.

And that's how Alice heard that her husband was alive.

And that's how Alice heard that her husband was alive.

She headed straight to the Bethesda Naval Hospital to meet with Hegdahl. Hearing the gruesome and painful firsthand story of her beloved husband's terrible treatment and life as a POW was devastating. The shocking reality of his situation slammed home in her head and heart. Her first instinct was to just shut down and keep it all internal. But her courage and wisdom came through, and she knew she would have to speak up and share Dick's story.

The story was already rattling cages in D.C., and on September 2, 1969, there was a major press conference at Bethesda Naval Hospital where a government spokesman read a statement from DOD Secretary Melvin Laird hammering the communists for their mistreatment of American POWs. The next day Ho Chi Minh died, and when the new leaders took over in Hanoi in October, a change for the better finally began in the treatment of Dick and his fellow POWs.

Meanwhile, strong and steady Alice spoke very effectively before many groups, including the media. As Dick later reflected on her actions while he was imprisoned, "Alice was prepared to fight the system all the way to the top!"

3,241,440 MINUTES…

…just over six years, is how long Dick was held captive by the North Vietnamese.

"My fellow POWs and I had many things in common. We had families that were cohesive; we grew up in actual neighborhoods; we took school (mostly) seriously; we attended church, and we had a good sense of humor—with a bias toward *self-deprecating humor*—all of which reinforced the common values of a free people.

"And, we were *optimists*. We knew that we could prevail over our enemies, that our families loved us, that God was looking over us, and that our country would come for us. Alice was an optimist, too. She overcame her natural shyness and was tremendously active in the League."

OPERATION HOMECOMING

On March 4, 1973, the C-141 transport plane full of just-freed POWs had just touched down at Clark Air Base in the Philippines. A color guard, red carpet, and more than a thousand people waited for the men to emerge one by one. The commander approached Dick and advised the scowling man to smile. "Why the hell should I smile? I'm tired, I'm dirty, I stink. The clothes don't fit, and I don't feel like smiling!"

"Well, just take it from a friend. If you love your family, you'll come off this plane smiling because they're going to be watching you." Dick pondered this advice.

He exited the plane and nearly ran down the ramp. And his smile was so dazzling that the media commentators remarked on it.

In Palo Alto, California, watching her TV, Alice saw her husband get off that plane. Seeing the walk, the salute, and the smile, she let out a cry of joy. Then the tears came—followed by an incredible feeling of relief. The desperate hours were over. More than six years—2,251 days, 54,024 hours, 3,241,440 minutes—of waiting, fear, sleepless nights, of raising sons without a father, of helping other wives in the same predicament, of loneliness and anger and frustration, of sleeping alone and fighting alone and hoping alone…were all finally at an end. Now she would wait for what she knew would quickly come next—his voice.

The phone rang once. She picked it up in mid-jingle.

"Hello?" she said automatically, even though she *knew* who it was.

"Hi, hon, I love you. How are you?" The Massachusetts baritone with its broadened A's was still the same, still strong, still *him*.

"Back in the years when Dick was away, it was the children who often had the most difficulty," says Alice. "Charlie, our youngest, didn't know his dad at all, as he had been only one year old when Dick went off to war. In second grade his teacher asked the class to write their three wishes and to draw a picture about them. Charlie wrote, 'I would wish for my Daddy to come home three times,' and he drew an elaborate picture of the helicopter bringing his dad home, and of Charlie's eyes popping out as he greeted his dad with arms uplifted. But he did not draw a head on his father—because he couldn't visualize him, even though I had pictures of him all over the house. The next day, the teacher told the class to draw a picture of their wishes come true. Charlie wrote, 'My Dad is home now,' and he left the rest of the page blank."

AT HOME & WORK

Dick continued serving in the Navy for several years. He worked on the Trident Program with Lockheed Missiles & Space Company; he worked in recruiting in New York City and Chicago; and he served as Director of the Naval Academy Preparatory School in Newport, Rhode Island.

At the same time, Alice became involved with the Navy's new concept of Family Service Centers. Then, in 1985, because of her unique experience as a POW wife and a social worker for many years working extensively with Navy families, she was invited by the Assistant Secretary of the Navy to take the newly created role of Deputy Assistant Secretary for the Navy's Department of Personnel and Family Matters. She accepted the post, and during her four-year Pentagon tour her office diary shows that she visited 89 USN bases here and around the world. Her job was to listen, report, and recommend. It was a perfect fit, and she accomplished her mission. Meanwhile, Dick was holding down the fort back home in Rhode Island. What a great example of two people who are committed to each other and supporting the mission that each is called to accomplish.

As he was winding down his military career, Dick realized that he also had a passion for helping people and families. He decided to fly formation with Alice…and he quickly gained a master's in social work and practiced as a clinical social worker from 1987 to 2001, specializing in psychological trauma and addictions.

Dick and Alice are retired and live in Atlantic Beach, Florida. In 2023 they will have been married 64 years. They are very proud of their three sons whom they believe "married up" to some smart and special women. These three families have given them six granddaughters. And what makes Dick and Alice especially proud is that they have taught the kids right from wrong, about duty, honor, country, about religion, about teamwork and sports, about sharing and contributing.

Dick summed his pride of his sons saying, "They all learned the value of an honest day's labor, the denial and delay of self-gratification, of when to keep their mouths shut and when to speak up. They have served their country in combat or in the slums. They are productive, contributing, employed, decent human beings who ask for little and give their all."

And he gives credit to the one who captured him by love saying, "If you believe as I do that a child's code of ethics is implanted in that child by the time they reach puberty (10 to 12), you can see how important Alice's efforts to provide a normal childhood in an abnormal situation (a single parent for seven years) were to enabling the boys to successfully compete in a rather cruel world."

And yes, Dick's call sign, "The Beak," was bestowed on him because of his generous nose. And no, it has never bothered him.

LOVE LESSONS

COMMITMENT

An unshakable commitment to each other is critical for all couples, and especially so for two people who both have strong personalities and are quite independent. Dick and Alice are great role models who are very different yet completely committed to each other and their life missions. Their story was a great example of the "give and take" that it is needed in a great marriage.

SENSE OF HUMOR

If you truly believe in yourself, you can laugh at yourself. When you have the ability to laugh *at* yourself and *with* others, you can weather the bad times and enjoy the good times. When you find a person who can laugh at themselves, and with whom you share laughs, you have found a treasure.

BE OPEN TO GOOD ADVICE

Know-it-alls don't learn from experience, nor are they able to act on good advice when it's given. You have to be open and trusting to learn from others who are wiser than you. Both of them understood this, and Dick gave a great example. He was smart enough to listen to his commander when he advised him to smile for his family upon returning home after being away for 3,241,440 long minutes. His smile sent a powerful ray of love to his wife, boys, and his country.

Dick & Alice Stratton

1 LCDR Richard A. (Dick) Stratton USN, A-4E Skyhawk, POW 5-JAN-67 – 4-MAR-73, Retired CAPT USN (0-6)

WELCOMED HOME WITH OPEN ARMS

Unlike most other Vietnam veterans, the returning POWs were warmly welcomed. Several things came into play to make that happen. The widespread effort by the National League of POW/MIA Families and the Go Public effort of the Nixon administration touched minds and hearts at every level of our society. Additionally, Pentagon leaders had been working for several years to plan for the return of POWs to their families. The process launched with the great name of "Operation Homecoming." Also, the war was over, so the anti-war groups were shrinking back.

It all started when we landed at Clark Air Base in the Philippines. There were crowds to greet us and crowds to say goodbye when we left two days later. And then there were crowds and parades waiting for us when we got home.

We were much healthier than expected. Thanks to the pressure from the League, our government, and related world pressure, our treatment changed drastically in the fall of 1969. Thereafter, we received minimal harassment and torture. Additionally, after the Son Tay raid, we were typically locked in large rooms with cellmates who had experienced worse treatment and been there longer. This environment gave us what turned out to be a subtle version of group therapy and catharsis. The emotional healing that came in the prison camps during our last three years was instrumental in our recovery from the pain and stress of the POW experience.

And then, when we were released, we were instantly transformed from being caged prisoners to being national heroes. The love we experienced brought much joy and more healing.

Amazingly, the data shows that POWs who returned from the Hanoi system had a lower rate of PTSD than soldiers who fought in the south. We POWs are extremely sad that most of our Vietnam veterans were not honored when they came home. We believe that would have helped them to find healing from their terrible war experience.

It's been 50 years since the war ended, but it's never too late to show appreciation and welcome home our Vietnam veterans.

HISTORICAL HIGHLIGHT

19 | A TALE OF TWO HEROES

THE STORY OF
Paul & Phyllis Galanti

While grinding through a somewhat boring "summer cruise" in the Great Lakes, Naval Academy Midshipman Paul Galanti[1] was struck by a romantic poem he ran across in a magazine. He was deeply moved by the message—as though it had been written specifically for him to share with the love of his life—Phyllis Eason. He gave it to her during their courtship, and it was treasured by both of them.

> "Lonely the days and nights, my love,
> that we have been apart.
> It seems almost forever since I held you
> to my heart.
>
> The moments are as restless
> as the waves that move the sea,
> but every second means a step nearer,
> nearer, my love, to thee."[2]

In retrospect, that poem was incredibly prophetic. Paul and Phyllis had been married for two years when his ship deployed to war in November 1965. En route, Phyllis met him in Hawaii for a romantic farewell. From there he headed into combat, and seven months later he was shot down and captured. Sadly, it would be seven years and two months before they would see each other again. This beautiful, heartfelt poem became especially meaningful when Paul regained his freedom. It was as though things came full circle when those were among the very first words he spoke to Phyllis.

On the plane headed to Virginia, Admiral Denton—the senior officer who spoke when the first group out of Hanoi landed at Clark Air Base days before—graciously asked Paul to speak when the plane landed. Paul, looking out of the plane window, spotted among the large crowd his parents and Phyllis. On the tarmac, after addressing the public, Paul recited the love poem he had given to her years before…and Phyllis broke ranks and ran to greet him. It was his first hint that "shy Phyllis" was not so shy anymore!

This is the story of two war heroes. One was a confident and gregarious Navy pilot fighting communism in Vietnam. The other was a once-shy woman fighting a battle on two fronts. First, the wives had to stand up and resist the passive "soft diplomacy" policy of the American government regarding the treatment and accounting for our POWs and MIAs. And second, they had to bring pressure to bear on the communist captors who were treating our men as "creeminals." These two war heroes were husband and wife, Paul and Phyllis Galanti.

Their story can be summed up in three famous scenes. The first is the photo portrayed on the October 20, 1967 cover of *Life* magazine. It was a communist propaganda photo, in which he undercut their disinformation campaign by flipping the bird to his unsuspecting captors. The second is Phyllis in a newspaper photo shown below. It shows her seated between President Nixon and Henry Kissinger as she and Sybil Stockdale insisted that they toughen their stance against North Vietnam to ensure that all POWs would be released. And the third is Paul and Phyllis together on the front cover of *Newsweek* (February 26, 1973). It shows them reunited and enthusiastically ready to resume their marriage.

BUT LET'S JUMP BACK TO THE BEGINNING...

Both Paul and Phyllis grew up in military families. Their fathers were both career Army officers who happened to be stationed together in Turkey in the 1950s. Paul had spent some time there, and the younger Phyllis had noticed him, but it was Paul's mom who brought them together. As Paul relates, "I met Phyllis when I was a rising high school senior at Valley Forge Military Academy in Pennsylvania and returned to Turkey to visit my family. My mother worked in the Ankara American School, where Phyllis was a sophomore. Out of the blue, my mom began promoting her and gave her total endorsement, saying things like, "She's beautiful, very nice, and very smart!" Paul, with an incredulous look that oozed sarcasm, responded, "Yeah. Right, Mom. And all the girls like her and she makes her own clothes!" Actually, both of those were true—but unimportant to a prospective Navy Midshipman. But Paul definitely remembers his first impression: "She was drop-dead gorgeous!"

And then providence intervened. Phyllis's dad was reassigned to Fort Meade, Maryland, a mere eight miles from the Naval Academy, where Paul would enter one year after his mother began marketing for her first daughter-in-law! Their relationship seems to have been preordained.

Paul and Phyllis began dating when he was a plebe (freshman) at the Naval Academy. Plebes were not allowed to date, but the academy held regular "tea dances." Phyllis somehow got herself onto the invitation list, and when the girls lined up to be asked to dance, Paul tactfully moved quickly to cut in when Phyllis appeared. Later, when she went off to college at William and Mary, she would visit with family and friends who lived near the Academy, which allowed them to date more frequently. The relationship grew strong. Paul says with a smile, "We used to make out till our jaws hurt! Then we'd rest up for our next date."

Paul graduated in 1962 and headed off to Naval flight school. It didn't take long to miss her companionship, so when there was a short break in training, he headed back east to ask for Phyllis's hand in marriage. For her engagement ring he bypassed the traditional diamond ring and chose something he knew was especially meaningful to her: a replica of his USNA ring.

As a military child she knew what the ring meant: commitment, hard work, and dedication to our country—qualities important in a good soldier and in a good mate.

You know the phrase "Opposites attract"? Phyllis and Paul were polar opposites in terms of personality types and natural talents. Phyllis described herself as an "extreme introvert," and came across as calm, patient, and kind. Paul was a supremely confident and boisterous extrovert. (Phyllis says, "He had a fighter pilot's personality long before he became an actual pilot!") The two of them made their differences work for them: They respected and even celebrated each other as individuals.

As a military child she knew what the ring meant: commitment, hard work, and dedication to our country— qualities important in a good soldier and in a good mate.

Paul says that Phyllis was his "great love" but his *first* love was flying! "I fell in love with flying when I was four years old. I knew what a P-38 Lightning fighter plane was before I could count to 38!"

PRISONER OF WAR

US Navy pilot Lt Paul Galanti deployed to Vietnam aboard the *USS Hancock* in November 1965. While flying his 97th combat mission, his A-4C Skyhawk fighter jet was shot down over Hanoi, and he was captured immediately by North Vietnamese citizens. He was hauled off to the Hanoi prison system where he spent nearly seven years in ten different POW camps.

Paul's fighter pilot nickname in the camps was "Wopppo." He explains, "That's my Italian heritage. And I always point out to people that the middle p is silent." "Wopppo was inflicted on me by my VA 216 Flight Safety officer LCDR 'Baldy' Baldwin. When I ran into him after the war, he confessed that he too is half-Italian. So, I made him an honorary Italian by adding an i to his last name, and 'The Great Baldwini' became his new nickname. He wore it well."

"Humor was one of the major factors that helped the guys entertain themselves and keep their sense of perspective. For example, at the infamous Hanoi March—during which 50 POWs were forced to march through the streets of the city while thousands of angry citizens beat them, threw rocks at them, and screamed and spit at them"—Wopppo remembers, "I was handcuffed to Len Eastman, and we were at the tail end of the parade. I had been a prisoner in Hanoi for only one week and had no idea what to expect. At one point I said aloud, 'Geez, I hope they don't do this *every* week!' Our buddy Jon Reynolds was right in front of us, and he cracked up—and was promptly banged on the head by a guard. Later he told me, 'It was worth it!'"

While in solitary confinement, Wopppo discovered an unknown talent. He was adept at creating off-color commercial jingles for fictional products. For a time, he composed a new one every day, then sang them to the guys when they lived in the larger cells. With the language classes and Paul's amazing skill, he could conduct commercials in four-part harmony by their version of a barbershop quartet—in English, Spanish, French, and German. He claimed that his jingles came from The Golden Guinea Advertising & Plumbing Company.

[Greg's coauthor note]
At 83 Paul still remembers plenty of his jingles. I can confirm that they are rather bawdy, they are very funny, and he is still a darn good singer!

Back to Paul: "An important thing that helped me survive was that I am an eternal optimist. The communists never understood that they had captured the biggest group of optimists in the world. Fighter pilots know that they can handle any challenge, defeat any foe, and that they are *not* going to be the guy who's gonna crash a plane or get shot down. And even after getting shot down, captured, and tortured, the suffering and deprivation over several years didn't shake our optimism. Of course, we all had tough times, but we always bounced back."

[Lee's coauthor note]
While Paul and I were roommates for two years, he acquired the new nickname "Pablo" while we were studying Spanish together. I was lucky, as he already had a year-and-a-half of experience dealing with our captors during the hard times. His toughness set the bar high, and his optimism helped us stay positive. Paul was a great cellmate—easy to get along with and always bubbling with humor and a quick wit. In the "big

room" years, we studied three languages together and practiced them so much we started speaking them in our dreams.

A WIFE AT WAR

For Phyllis, waiting passively while the love of her life suffered made the early years a slow burn. Like many of the other wives her patience eventually wore out. In 1969 she reluctantly but confidently spoke up. She could no longer tolerate the US government's "keep quiet" policy for families and its hesitancy to publicly confront the North Vietnamese about the treatment of our men they were holding in prison. To step up and step out, she had to overcome an intense shyness. She had majored in French but considered herself "way too shy to teach" or to stand up in front of a group of people. But, her love for Paul and her frustration with the government's inaction roused an unexpected fierceness inside her.

Just as the POWs were hanging tough with close camaraderie and secret communications, Phyllis had amazing support as she fought for the POW/MIA cause. Like all great warriors she did not fight alone. There were two women beside her every step of the way, Judi Clifford and Connie Richeson. Together with their husbands and Phyllis, this small group would sit down and plot out necessary steps to promote awareness for their mission to make it a national cause. They came up with the wonderfully creative idea to get PO Box 100,000 as an attention-getting tactic that generated three-quarters of a million letters to Hanoi leaders from Virginia citizens.

Phyllis was blessed by the camaraderie provided by these two ladies and their families. Judi lived in England for six years and Phyllis visited her 30 times in those six years. Every week she would mail Judi a package of newspaper clippings to keep her up to date.

Connie had two kids and Judi had five, and they all vacationed together every year. They have hysterical pictures of those kids hanging on Phyllis and loving on her. She spent so much time with these two families and became so close to those seven kids that they were like a medicine for her loneliness and for the anxiety over Paul's uncertain future. A crucial message comes through loud and clear from both the cells of Hanoi and the homes of the prisoners' families: Strength, hope and resilience come from love, camaraderie, common cause, and heart connections.

As the Virginia state chairman of the National League of POW/MIA Families in February 1971, Phyllis announced her "Write Hanoi: Let's Bring Paul Galanti Home," campaign during her speech to the Virginia Senate. She secured financial backing, gathered a team, and worked tirelessly.

A decade later journalist Don Dale wrote in the *Richmond Style Weekly*:

> "Early on, Phyllis had walked into the *Richmond Times-Dispatch*'s newsroom straight out of a meeting with the governor and asked if the paper was interested in doing a story. It wasn't. Phyllis asked bluntly whether fashions and furniture were more important than the POWs, then left.

> "A few hours later, a T-D reporter was asking for an interview and Richmond had its own, self-described 'token POW wife.' Richmonders got to know Phyllis well, in print, on the radio and on TV. She told us Paul's story to make us care. And it worked. More than 450,000 Richmonders sent letters in a Write Hanoi campaign to urge North Vietnam to release the POWs."

The "Write Hanoi" campaign caught on quickly and soon Phyllis' team efforts had collected more than 750,000 letters from Virginia (452,000 from Richmond) demanding that they comply with the guidelines of the Geneva Conventions on treatment of POWs. Phyllis and a group of POW wives then hand-delivered them to the North Vietnamese delegation at the Paris Peace Talks.

In March 1971, Phyllis and a small delegation traveled to Stockholm, Sweden to meet with the chargé d'affaires at the North Vietnamese Consulate. During a pre-meeting phone call, they were specifically told that only men could attend. Phyllis would have none of it! She raised her voice and defiantly said, "No way! Either meet with me or I'll bring the press." Fifteen minutes later the North Vietnamese agreed to meet with her.

A few months later, Phyllis was one of four POW wives who met with President Richard Nixon and Secretary Henry Kissinger in the Oval Office to discuss the US government policies relating to the POWs. In October

1972, Phyllis was selected as Board Chair of the League. In this role she tirelessly petitioned US congressmen, senators, and President Nixon for the release of all 591 POWs.

After the end of the war, in 1973, President Nixon said of Mrs. Galanti and other League members:

> "The reason that I said these are some of the bravest people America has ever produced is that they never wavered. They always said, 'We want our men back, but we also want peace with honor for what they fought for.'"

In 2018, writing in the *Bearing Drift*, journalist and political commentator Lynn Mitchell remembers:

> "I was a student growing up in Richmond during those Vietnam years when it became the epicenter of the POW movement. Mrs. Galanti appeared to be all over the news to my young eyes, but I didn't realize the huge significance of it all at the time…

> "In 1971, when women were still finding their way in a man's world, she was a shining example of what was possible through hard work, perseverance, determination, and a plain old never-give-up attitude. For my generation, Phyllis Galanti was a role model of what women could do… for me as a shy introverted teenager, she was a role model who proved that even the quiet warriors among us have a place in battle and, sometimes, history."

Phyllis met and worked with many influential people through her work with the League. She remained friends with Ross Perot for the rest of her life.

REUNITED

Paul was released on February 12, 1973, and after three days at Clark Air Base he returned to America. And, as mentioned earlier, he and Phyllis graced the cover of *Newsweek* under the banner headline, "Home at Last!"

When Paul began responding to media requests for interviews, he said he'd love to, but he doubted that Phyllis would participate, saying that "Phyllis is *so* shy—you'll see!" She arrived for their first interview together dressed in her gorgeous navy-blue dress (that she wore for the *Newsweek* cover). Paul noticed that she was unusually calm and confident. The reporters seemed to know her, and she called them by name. Paul was very confused. He answered the first few questions, but when he paused for a moment Phyllis took the microphone and said, "I'll take the next one." Paul later marveled, "My shy kitten has evolved into a tiger!"

Shortly after all the POWs were freed, they were all honored at a gala dinner at the White House. At one point Henry Kissinger leaned over to Paul and said, "Your wife, Paul. She caused me so much trouble!" Paul smiles when he remembers this. "I'd never been more proud of Phyllis!"

She believed and often said, "The circumstances of life don't make you who you are, they reveal who you are," quoting Rev. Dr. Sam Peoples.

In their first few weeks together, Phyllis shared with him the many changes, stories, and adventures she had experienced over the previous seven years. Paul was astounded! But Phyllis soon took a step back out of the spotlight. She was comfortable and happy to let Paul take the lead. And while she had good friends, she also enjoyed being alone. And although the two of them were totally opposite in personality, they were "very easy" with each other. They both loved to laugh, read, and keep up with current events,

And when Phyllis found that she couldn't escape the spotlight altogether, she decided to use it for doing good. She raised money for her favorite causes, including The Virginia Home and other local groups that help women.

Phyllis and Paul worked well as a team. But their professional partnership was very different from their personal partnership. They didn't go in for PDAs (public displays of affection) and they didn't hold hands. But they were both extremely affectionate, complimentary, and supportive at home.

When asked what he learned from his time as a prisoner of war, Paul said, "The first was that I wasn't as tough as I thought I was. And I learned that no matter how bad I had it, somebody else always had it worse. But the most important thing I learned came from solitary confinement: *There is no such thing as a bad day when there's a doorknob on the inside of the door.*"

And here's a little background on *Life* magazine's cover photo of Paul in prison. He had posed with both middle fingers extended. His captors didn't know what the gesture meant. The editors at the magazine decided that this was inappropriate—so they air-brushed out the offending fingers. But the uncensored photo made its way into newspapers and magazines around the world. Ultimately Paul's message of defiance came through loud and clear!

One of Paul's curious claims to fame is that he has a comic strip character based on him. The characters in the cartoon Shoe are anthropomorphized birds. "Loon" is a mail carrier whose lack of aeronautic skills are the subject of recurring jokes. Paul's friend, Jeff MacNelly, was an award-winning cartoonist who honored him in this unique way.

Phyllis passed away in April 2014 after a short battle with leukemia. She was interred at Arlington National Cemetery. "We were happily married for 51 wonderful years. I'm surprised I didn't go first—because I did everything wrong. I smoked till I was 60, and I haven't exercised much. Phyllis walked every day. She could wear out a dog!"

Paul has spent the last several decades in a variety of public service activities. In 2010 he and Phyllis were honored when the Virginia War Memorial in Richmond named a new wing "The Paul & Phyllis Galanti Education Center." Paul is currently active in the Families of the Wounded Fund, a nonprofit that raises funds for the primary next of kin for post 9/11 wounded service members. He says, "It's the most rewarding thing I think I've ever done."

And so, Paul's work and dedication to helping others has become a wonderful way of honoring Phyllis's memory and her heroic work on behalf of all our POWs.

LOVE LESSONS

OPTIMISM

After the war Paul often spoke on optimism. He knew from experience that "truly believing that 'It's all going to work out' will give you the faith and dedication to make it work out." Optimism has been identified by psychologists as the most important factor in Vietnam POW survival and returning with good mental health. This same optimism enabled Phyllis to endure without Paul for almost seven years, and then it carried their marriage throughout the rest of their lives.

THE HEALTHY COUPLING OF CONFIDENCE AND HUMILITY

Leadership is sometimes overt and loud, and sometimes quiet and firm. Underneath is the foundation of the somewhat paradoxical qualities of confidence and humility. True self-confidence enables a person to make the difficult decisions, while humility enables them to own their mistakes and respect the roles of others and value their contributions. Paul and Phyllis were opposites in many ways, but in their marriage, they both displayed a healthy combination of inner confidence and genuine humility.

COMPANIONSHIP

Companionship is often assumed away. But in great marriages the partners learn to intentionally flex to the other's interests in order to find ways to enjoy time together. As the years go by and the infatuation fades, it is companionship that is a constant background to the peaks and valleys of a strong marriage.

Paul & Phyllis Galanti

1 LT Paul E. Galanti USN, A-4C Skyhawk, POW 17-JUN-66 – 12-FEB-73, Retired CDR USN (0-5)
2 Author unknown.

BLACK AND WHITE BROTHERS IN THE CAMPS

Since all the POWs grew up in the era of segregation in the south and many of us were raised in that region, you might think that race issues would have been a problem in the camps. After all, we were all locked up together, in tiny cells, for many years. Yet, we never had a single problem. In fact, there are many inspiring stories of our unbreakable relationships. Here's one.

During his shoot-down and capture, Major Fred Cherry (Virginia), a black man, was so seriously injured that he could not care for himself. They put Fred in the cell with a "white boy," Navy Lieutenant Porter Halyburton (North Carolina) who fed, bathed, and dressed Fred and helped him survive. You can read about their story in the great book *Two Souls Indivisible* by James Hirsch.[1]

But there was a "race problem" in the camps. It was the attempt by our communist captors to exploit the race issue with our black teammates. In an effort to divide us, they ranted to them about their victimhood. When the communist captors could not get them to turn against their country and their white teammates, they tried to bribe them, offering to help them and their families escape from America and go to a safer country. (That's how little they knew about America!) They threatened that if the men didn't cooperate, they would likely never go home.

My black cellmate, Major Tom Madison, was one of the most highly respected men among the 52 POWs in Room 3 during the "big rooms" era. He was wise, courageous, and deeply loyal to our country and his teammates.

Recently in a conversation with my friend Colonel Norm McDaniel, the only remaining long-term POW who was a black person, he said simply: "We were brothers and a great team."

---

1   For more on their inspiring story, search "Fred Cherry and Porter Halyburton" online and on YouTube.

20 | WHEN YOU FIND "THE ONE"

THE STORY OF
Lee[1] & Mary Ellis

Lee

When I look back at our marriage journey, I think it's amazing—but probably typical of great marriages—that we flew safely through the turbulence of our early relationship. Now, we're cruising smoothly as we head toward our Golden Anniversary.

Mary

Well, there was never a question that we were meant for each other. But we did have some challenges, didn't we?

Lee

"Challenges?" I think you're being overly polite. Thank you for that, but...I came into this relationship with an extremely confident personality. I assumed that I was right about everything—unless confronted. I assumed that everybody thought the way I did. And that you were basically a female version of me!

Mary

That's true. But we've both grown a lot; we've both become more self-aware. Gosh, we were extreme opposites, with you being a take-charge, expressive extrovert, and me being a cooperative and quiet introvert.

Well, we are still extreme opposites, but we've learned to accept—and appreciate—each other's differences.

Well, we are still extreme opposites, but we've learned to accept—and appreciate—each other's differences.

Lee

I now understand why you didn't push back harder when I insisted that we get married quickly, which meant a ceremony just four days before Christmas! All I could see was that the chapel was beautifully decorated—at no cost to us!

Mary

Yes, that was a big one. And it set the stage for the early years of our marriage.

Lee

You could have pushed back and gotten my attention right then!

Mary

Well love is blind, you know! But while on the surface our personalities and styles were wildly different, on a deeper level we shared all the important things. Like our values, our spiritual beliefs, our belief in each other, and our commitment to each other. And deep down we simply knew that we were meant for each other.

Lee

We've had a great marriage, but I think our big breakthrough came some 16 years later when we explored our behavior styles and came to understand just how radically different we really were. I remember the assessment showing that on most factors of natural behavior (like people and details) we were two standard deviations apart on the factors except *one*—and on *that* one we were *three* standard deviations apart!

Mary

And that factor was…

Mary and Lee together

…*Patience!*

Lee

Yup! You had a lot, and I had virtually none!

Lee

Yes, through it all, we were both confident that we were meant to be together, and therefore completely devoted to each other. My love for you was so strong that I never in any way doubted that you were "the one." And I'd dated lots of nice ladies by the time I was 30 and met you.

I had always loved meeting and being with girls, but during my five years in the POW camps, I didn't think about them very much. Maybe it was because I had not yet met "the one," or because I was still so young—in fact, the youngest in the POW camp at that time.

Being the "kid" of the camps turned out to be a great advantage for me. My nature is to get bored easily, and I perform better with a challenge, so in the camps, taking risks to communicate covertly was right up my alley, and I became a trailblazer in that risky, but important function. Also, our captors focused more on the older and senior ranking guys, and though I was tortured a couple of times, it was lightweight compared to what some of the others experienced—especially our leaders.

For the first couple of months, I *did* have nightmares. I was always in a gun battle with the enemy, which ended up in fierce and frightening hand-to-hand combat. I would jerk awake just as I was about to be stabbed. Thankfully those began to subside. But then I had a dream that changed my life! My ninth grade science teacher, Mrs. Jordan, leaned over, looked down at me with a caring face and said, "Leon, you could be a good student if you would just do your homework!" I got the message, and it has kept me on course ever since. I'm sure that nightmare lesson played a role in my actually writing six books since retiring from the Air Force.

When I returned home, I initially spent most of my time with my parents and family on our farm near Athens, Georgia. But I also started dating immediately—mostly single girls from my home area. They were nice and we had fun, but nothing serious came of it. I was not interested in getting married right away. While spending time with my family and adjusting to freedom, the Air Force asked me if I wanted to return to flying. Of course, I said absolutely, and it was not long until I headed west to San Antonio to get requalified. Thankfully, for me flying was like riding a bicycle; it didn't take long to get back in the saddle, even after all those years in prison. And

I dated a lot of girls during my first year home, but unlike most of my single POW buddies—I didn't meet *the one*.

I became a T-38 Talon supersonic jet instructor pilot, and headed back to Moody AFB in Valdosta, Georgia. Moody was the base where I had begun my Air Force career in flight school as a single 22-year-old. Back in those days, I dated many young ladies from Valdosta State College, and often took them to the Officer's Club.

Now, eight years later and on the Friday night before Memorial Day weekend, I went to the Officers Club for a drink and some social time. I had no idea what was about to happen.

Now, eight years later and on the Friday night before Memorial Day weekend, I went to the Officers Club for a drink and some social time. I had no idea what was about to happen.

Mary

My part of our romance story began when I moved to Valdosta to resume my college education. I was separating from my first husband and needed a college town with a military base so I could have medical care for my two young children, Pat and Kristy. Valdosta State fit the bill, and I decided I would get my degree in education so I could support myself. Additionally, my parents lived fairly close, in Albany, Georgia.

I remember feeling very lonely, as I was a nontraditional older student (27) with few friends. One night I was really feeling sorry for myself and prayed that God would bring someone into my life to love. My marriage had been unsuccessful, and I had finally decided to walk away. Our parting was amicable, but the divorce proceedings dragged on, as he was deploying for an overseas tour with the Navy, and I was headed back east to be near my parents and other family members.

All I can say is that God works in mysterious ways. Sometimes He uses our troubles and worst times to answer our prayers. I was somehow "inspired" to go to the Officers Club with a friend one Friday night.

Lee

The club wasn't crowded, but there was good music playing. From the bar

I surveyed the landscape (like young fighter pilots tend to do) and saw two young ladies walk in. One of them caught my attention—or in pilot terms, my eyes immediately locked onto the target. She was absolutely beautiful! Shortly after they sat down, I strolled over and asked her to dance. She said, "Yes" and, as though divinely inspired, she soon became my dance partner for life! And that's how it began.

We danced and talked and eventually I invited the two girls to come over to my house nearby for a nightcap.

Mary

I was very impressed that you were a perfect gentleman.

Lee

I guess my behavior was anchored in my upbringing and military training. Anyway, as we listened to music and chatted, I could feel my heart and head being drawn to this lovely lady. I wasn't thinking anything serious, yet I felt a magnetic attraction, which made me want to get to know her better. We dated several times over the next few weeks. But I was soon faced with a big decision. Three months earlier I agreed to tour Europe with a former girlfriend. As a fighter pilot you learn to be good at evaluating risk versus reward. So, my aviator logic kicked in, and I quickly decided that the risk of losing Mary was too big to take.

Mary

Wise decision!

Lee

And even though she wasn't what I had expected, nothing dented my interest. She was separated, but still married and had two children. These were two big shifts from my idealized picture of what my romance and marriage would look like. Yet her situation never caused me the slightest pause. My love for her was growing rapidly. Now, it's important to emphasize that neither one of us had ever noticed or thought about the fact that we were totally different personalities. As they say, love is blind to many of the natural personality differences of the other person—especially romantic love.

Mary

That's quite an understatement!

Lee

I am a spontaneous, impatient, logical, big-picture, and directing kind of guy, while Mary is a patient, detailed, planful, sensitive, and cooperative woman. But as most of us have learned over time, when you meet the "right one," you simply don't see the potential road bumps in your relationship.

Mary

If I had any reservations about Lee, it was that he was too good to be true! He was genuine, mature, professional, and comfortable with himself. We just "clicked." He had no baggage from a marriage, *and* he owned his own nice home. Oh, and he was also crazy about me! I trusted him totally from the very beginning, and that was especially important to me.

We were getting closer and closer, but our first deep bonding occurred when he saved my little boy's life. We were picnicking by a river with my four-year-old daughter, Kristy, and seven-year-old son, Pat. One minute the kids were playing in the water—and a second later they disappeared! Lee and I both rushed to the water, when Kristy's head popped up. I pulled her to safety. Without pausing for a second Lee dove under the water. My feeling of panic in the next few seconds was the worst experience of my entire life. But Lee soon surfaced with Pat safely in his arms.

Much of the rest of that day is a blur to me, but thank God both kids were fine. It was frightening and sobering, but it was also unifying for me and Lee. Our relationship went up a notch.

Lee

Going to church together was important to both of us, and soon it was obvious that our spiritual beliefs were quietly entering our relationship, too. I had grown up in a home where our Christian faith was the bedrock of our worldview. Knowing that Mary was interested in deepening her faith added another strong pull in her direction. Also, during our time together it became clear that she was a person who valued honor and integrity.

Mary

By the end of the summer, we both had separately and secretly told our families and closest friends that we thought we had met "the one"—our one true love. My divorce was finalized in the fall, and one week later Lee proposed to me, and I happily accepted! Now Lee, why don't you tell them about how "romantic" you were with my engagement ring!

Lee

I wasn't trying to be romantic. I was simply being logical!

Mary

You *see*?

Lee

Let me explain. During the war, it was a common practice for guys to go shopping during their week of R&R (Rest and Recreation). Many Asian cities were great places to buy all kinds of items (like clothing, art carvings, watches—and especially jewelry) at fantastic prices. Since I had missed that opportunity due to my years in prison, I headed back overseas before returning to active duty. While shopping, I decided that buying a diamond—for my future fiancée—would be a great investment.

Mary

His pragmatic, logical mind thought it was a good investment!

Lee

Yes, an investment! Anyway…I proposed to Mary, she accepted, we went to the jewelry store, she chose a diamond she liked, and I upgraded her choice to a larger one that was near perfect in the "four Cs of diamond rating." This was possible because I traded in my *investment diamond* and it had increased in value! Any complaints?

Mary

No, I've never complained, dear. I love it and am very appreciative.

To give you a balanced picture, here's another jewelry-related story that shows that Lee can be very romantic! For our 40th anniversary he suggested we go to New York City to celebrate. He reserved a room at a nice small hotel near Macy's and Herald Square. That afternoon he took me to see "Jersey Boys," a Broadway musical about the Four Seasons. I've always *loved* their music! The next day we went to the Rockettes' Christmas performance at Radio City Music Hall. Afterwards, as we strolled back south, he subtly steered me over to the nearby Diamond District. "Let's go in and just look around," he said at one shop. An hour later I walked out wearing a stunning ruby ring that was set among small diamonds! (Note: Ruby is the traditional gift for a 40th anniversary.)

Lee

Don't forget to tell them that I negotiated the price down to almost half!

Mary

That's my Lee…romantic with a logical, practical twist!

Lee

Now that people can see how romantic I can be, let's go back to the early stages of our marriage. I was building a good relationship with Mary's kids. (Pat was interested in football, and Kristy was cute as a button.) I had never been around small children much, but I really enjoyed being with them. With time I would learn that children are *not* small adults. (A blinding flash of the obvious, but there you go.) I regret that I was a slow learner in that area.

Mary

I have grown and changed a lot in our 48-year marriage. As I said earlier, I was not assertive enough to express my feelings that a wedding four days before Christmas day would be—to say the least—stressful. Yes, I mentioned that it was not a good idea, but I had not yet learned that soft, non-direct talk does not register in Lee's brain. Nowadays, we know we are different and, I'm happy to say that I do speak up and he does listen well.

I so wanted to have a nice, happy, "normal" family. I wanted Lee to be the kids' dad, and I wanted him to discipline them as I expected a father would. I did not know that this was the worst thing to happen to the kids' relationship with Lee. He became the disciplinarian, the "bad guy," and over those early years he missed some opportunities to really connect with their hearts. Eventually, Lee suggested that I should determine boundaries and punishment, and he would support me. I stepped up, and he stepped back, and as we learned to adapt, it worked very well. Fortunately, we have all experienced a lot of growing and healing through the years, and Pat, Kristy, and Lee have a close relationship.

Lee

I had a great military career, and Mary always did a fantastic job as an Air Force wife. Her father had been an Army officer during her childhood, so she understood the role of military wives in that era. Her duty-bound nature overcame her introverted personality, and when I was the T-38 squadron commander, she led our Squadron Wives Club. She took on this responsibility while juggling our four children (Pat and Kristy and now Lance and Meredith). Much later, as I learned about her natural strengths and struggles, I realized that Mary was putting a *huge* amount of energy into adapting to be a social leader.

At the time I hadn't recognized the magnitude of her dedication to being a great wife.

At the time I hadn't recognized the magnitude of her dedication to being a great wife.

But as Mary approached mid-life it became even more challenging for her. I think I had a subconscious awareness of this, and in 1986 this was a contributing factor to my decision to step sideways on my next assignment, and head toward retirement. I took the commander slot at the Air Force ROTC detachment at my alma mater, the University of Georgia, located just ten miles from my parents.

After retiring from the Air Force in 1990, I took on a startup venture with a not-for-profit to build a career assessment program for teenagers. It was a perfect fit for me. (I love a new challenge!) I was doing meaningful work, and it gave me the opportunity to learn much more about human behavior and to develop tools and models to help others. I worked with University of Georgia IO psychologists to develop and validate in-depth assessments, and over time I became very knowledgeable in human behavior.

Mary

Lee's foray into career assessment, which led to career counseling, piqued my interest. I found that my natural traits and talents were a perfect match for personal counseling. I soon got my master's degree and professional license and have been practicing for more than 20 years now.

Lee

And guess what? Some of her client work is marriage and relationship therapy. Mary found a perfect career fit...and so did I! With my focus on human behavior (related to leadership and team development) for more than 25 years, we have found a great overlap. She is a counselor, and I am a coach. We often read the same books and discuss the impact of differences on relationships.

Mary

It is now quite normal for us to focus on each other's natural personality strengths and not each other's struggles. Most of the time we find humor and good reminders in reflecting on our struggles. We laugh and joke: How could any rational couple get married on December 21st? It's always been a good reminder of how different we are, and how much we love each other—and how great it is that we are different!

Lee

Mirror opposites can be a great team and do great work when they come together in love and respect. And through it all we have never doubted that we were married to the right person—the love of our life—"the one"!

LOVE LESSONS

COMMON VALUES

Common faith and values provide a powerful foundation. When they are aligned, you can withstand and work through your other challenges and differences.

LOVE IS BLIND...

...and marriage is an eye-opener. Research shows that most couples come to this realization within two years. Don't be a slow learner! When personality and natural behavioral differences show up, focus on and celebrate your partner's strengths and talents—and ignore their natural struggles that irritate you. You can't change them. And most likely—with your affirmation, love, and respect—they will try to adapt in those areas.

ALIGNMENT

Spend time on your areas of alignment. Find the interests and subjects that the two of you share. Then spend time together discussing and sharing your knowledge, feelings, and insights. If you listen with love, you will learn a lot from each other, and this will build a deeper intimacy.

Lee & Mary Ellis

1   1st Lt Leon F. (Lee) Ellis, Jr. USAF, F-4C Phantom, POW 7-NOV-67 – 14-MAR-73, Retired Col (0-6)

"TIE A YELLOW RIBBON"— THE ANTHEM FOR VIETNAM VETS

Early in 1973, just as we were coming home, the song "Tie a Yellow Ribbon Round the Ole Oak Tree" by Tony Orlando and Dawn, became the number one hit in the US. It became the top-selling single of the year. Billboard ranked it as the 37th biggest song of all time! This touching love song became a heart-warming anthem for returning Vietnam soldiers, our families, and our nation.

As long-term POWs, we never imagined how much of America's attention had been focused on us over the years. But we were about to learn. As my parents were driving me home from the Atlanta airport, the closer we got to our home the more I saw yellow ribbons on trees, buildings, fences, and posts. I asked them what that was about. They explained—and I was deeply touched. It was very uplifting, and to be honored this way brought healing—something that was denied to most Vietnam veterans. It is tragic that our brothers-in-arms were largely scorned and disrespected by so many.

You cannot imagine the impact this song had on the POWs who had been locked up away from our homes and families—our wives or girlfriends or fiancées. But in the stories we have collected in this book, you can see why this song became "Our Song" for so many loving couples.

We POWs still have a strong bond with Tony. He attends our reunions and inspires us. At our 25th reunion, Mary and I were on a bus loaded with POWs and wives about to shuttle back to the hotel—then Tony climbed aboard. When the group saw him at the front several people called out "Sing it for us!" And as we were riding the bus through the streets of Dallas, Tony stood up front and sang it! And we all joined in. That was exhilarating and a special memory for a lifetime.

Tie a Yellow Ribbon Round The Ole Oak Tree

I'm comin' home, I've done my time
Now I've got to know what is and isn't mine
If you received my letter telling you I'd soon be free
Then you'll know just what to do
If you still want me, if you still want me

Whoa, tie a yellow ribbon 'round the ole oak tree
It's been three long years, do you still want me?
If I don't see a ribbon round the ole oak tree
I'll stay on the bus, forget about us, put the blame on me
If I don't see a yellow ribbon 'round the ole oak tree

Bus driver, please look for me
'Cause I couldn't bear to see what I might see
I'm really still in prison and my love, she holds the key
A simple yellow ribbon's what I need to set me free
And I wrote and told her please

Whoa, tie a yellow ribbon 'round the ole oak tree
It's been three long years, do you still want me?
If I don't see a ribbon round the ole oak tree
I'll stay on the bus, forget about us, put the blame on me
If I don't see a yellow ribbon 'round the ole oak tree

Now the whole damned bus is cheerin'
And I can't believe I see

A hundred yellow ribbons 'round the ole oak tree

I'm comin' home
Tie a ribbon 'round the ole oak tree
Tie a ribbon 'round the ole oak tree
Tie a ribbon 'round the ole oak tree
Tie a ribbon 'round the ole oak tree

Source: LyricFind
Songwriters: Irwin Levine / L. Russell Brown
Tie A Yellow Ribbon Round The Ole Oak Tree lyrics
© Peermusic Publishing, Spirit Music Group

Tony Orlando—Dallas Salutes June 2, 1973

FROM STORIES TO ACTION

We hope that you have been touched by the powerful stories in this book, and now the next section is about your story. If you are inspired to take positive action in your own romantic relationship, we have gathered some resources to help you.

By applying the principles and advice that these couples have shared, you can continue to create your own epic love story with your special someone. The following sections listed below will help you in your journey to become ever more captured by love.

A. Love Lessons Summary

B. Recommended Books about Love and Marriage Relationships and Personal Development

C. POW/MIA Related Vietnam War Books

D. The N8Traits Relationship Report to Clarify and Help You Understand Your Differences

E. A List of Additional Subjects Shared on the *Captured by Love* Website at powromance.com.

A. LOVE LESSONS SUMMARY

There are many love lessons in this book, and the key ones are highlighted at the end of each story. We hope you were able to reflect on them as related to the story and then perhaps to your own life and family. Here we have summarized all the love lessons into eight overarching principles or concepts for lasting relationships.

It is amazing, but probably should be no surprise, that these align very closely with the conclusions of some of the best-known love/romance/marriage experts. (See the Recommended Books in the next section for that list.)

We think you will see how fundamental and seemingly obvious these love lessons (marriage principles) are, but of course, simple and obvious do not mean that implementing them is easy. We are all imperfect humans, and lasting love is usually the rewarding results of putting our mate on a pedestal and accepting ourselves as a work in progress.

Before we jump into the love lessons, there is one more important aspect to consider.

Romantic attraction. Romantic couples have great chemistry—an attraction that, in retrospect, can seem somewhat beyond logic. It's typically more of an intuitive and feelings-based type of attraction. Romantic attraction was evident in most of the stories but not really featured in the love lessons. It's hard to define it, but you know it when you feel it—or for those who are still learning about feelings—when you sense it. It's a reflection of many connections that reside at a deep level, a place where physical attraction, core values, trust, and personalities click and result in an amazing, almost magnetic pull.

Brain scans show an unusual flurry when this romantic attraction hits. Somehow, in the early stages of romance (typically lasting no more than two years), this brain flurry tends to overshadow or shut down your ability to notice the differences and potential struggles of your romantic lover. That's why the following love lessons are so important, because it turns out there is scientific truth in the old saying that "Love is blind, but marriage is an eye opener." These lessons will help you make the transition from the magnetic attraction that fades, into the powerful connection that committed love brings.

LOVE LESSONS

The great reward of these lessons is that they enable us to slide—even glide—through the eye openers, wake-up calls, and challenges of marriage to establish devoted, long-term love relationships. These are the principles that have enabled these 20 couples to survive and thrive through more than 1,000 years of combined successful and happy relationships.

1. Companionship. Human beings are designed for relationships. We all want to have good relationships—they make us feel valued, special, important, and happy. Romance takes it a step further to an even deeper connection of the heart. How wonderful it is to know that someone is emotionally, mentally, physically, and even spiritually attracted to us. When we want to spend time together, listen to each other, and care for each other, we become friends and teammates at the deepest level.

Harvard University conducted a 75-year study to determine what makes a person happy and successful in life. The results showed that good relationships keep us happier and healthier. The study concluded that regardless of all your other worldly accomplishments, the biggest predictor of your happiness and fulfillment in life is, basically, love.[1]

Committed companionship facilitates true love and enables a couple to enjoy being together so much that they become soulmates—sharing life together, enjoying humor. Soulmates are equipped to work through the challenges of life and marriage. And this companionship creates the foundation for both spontaneous and intentional affection and the joy of sexual intimacy.

2. Common Values/Shared Faith. Values are the foundation for our character and sense of right and wrong. They provide the guard rails for our travel through life and form the framework for our view of the world and the individual ethics of others. A couple with similar/shared values tends to have a common mindset on the most important areas, and that makes it easier for them to align their worldview on issues that arise.

Closely connected is our spiritual faith. As you saw in the stories, it was the anchor for most of the relationships. Their faith in God enabled them to know they were loved by a divine higher power. Their faith helped them deal with their life challenges, and also helped them believe that they were not alone and would somehow make it through their pain and suffering.

Interestingly, most of the key marriage books featured in the next chapter point out that a good marriage relationship helps each partner in their spiritual growth and refinement. And of course, all these aspects of values, character, and faith are foundations for many of the other key love lessons here. Common values and shared faith help improve trust, inspire love, and ultimately produce a healthy family, which is the greatest contribution one can make to the next generation.

3. Respect. The concept of respect is broad and powerful. Every human has a deep need to be respected, and we tend to experience great pain and negative emotions when disrespected. We saw in the stories many ways in which great marriage partners respect their beloved. Most of us have heard the idea of putting someone on a pedestal. In many ways we believe that's a good way to look at your mate. Put them on a respect pedestal and work hard to keep them there so they feel special and know that you see them as special.

Several of the Love Lessons emphasized this pedestal approach. For example, our couples were intentional about showing appreciation and gratitude. They love and believe in the other person so much that they show them patience and empathy, even in challenging situations. And when they didn't, they reflected on it and came back to apologize and respond with different words and emotions. Respecting each other in this way makes it easier for them to give and take and negotiate, which research shows are key aspects of great marriages.

4. Focus on your love's unique strengths, and ignore their struggles. One of the most obvious and important lessons was the way these strong couples learned to honor and celebrate their partners' natural talents (personality, innate traits, bent) and ignore their struggles. Interestingly, the famous management and leadership author Marcus Buckingham begins his book *The One Thing You Need to Know* with an example of "The one thing you need to know" about a marriage relationship. He says, "Find the most generous explanation for each other's behavior and believe it." He points out that research shows that the most lasting and happiest love relationships come when we identify our partner's talents and project them into what he calls "positive illusions," so that we believe in them even more than they believe in themselves. We agree and believe that when you intentionally notice and affirm the talents of your teammate, it's like a strong ray of love that helps them feel worthy and accepted. In the stories you saw how it enabled couples to achieve the remarkable status of being both independent and interdependent. We share some specific ways to do this using the Relationship Report, which we introduce in a later section of this book.

5. Trust. Whether it's friendship, leadership, teamwork, politics, or marriage, trust is essential; you might think of it as the glue that holds things together. Trust means safety, and that facilitates vulnerability, which allows others to be genuine. Even though it seems to be the key bond that holds couples together, it also seems that trust is like a channel that contains the flow of all these other lesson attributes. Regardless of how you look at it, trust is essential to all relationships, and even more so in a loving marriage relationship.

6. Optimism. This came up in several of our stories, perhaps because it was a lesson learned during our hard times. Research shows that keeping a positive outlook was essential for the POWs' resilience and survival. The same is true in marriage. Life is tough, and every relationship will undergo difficult times: disagreements, disappointments, losses, and suffering. But, allowing negative emotions to persist creates a negative outlook, and negativity undermines all relationships. Just like good teams, loving couples learn to address problems, accept losses, overcome challenges, and bounce back.

One of the key lessons that we POWs brought home was not only to think positively and be optimistic, but to deal with the issues as a team. If you collaborate and listen to the ideas of others and then come up with a plan, you can walk it out step by step until you come out the other side successfully. Or, as it was in our case, we walked out the gates of the Hanoi Hilton and headed home after many years of keeping the faith. Couples who stick together and work through issues with a positive attitude, believe in each other, and are resilient can create good outcomes.

7. Commitment. What typically enables our perseverance through the challenging times in life is pure commitment. Take a look at these synonyms: promise, pledge, vow, word, duty, devotion. This type of commitment was essential for the Vietnam POWs to serve honorably. And it's the same in marriage. When you commit to something that is dear to you and part of your life purpose and mission, you don't turn your back and walk away. Rather, you humbly find a way to work through the issues that have made it challenging.

In marriage we often refer to it as devotion. When you are devoted, you are willing to courageously confront your doubts and fears and walk into the painful sacrifice that may be needed to achieve your goal. Life (and marriage) is going to have difficulties—there are no exceptions. That's why we all need the perseverance to work through issues even when it feels sacrificial. With optimism and commitment, great mates turn toward the problem and humbly do their duty to follow the process, and overcome the barriers and issues, getting help as needed.

8. Healthy and Authentic. This was not specifically identified as a love lesson, but the concepts of being healthy and authentic are foundational for all the rest. From my leadership coaching and Mary's counseling experience, we know that emotionally healthy people tend to be more authentic; they are more comfortable with themselves and therefore can be more focused on giving their love and attention to others. Healthy, authentic people have the best relationships—at home and at work.

But none of us grew up in a perfect home, with perfect parents, perfect neighbors, perfect friends, teachers and role models. We all have some emotional scars of fear, shame, guilt, and false pride from our childhood and teenage years. And we continue to learn more about the PTSD related struggles of war veterans. So, we are all a bit unhealthy, and thus for love relationships to thrive, we must work at growing healthier—which means becoming more secure about our own inner self. I encourage you to take a look at the Insecure to Secure Model on powromance.com to see the power of growing more comfortable with who you are.

I think you'll see that one of the most important contributions to growing healthier is to have people around us who believe in us, who focus on our unique talents and strengths, and encourage us often. This is evident in our stories, and when you reflect back on those who have had the most positive impact on your life and career, you'll see how important it was. So, listen to them, receive those rays of love, believe in yourself, and then become a giver, sending similar rays of love to others.

* * * *

Well, there you have the lessons all compiled for your reflection and discussions. In the next section we introduce you to some of the most famous marriage and love experts. And in the final section, we introduce our N8Traits Relationship Report, based on natural behavior. It enables two people to see how they are similar and different in eight factors of natural behavior (personality). We think you will enjoy all of these very helpful resources.

---

1   https://www.fastcompany.com/90274181/secret-to-fulfilling-life-harvard-study

B. GREAT MARRIAGE AND ROMANCE BOOKS

The Love Lessons in the previous section align with the observation and advice from some of the most famous love and marriage experts. In case you would like to read more on this subject, we have included several great books here.

They all emphasize the importance of having healthy and respectful dialogues for developing and maintaining good relationships. Four of them go into great detail about how people naturally tend to share and receive communications differently—and others talk about our different love languages. And as you will see in the next section, relating to people who have different talents and communication styles is one of the focal points of our Relationship Report.

1. *The Seven Principles for Making Marriage Work* – John Gottman Ph.D.

Drs. John and Julie Gottman are two of the most famous marriage researchers in the US. This book provides a short summary of the key principles they have learned over the years. There are many great articles online that share insights from the Gottmans' research. My wife Mary has attended several Gottman-based workshops and has used their concepts for many years. Reading about their laboratory observations of couples is quite enlightening.

In describing their Seventh Principle of Marriage, Dr. Gottman says that "Creating Shared Meaning" has a spiritual dimension that is important for a couple's growth.

In addition to the seven principles, this book shares the Four Horsemen that destroy marriages: Criticism, Contempt, Defensiveness, and Stonewalling. These endanger a marriage very quickly.

2. *Love and Respect* – Dr. Emmerson Eggerichs

Throughout this book we have talked about the importance of learning to respect and celebrate differences. *Love and Respect* takes on that mission very specifically to show couples how they typically are different. His premise is that communication between a husband and wife is often frustrating because of the vastly different ways in which men and women perceive love. Women are wired to need unconditional love, while men need to feel unconditionally *respected*. But giving those freely is not natural to many people. In the book, Dr. Eggerich shares many stories of how these concepts play out (with failure and success) using examples from his counseling clients and in his own personal experience in his relationship with his wife Sarah.

3. *The Meaning of Marriage* – Timothy and Kathy Keller

Drs. Timothy and Kathy Keller provide a great foundation for understanding the reality and purpose of marriage. They are both highly educated, very experienced, and both are bestselling authors. This book looks at marriage from a biblical perspective and delves into themes of friendship and commitment; the completion of men and women in each other; singleness, sex and divorce; and ministry and discipleship within the context of marriage.

Timothy and Kathy founded Redeemer Presbyterian Church in New York City in 1989, where for many years most of the members were single professionals. With so many moving toward marriage in this modern era, they wrote this book to really clarify what marriage is and how it works best. They also address the challenges for both young and older singles who are romantically moving toward marriage.

4. *Love Talk* – Drs. Les and Leslie Parrott

Les is a clinical psychologist; Leslie is a marriage and family therapist; and both have many years teaching in this field. Together, their writings and workshops have had a huge impact on couples. This book focuses on building strong relationships through healthy and vulnerable communications. They make it simple and give lots of exercises to help you connect with each other's heart to grow closer. In the process each person becomes more healthy and secure, which builds the foundation for a couple to truly be captured by love.

Additionally, Les and Leslie have developed an extremely helpful website called loveology.org that has short videos in which some of the most famous love and marriage experts answer questions. It's one of the best resources available for couples and families. It's simple to use, questions are organized by category and subject, and when you pick one, you'll get a lot of insight in two to three minutes.

5. *Receiving Love* – Harville Hendrix, Ph.D. and Helen Lakelly Hunt, Ph.D.

Harville and Helen were two of the most famous marriage teachers, counselors and writers—specializing in Imago therapy. They had written a world-famous book called *Getting the Love You Want*—and then one day they came very close to divorce. That was when Helen discovered the research on two different brain perspectives. As she shared it with Harville, he realized that he had not been able to receive her love, and in fact, he had a built-in barrier to receiving love—called "separate knowing." His logic was not able to receive her feelings, while her natural "connected knowing" made it difficult for her to express love in a way that connected well with him.

Receiving Love also includes their famous Imago Dialogue and Relationship Therapy. The insights they present, of listening and sharing by using both rational/logic and feelings/emotions, was something Mary and I learned a few years ago that has been extremely helpful.

6. *The Five Love Languages* – **Gary Chapman**

This book is so famous that you probably have already read it and clarified your own top love languages. If not, you'll want to get it soon. We love Dr. Chapman's concept of the five love languages because it's so simple and yet so very powerful. As we have mentioned in a couple of places in this book, it is really important to "give the dog what the dog wants to eat." Because most of us are slow learners and quick forgetters, if you have already read this book, we suggest that you circle back and dig in at least every couple of years. By the way, Mary's two love languages are Quality Time and Acts of Service. I try to keep that in mind and feed her those often. Mine are Words of Affirmation and Physical Touch. As a writer and speaker, I get a lot of affirmation, so Mary focuses on giving me a ten second hug in the morning and evening—that feeds me well and I feel very loved.

7. *Beyond Mars and Venus: Relationship Skills for Today's Complex World* – **John Gray**

More than 20 years after his world-famous Mars and Venus book for couples, John Gray has now brought us an updated perspective for today's culture—a culture where women are operating much more on Mars and men are operating more on Venus. Gray shares research on how our male and female hormones still play unique roles, but with awareness we can adapt to successfully improve our lives and especially our relationships as couples. He also emphasizes the importance of pulling back to restore your hormones to their most effective level.

Research shows that to be a great leader, you must learn to adapt beyond your natural "go to" talents and gain a leadership balance between *results* behaviors and *relationship* behaviors. This book shares a similar concept—individuals must learn to adapt their male and female tendencies to appropriately fit the situation.

Gray consistently points out that our hormones drive our emotions and behaviors, and with greater awareness we can learn how to relate to our partner in a powerful way that brings us the love of great soulmates. The book offers lots of coaching and lists of examples of how to adapt and love your mate.

Keep in mind that all these books are by well-established authors with years of practical experience in the field of relationships, love, and marriage. They also have great websites with lots of information and tools for your further insights. We have links on powromance.com.

* * * *

PERSONAL GROWTH IS THE KEY TO A MEANINGFUL AND HAPPY LIFE.

I may have heard this from someone many years ago—I'm not sure, but since I don't know who came up with it, I call it Lee's law of marriage: We tend to marry to our own level of dysfunction—usually a different dysfunction but an equal level. As mentioned earlier, no one is perfectly healthy—no one grew up in a perfect home or a perfect neighborhood. We all have some pain, shame, doubts, fears and false pride. So, we all have some dysfunction. The earlier we can start growing healthier as human beings, the more likely we'll find a good mate. Beyond that, all these books point out that the healthier the person, the easier it is to work through the issues of love and marriage. And as we discussed earlier at the summary of the Love Lessons, in a healthy marriage each person in a couple helps the other grow healthier.

In more than 25 years of leadership coaching, I have observed that secure, healthy people (both confident and humble) become the best leaders. So, I encourage you to make personal growth an ongoing part of your life.

There are many personal growth books that I re-read often. Here are the three that I study the most. I've read all of them at least five times, and some of them ten times. Sometimes it's a blessing to be a slow learner!

- **Surrender to Love**, **The Gift of Being Yourself**, and **Desiring God's Will** (a trilogy of short but powerful books), by David Benner, Ph.D., a Christian Psychologist and spiritual director/therapist.

- **Man's Search for Meaning** – Victor Frankl, M.D. (an Auschwitz survivor who was a young psychiatrist in Vienna before being incarcerated). After the Paris Peace Agreement was signed, ending the Vietnam War, each cell was given a book to read, and they rotated them across the camp. (They had been sent years earlier by our families.) One of those books was this one, and we read our copy out loud sitting in our cell.

Shortly after I returned home, I learned that Dr. Frankl was speaking on campus at the nearby University of Georgia. I attended the event and met him after his presentation. We spent a few very inspiring minutes visiting. I learned that he had been on the board to advise the Department of Defense on how to handle the returning POWs.

• ***The Road Less Traveled*** – M. Scott Peck, M.D. Psychiatrist and therapist. Like David Benner above, Scott Peck uses his brilliance to transform the abstract issues of human nature into real-world stories with lessons we can understand and use in our day-to-day lives.

* * * *

Life is a journey, and continuing to learn and grow can make it an exciting and rewarding experience. Don't quit. No matter what age you are, keep learning and growing.

To make that point, let me remind you that when this book is launched, the average age of the 20 POWs in these romance stories is 87, and four of them are over 90 and still attending our reunions. The greatest lesson from life is that love conquers all. The more you feel loved, the more love you are able to share. And the more you give to others, the healthier you both will be.

C. ADDITIONAL BOOKS

BOOKS RELATED TO *CAPTURED BY LOVE* STORY CONTRIBUTORS

- **Everett Alverez** – *Chained Eagle: The Heroic Story of the First American Shot Down over North Vietnam*, Everett Alvarez, Jr., and Anthony S. Pitch, Potomac Books 2005, (1989 Donald I. Fine)

Code of Conduct: An Inspirational Story of Self-Healing, Everett Alvarez, Jr., Dutton Adult 1991

- **Mo Baker** – *Serve with Pride & Return with Honor*, Colonel Elmo "Mo" Baker USAF (Ret), 2014

- **Jim Bell** – *The Heroes' Wife*, Dora Griffin Bell, 2006, Authorhouse

- **Dave Carey** – *The Ways We Choose*, Dave Carey, 2000, Bookpartners Inc.

- **Lee Ellis** – *Leading with Honor: Leadership Lessons From the Hanoi Hilton*, Lee Ellis 2012 FreedomStar Media

Engage with Honor: Building a Culture of Courageous Accountability, Lee Ellis 2016, FreedomStar Media

- **Ralph Gaither** – *With God in a P.O.W. Camp*, Commander Ralph Gaither as told to Steve Henry, Broadman Press 1973, Ralph Gaither 2004

- **Smitty Harris** – *Tap Code: The Epic Survival Tale of a Vietnam POW and the Secret Code that Changed Everything*, Col Carlyle "Smitty" Harris (Ret) and Sara W. Berry, Zondervan, 2019

- **Ben Purcell** – *Love and Duty*, Ben and Anne Purcell, 2006 (Expanded Edition)

- **Dick Stratton** – *Prisoner at War: The Survival of Commander Richard A Stratton*, Scott Blakey, Anchor Press/Doubleday, 1978

HISTORICAL BOOKS OF THE VIETNAM WAR POW/MIA EXPERIENCE

• *POW: A Definitive History of the American War Experience in Vietnam 1964-1973*, John Hubbell. Readers Digest Press 1976 (633 pages)

• *Honor Bound: American Prisoners of War in Southeast Asia 1961-1973*, Stuart I. Rochester and Frederick Kiley, Naval Institute Press. Originally published in 1998 by the Office of the Secretary of Defense. Naval Institute Press Edition 1999 (706 pages)

ABOUT THE GOVERNMENT EXPERIENCE

• *The Long Road Home: US Prisoner of War Policy and Planning in Southeast Asia*, Vernon E. Davis, Historical Office, Office of the Secretary of Defense, Washington, D.C. 2000 (613 pages)

ABOUT THE WIVES' EXPERIENCE

• *League of Wives: The Untold story of the Women Who Took on the U.S. Government to Bring Their Husbands Home*, Heath Hardage Lee, St. Martin's Griffin, 2019

• *Saved by Love: A True Story*, Evelyn Guarino, Blue Note Books, 2001

• *In Love & War: The story of a family's ordeal and sacrifice during the Vietnam years*, Jim and Sybil Stockdale, Harper and Row, 1984

BOOKS BY FOREWORD AUTHORS

• *Halfway to Paradise*, Tony Orlando and Patsi Bale Cox, St Martin's Press, 2002

• *Grateful American: A Journey from Self to Service*, Gary Sinise, Thomas Nelson, 2019

D. THE RELATIONSHIP REPORT

UNDERSTAND AND CELEBRATE YOUR DIFFERENCES
POWRomance.com/Report

As you have seen in our love stories, it is very common for couples who have great long-lasting marriages to be very different in personality—meaning they have very different natural talents, with different strengths and struggles. Learning to celebrate these types of differences is crucial to great relationships.

In our story, both Mary and I shared how the biggest challenge we had in our marriage was that we were wildly different. In the early romantic stage, I only saw her strengths (and of course, assumed that I had all those too—which I didn't). Soon after we were married, and our romantically quivering brains calmed down, we started to notice each other's struggles. "How can she/he be that way?! No one should act like that, *especially the one.*"

We had a strong marriage, so we endured those issues, but we now celebrate the breakthrough that came when we discovered our natural behavioral talents, and came to understand just how radically different we really were!

BEHAVIORAL ASSESSMENT INSIGHTS

The good thing is that even though I had been a *slow learner* about our *personal* differences, I had a big turnaround when I began working to develop behavioral assessments. Once I saw scientifically and statistically how we were different, I began to accept Mary's unique style, and then to celebrate her talents. And at the same time, I began to coach myself to adapt my own behavior to relate more effectively to the love of my life—my polar opposite—my sweet Mary.

Since 1990, I've been involved with developing and deploying behavioral assessments—first as part of a career assessment package, and then for leadership development, coaching, training, and hiring. Millions of people have used these assessments, and I've written two books on the subject (related to discovering and understanding natural talents). Mary has used this type of assessment in marriage counseling for many years, and it has proven a powerful tool.

If you've struggled with differences in your romantic relationship or would just like to gain a clearer picture of your strengths and struggles, then I'd like to offer some help and insight for you.

COMPARING TWO PEOPLE

The N8Traits® Relationship Report provides a scientific explanation of each person's unique talents (strengths and associated struggles) and supporting graphics that make it easy to see areas where the two may be similar or different.

Three of the most important aspects are that each person:

- Has natural traits (their natural talents).

- Has strengths and struggles that go with their talents. Yes, we all have an equal number of struggles that go along with our talents.

- Likes to be related to, and communicated with, in their unique way—which is often very different from the other.

Typically, people know they are different, but with an assessment, they can see very *specifically* how they are different, and understand that these differences are "natural born" and of equal worth.

The goal is for each person to gain an objective view of themselves—which means they will now see their own struggles (which they may not have noticed or accepted) that typically stand out to others. At the same time, they learn to focus on the other person's strengths, and ignore their struggles. We all know that can be a challenge—at work and at home. Remember what we said back in our story—love is blind, and marriage is an eye opener.

To show you how the report can open our eyes more quickly, check out this graphic of just one factor of natural behavior for Mary and me. This will give you a quick picture of the differences that we now celebrate. This is the Patience Factor. You can see that she is on the Patient side and I'm totally opposite. Ten points is a standard deviation in this statistical based scoring system, and we are almost 30 points apart! Three standard deviations is an extreme difference, but it's just how we are wired. You can see that the graphic and numbers make the assessment a great "eye opener."

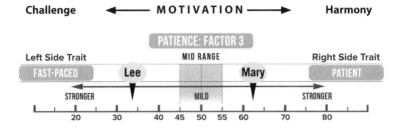

Strengths

1. Able to handle conflict
2. Objective and detached
3. Prefers to take action
4. Works at a fast pace and responds quickly

Struggles

1. Can be argumentative
2. May be abrupt or interrupting
3. Can be judgmental and critical
4. May lack needed patience

Relationship Essentials
How to relate to this person:

1. Remember their need for **Quick Action** and **Logic**
2. Speak/move at a quick pace
3. Expect them to confront you to provide facts

Strengths

1. Operates best in harmony
2. Compassionate and warm, displays empathy
3. Listens well and receptive to others
4. Patient, willing to wait

Struggles

1. May compromise too much
2. Does not like to challenge or confront
3. May be too trusting
4. May lack needed objectivity

Relationship Essentials
How to relate to this person:

1. Remember their need for **Stability** and **Compassion**
2. Soften the tone of communication
3. Slow down the pace of communications

Coaching

Lee, celebrate Mary's warm and sensitive nature. Remember her radar for feelings is much stronger than yours, so slow down, reduce your intensity, and soften the tone. Be sensitive to her need for peace and harmony, and give her more time to adjust.

Mary, you have a gift for the soft side of love, but don't forget the tough side is also important. And remember, Lee listens better to direct firm challenges. Also, when needed, coach yourself to toughen up, set firm boundaries, say no, and hold others accountable.

Keep in mind that these opposite traits are God-given, or natural talents—and are of equal value. (But not equal in performance in certain situations.) Notice the difference in our strengths and struggles shown below the continuum.

Can you see how powerful it is to know that someone you love is naturally designed to be very different from you, and that each of you has arenas where your talents are more suited? But in a relationship, our first reaction to our opposites is often to be turned off, to judge them, to try to get them to change and act more like us.

These visible, scientific insights help us to accept our differences. They give us the tools to think differently and celebrate traits—theirs and ours. Mary's patience, kindness, good listening ability, steadiness, and radar for the emotions of others makes her a wonderful teammate. And I know that in communicating with her, I've got to turn down my natural intensity and soften the tone of my voice.

* * * *

This is just a quick overview, but you can see much more on our website at POWRomance.com/Report. There you will see an example of the full report, and the specifics on the Factors with their associated Traits, Strengths, and Struggles.

Then, consider purchasing your report. As soon as you complete it, you can instantly download your report and review your results. You could be coaching yourself to a much smoother relationship before bedtime. Now wouldn't that be nice?

E. ONLINE APPENDIX

Rather than a lengthy appendix section in the back of this book, we've created a section on the **powromance.com** website that provides the following supplemental resources to go deeper and get additional insight.

Please explore this webpage to see more information on items such as –

- More photos, videos, and insights about the POWs and the couples in this book

- More historical insights about the war

- Illustrations and artwork about the war and those who fought in it

- Practical tools such as the Honor Code and Courage Challenge Card

ACKNOWLEDGMENTS
FROM LEE ELLIS

First and foremost, God has blessed me in so many ways—I'm sure in more ways than I realize or could ever imagine. I have always felt and now feel even more that I am greatly loved by my Heavenly Father, His Son and Holy Spirit. In good times and bad, He has always placed people around me to share rays of His love, and that has been a gift that has helped me grow in both confidence and humility. I will always be a work in progress, but His love helps me grow more humble and vulnerable, which in turn helps me become authentic as a human being.

Family

For more than forty-eight years, I've been captured by the love of my dearest Mary. She has exceeded all my expectations of what a great wife would be. I am so thankful to her for her loving kindness and partnership. Our children and grandchildren are all very special to us and we appreciate their contribution to our lives.

My mom and dad were amazing "warriors" during my years as a POW, and my brother Robert and his wife Pat were by their side, supporting them and actively getting signed petitions for the National League of POW/MIA Families to demand humane treatment and a full accounting for those captured or missing.

NAM-POWs

Our organization of NAM-POWs (Vietnam POWs) has stayed together, and we celebrate reunions more frequently as we have advanced far down the path of senior citizenry. This year (2023) marks the 50th anniversary of our return home from the War. We will celebrate our reunion in California with a very special event on May 24th when we will gather at the Nixon Library to celebrate the 50th anniversary of that still-famous White House Dinner.

It was at our NAM-POW reunions where I was struck with the great love stories of my buddies and their ladies. Sharing at those gatherings was the source of the idea of a "POW Romance" book.

The Couples

I'm so grateful to the 20 special couples who have shared their stories in this book. After all, the book would not have been done without them. They have been very forthcoming, honest, vulnerable, and patient as we worked together to bring you their stories. They were and are heroic couples.

The Foreword Authors

We are especially grateful for the support of Tony Orlando and Gary Sinise. Tony has been a loyal friend of the POWs since we came home, and he sang the "Tie A Yellow Ribbon Round the Ole Oak Tree" song at the Dallas Salutes Cotton Bowl event for veterans and POWs. Tony comes to our reunions, sings on stage, and hangs with us in our hospitality room.

Gary has been a friend since we met ten years ago at Randolph Air Force Base in San Antonio, Texas. Of course, he is also nationally famous for his dedicated service to veterans through the Lt Dan Band and The Gary Sinise Foundation. Read more about them in the Biographies section.

Our Team

Our Leading with Honor Team is always ahead of me, clearing the path and making the various steps of my work and life easier. For more than ten years, Kevin Light has served fabulously as the managing director of both our leadership consulting company and our publishing company FreedomStar Media. And Stormie Knight-Ellwanger has been my faithful executive assistant for almost that long. They are experts in their field—thoughtful and efficient in getting things done and always striving to make me look good, which is not easy. Liz McKenzie manages our online assessment program and supports our clients. Matt Wojteczko is our master facilitator for our online Courageous Accountability Course, and Kristi Deutz keeps our financial records. Their talents and dedication exceed all expectations. I'm grateful to all of them for their performance and service. Also, being a small company, we are served by many other great contractors, each using their talents and resources to help us succeed.

Military

I began Air Force ROTC in college at age 18, and the military was the perfect place for me as a young man. I learned so much about discipline, responsibility, and accountability. My Air Force leaders, especially then Maj Bill Garner (Col USAF Ret), were outstanding role models, and I still remember and coach myself to operate with some of the key leadership principles they taught me.

I retired from the Air Force in 1990 and launched into developing the Career and Life Pathways assessment program and then launched my first leadership consulting and training program in 1997. It was not until the *Leading with*

Honor book launched in 2012 that I reconnected with the Air Force and military. My friend, Joe DiRago, who had worked for me back when I was the T-38 squadron commander at Randolph AFB, was invited by his close friend General Mike Hostage, four-star commander of Air Combat Command, to go out west with him to visit a couple of bases. Joe took some of the new LWH books with him and gave one to 12th AF commander, Lt Gen Robin "Baba" Rand. When Gen Rand read the book, he brought me out to speak to his senior leaders conference on Friday and the 12th Air Force 70th anniversary banquet on Saturday evening. Then he began to buy books and use them with his senior leaders across the command. He also shared them with other general officers and continued to do so after gaining his fourth star and command of AETC and AFGSC. Since that launch, I've been speaking and training at Air Force military bases and Academies for the last 12 years. What a blessing that was from Joe DiRago and Gen Rand.

Business Friends and Clients

Business friends are also critical to our success. Hugh Massie, founder, CEO and Chairman of DNA Behavior, has been a loyal friend and strategic partner for more than 20 years. His wisdom and encouragement have been a big influence on my life and work. Others, like Greg Stipe, Jack Hodge, and Gary O'Malley, have shared their business wisdom and social friendship.

I've been a member of USAA for 58 years and have benefitted from their loyal service in all types of insurance. Their support of military families is unique and special. And, they have been a very special client for my speaking and our training in recent years. I appreciate all they do for veterans and their families and especially for me for almost six decades.

Over the years, I've worked with many great leaders from various Fortune 200 and Fortune 500 companies, small businesses, and not-for-profits. As a coach, trainer, and speaker, I've helped them, but they have also helped me to continue to learn and grow—great companies like AT&T, Southern Company, Georgia Power, Farm Bureau Insurance, Prudential, and several major healthcare companies. Many of their stories were the foundation for my previous books, illustrating how leadership principles from the POW camps are equally essential in the everyday workplace.

Great Organizations

The Wellspring Group. My friend Larry Bolden founded Wellspring Group, a Christian organization that has helped so many learn to connect with their hearts and the hearts of others. My first long weekend retreat was back in 2008. It was such a powerful, life changing experience in helping me grow as a person that I attended again and then became a facilitator for men's small groups at retreats. Larry's development of these great retreats has now expanded into women's retreats that Mary has been involved in with similar powerful experiences.

CEO Netweavers. I've been in this organization for many years, and we have a great community of business leaders here in Atlanta as well as another group in Houston. We are learning from our fellow business executives and our monthly speakers. Perhaps most important is that we are committed to serving and helping others grow and succeed. Mentoring and networking with others is the key.

National Speakers Association (NSA). When my book came out in 2012, my friend Dick Bruso, long-time speaker and formerly head of the NSA Colorado Speakers Association, suggested that I join NSA Speakers. That turned out to be a great learning experience for me and, perhaps just as important, was the great camaraderie I formed with so many great speakers. Their encouragement and promotion helped me develop the skills and strategies to become a Certified Speaking Professional (CSP).

Red River Valley Fighter Pilots Association. The "River Rats" began in 1966-67 under the leadership of Col. Robin Olds, the 8th TAC Fighter Wing Commander at Ubon Air Base, Thailand during the Vietnam War. Robin Olds was an ACE in WWII and a great leader. He brought together representatives from fighter/attack squadrons from the Air Force, Navy, and Marine Corps flying combat missions over North Vietnam, especially near Hanoi and Haiphong—hence the name Red River Valley Fighter Pilots Association. Sharing the combat tactics of the day was important, but over the long haul, it's been the camaraderie that has kept us connected and enabled us to provide scholarship funds for the young men and women who were children of our buddies who were lost in combat and now in any military air crash.

* * * *

These are just a few of the amazing people and organizations that have helped me become a better leader, speaker, coach, and author. And through that process, I've become a better person and most important of all, a better husband to the love of my life, Mary.

For all these blessings, I will forever be grateful.

ACKNOWLEDGMENTS
FROM GREG GODEK

First and foremost, I am forever and ever—and six weeks and a day, and maybe three more—grateful for, and beholden to, my bride/soulmate/best friend/person, Karyn Lynn Buxman-Godek. A close second is Dick Bruso…friend, colleague, consultant and consummate punster. Dick is to blame for this book, as he introduced me to my coauthor Lee.

And in approximately chronological order…Thanks to my mom, who was 100% supportive when I announced that I was going to marry my kindergarten teacher, Miss Fletcher. And to my dad, who was a Good Guy, but who wasn't at all romantic, which inspired me to make it my mission to cure the romantically impaired. A heartfelt thanks to all my girlfriends, who taught me so much about love…C.K., W.W., L.H., J.C., I.F., K.L, and J.R. And here's a hug to my high school group (Betsy, Butch, Connie, Jody, Kathy, Laurie, Katy, Katie and John), who were patient with me when I drifted in and out of active participation while I was infatuated with a series of girlfriends who weren't "One of us." I need to acknowledge the Boston Center for Adult Education, which, way back in 1981, welcomed me to teach, as a lark, "1001 Ways to be Romantic." Then there is the National Speakers Association, where I learned that I could actually make a living out of my little class! (NSA is also where I met my bride, Karyn…but that's a story for another time!)

Thanks also to the Holiday Rambler company, maker of the 36-foot RV which carried me across America four times, while I conducted a two-year, 43-state book signing tour. And warm thanks to John Bentz, a work friend turned great buddy, who encouraged me from the start of my little class, to publication and beyond! And a thousand (and one) thanks to graphic designer and great friend Bruce Jones who designed my first several books, and who graciously allowed me to camp out in his office for three months. And a gajillion thanks to artist Maria Thomas, whose amazing illustrations allowed me to publish the first edition of the book with a four-color cover on a black-and-white budget—and for creating Zentangle, which keeps my creative juices flowing. And then there's John Kremer, who's book *1001 Ways to Market Your Book* was, and still is, my bible (for 30+ years John and I have jokingly threatened to sue each other over the use of the phrase "1001 ways to…"). Many thanks to my friend and favorite baritone Carl "Doc" Martens, who happens to be the best Mark Twain impersonator ever. And to Mark S. A. Smith, for his friendship and his support through his killer business summits. Thanks also to my cheerleaders Dave Casdan, Kathy Dempsey, LeAnn Thieman, Jim House, Brian Lee, Terri Lonier, Pam Reed, and Marcelo Almeida.

I'm sending a virtual standing ovation to three comedians/actors who have inspired me greatly: One, Paul Reiser, for his insights and humor in his bestseller *Couplehood*, and for his role in *Mad About You*, the most romantic sitcom of all time. Two, Mike Birbiglia, whose comedy specials tickle me and Karyn endlessly; we have 86 Birbiglia-isms that are a daily part of our personal lexicon. And three, John Finnemore, for his brilliant BBC radio sitcom "Cabin Pressure" (we pretty much have all 27 episodes memorized). And then there are the musicians who have written and sung the soundtrack of our lifelong love affair…Jason Mraz for "I'm Yours"…James Taylor for "You and I Again"…Cat Stevens for "If You Want to Sing Out"…Billy Joel for "Just the Way You Are"…Paul McCartney for "Two of Us"…and Jacob Collier for "The Sun Is in Your Eyes."

Finally, a huge thanks and a formal salute to my coauthor, Col Lee Ellis, who invited me to be his copilot in creating this book…and who honored me with an actual military medal from the 4th Allied POW Wing.

INDEX

INDEX

P

Palm Sunday, 212
Pan Am, *see* Pan American Airways
Pan American Airways, 193, 196, 197
parenting, 33, 36, 39, 56
Paris, *see* France
Paris Peace Accords, 72, 82, 112, 184, 191, 270
Paris Peace Agreement, *see* Paris Peace Accords
Paris Peace Talks, 71, 79, 106, 111, 112
  and H. Ross Perot, 215
  North Vietnamese delegates to, 111, 122, 123, 237
Parkinson's disease, 89-90
parole, 18
Parrott, Drs. Les & Leslie, 268
  Love Talk, 268
partnerships, 6
patience, 6, 47, 62, 246
  and God, 113
  and trust, 165
patriotism, 10, 12, 31, 148, 161, 183, 193
  of Booncy Fullam, 35
  of Doug Hegdahl, 221-22
  of Ralph & Bobbi Gaither, 82, 83
  of Steve Hanson, 68
Paul the Apostle, 6
PBS, 46
  Return with Honor, 46
peace, 3, 33, 35, 47, 89, 90, 115, 156
  "with honor," 238
Peace Corps, 58
Peck, M. Scott, 271
  The Road Less Traveled, 271
penicillin, 95
Pennsylvania, 43, 131
  Pittsburgh, 56
  Valley Forge Military Academy, 233
Pensacola, 87, 88-89
Pentagon, the, 6, 10, 46, 58, 147, 175, 199, 208, 225
  and Operation Homecoming, 229
  International Affairs Division, 208
Peoples, Rev. Sam, 239
Perot, H. Ross, xxi, 238
  and the Paris Peace Talks, 215
  POW/MIA support from, xxi, 73, 111, 123, 208, 215, 238

Perot, H. Ross, Jr., 215
perseverance, 109, 116, 264
  and strength, 58
  in marriage, 116
persistence, 120
personal computers, 209
personal growth, 270-271
  books on, 270-271
pets, 100
Ph.D., 46
Philippines, the, 14, 24, 45, 73-74, 99, 100, 172, 191, 209, 223, 229
  Clark Air Base, 99, 100, 112, 172, 191, 209, 223, 229, 232, 238
physics, 180
piano, 180, 212
Pittsburgh, *see* Pennsylvania
poetry, 61, 81, 87, 91, 98, 139, 180, 185
  "High Flight" by John Gillespie Magee, Jr. (1941), 176
  Paul Galanti's gift poem to Phyllis, 231
  poem by Dora Griffin Bell, 187
  poems by Dave Carey, 134, 135
  poems by Ralph Gaither, 81-82, 89-90
  purpose of, 139
  writing at "Hanoi University," 207
police, 110
politics, 76
Pontiac Catalina Convertible (car), 131
Pope Paul IV, 71
Popeye, 75
post-traumatic stress disorder (PTSD), 170, 265
  rates of, 229
pot, *see* marijuana
Potomac (census-designated place), *see* Maryland
Potomac River, 57
  Le Bâteau (floating nightclub), 57
POW, *see* prisoners of war
POW/MIA bracelets, xxi, 5, 15, 71, 72, 81, 129, 171, 197
  Brown, Carol Bates, 129
  campaign for, xxi, 5, 15, 71, 72, 171
  cost of, 129
  Dornan, Bob, 129
  Hunter, Kay, 129
  materials of, 129
  number of bracelets worn, 129

S

sadism, 30
St. John, Washington, *see* Washington (State)
St. Jude Children's Research Hospital, 188
St. Mary's College, *see* colleges and universities
St. Patrick's Day, 127
Sanford (Maine), *see* Maine
San Francisco, *see* California
sanity, 22, 23, 44, 195
  and humor, 104, 108, 148
  and optimism, 139, 169-170
Sawyer, Tom, 144
Schierman, Wes & Fay, 7-15
Schweitzer, Albert, 13
science fiction, 32
Scotland, 197
  Prestwick, 197
Sea Knight helicopters, *see* helicopters
seasons
  autumn, 89
  spring, 89
  summer, 89
Seattle-Tacoma International Airport, 8
Secretary of the Air Force, *see* US Air Force
segregation, 243
self-respect, *see* respect
Senior Ranking Officer (SRO), 119, 153
September 11, 2001, 240
service, 37
service number, 18
Shakespeare, William, 61, 180, 207
shared values, *see* values
sharing, 62, 119
Shields, Dr. Roger, *see* Department of Defense POW/MIA Task Group
Shumaker, Bob & Lorraine, 43-48
Singapore Strait, 2
single moms, 1, 5
Sisson, Jerry, 171
60 Minutes, 74
Skelton, Red, 215
skiing, 207
Sleepless in Seattle, 57
Smartt, Ford, 32
  Red River Valley Fighter Pilots, 32
Smith, Gene & Rae, 95-101
Smith, Gene & Lynn, 101-103
  marriage of, 102

Smithsonian Institution, 149
  National Air and Space Museum, 149
smoking, 240
soccer, 211
Social Security, 222
soldiers, xxi, 2-3, 17, 30, 73, 85, 101, 109, 141, 148
  foot soldiers, 170
  homecoming of, 121, 170
  qualities of, 233-234
  resilience of, 2, 110, 148
  returning from Vietnam, 257
  US troop strength, 106
  Vietnamese, 110-111
solitary confinement, 1, 4, 12, 30, 49, 159, 187, 207
  of Ben Purcell, 108, 109, 110
  of "Bill" Bailey, 195
  of Bob Shumaker, 44
  of Everett Alvarez, 54
  of Paul Galanti, 235
  of Roger Ingvalson, 34
  of Wes Schierman, 12
Sonny & Cher, 129
sons, *see* children
Son Tay POW camp, 153, 215
  raid of, 167, 180, 215, 229
soulmate, *see* marriage
South Africa, 194
South Carolina, 175
  Anderson, 199
South Dakota, 221
Southeast Asia, 2
  deployment to, 183, 194
  missions over, 194
  shoot-downs over, 194
Southern, 22
Southern California, *see* California
South Korea, 75
South Pacific (Broadway musical), 180
South Vietnam
  Communist takeover of, 2
  invasion of, 2
  service in, 109, 229
  support of, 2, 68
Soviet Union, 71
space program, 58
Spanish, *see* languages
Spokane, *see* Washington (State)

INDEX

Lee Ellis is Founder and President of Leading with Honor® and FreedomStar Media®. He is an award-winning author, leadership coach, and speaker in the areas of leadership and human performance. His past clients include Fortune 500 executives and C-Level leaders in a broad range of business and military sectors. His media appearances include interviews on CNN, CBS This Morning, C-SPAN, ABC World News, and Fox News.

Early in his career, Lee served as an Air Force fighter pilot flying 53 combat missions over North Vietnam. In 1967, he was shot down and held as a POW for more than five years in Hanoi and surrounding camps. For his wartime service he was awarded two Silver Stars, the Legion of Merit, the Bronze Star with Valor device, the Purple Heart, and POW Medal. Lee resumed his Air Force career, serving in leadership roles of increasing responsibility, including command of a flying squadron and two leadership training organizations before retiring as a colonel.

Lee has a BA in History and an MS in Counseling and Human Development. He has authored or coauthored six books on leadership and career development; two of which have received multiple awards. One is now available as an online leadership and team development course for in-house training of teams and leadership groups.

In 2014, Lee was inducted into the Georgia Military Veterans Hall of Fame, and in 2015 was a DAR Medal of Honor Recipient for a lifetime of patriotic service.

Lee and his wife Mary celebrate their differences. By respecting each other and listening to the other's perspective they make a great team. They are now celebrating 48 years of a very happy marriage. They reside north of Atlanta, near the Blue Ridge mountains. They have four grown children and six grandchildren.

Greg Godek. "I had a girlfriend when I was in kindergarten. It simply seemed natural to me that people belong coupled-up." And so the die was cast. Nine girlfriends and 30 years later, Greg wrote a #1 bestseller, selling three million copies. He taught romance classes on *Oprah* and *Donahue*, and Jay Leno joked in his monologue: "There's a new book called *1001 Ways to be Romantic*. That's an *awful* lot of ways! I mean, guys—if the first thousand don't work…what are the chances she's gonna stick around when you say, 'Oh wait! One more!'?!"

The themes and threads of Greg's life are love and creativity, with a big dose of humor. In the world of love his guiding belief is that "Love is an *emotion*. Romance is an *action*. Romance is what brings love alive in the real world." Greg retired from the romance biz at the turn of the millennium to teach creativity, based on his underground bestseller, *How to be Mildly Brilliant*. Recently he began coauthoring a unique take on romantic relationships, with *Captured by Love: Inspiring True Romance Stories From Vietnam POWs*. This, in turn led to his coming out of retirement from the romance biz, and to his upcoming book *1001 Ways to be Romantic: The Baby Boomer Edition*.

Greg earned a creative writing degree…spent 15 years in "Mad Men"-like agencies…then got inspired and wrote and self-published his first book in three months…undertook the biggest book signing tour in history (two years aboard a custom RV, visiting 287 bookstores in 43 states)…and has never looked back.

Greg and his wife/muse, neurohumorist Karyn Buxman, both write and speak professionally. They live a never-ending honeymoon, they are two peas in a pod, and their motto is, "Nobody will ever be as entertained by us, as us." Greg credits POW Tom McNish and his wife Yona for this motto. "I saw this on a plaque in their home, and it resonated with me and Karyn instantly! They explained that it reflects their deep and intimate bonds—bonds that extend to their entire family, all of whom display this plaque in their homes."

Tony Orlando is one of America's most endearing and iconic entertainers. He continues to bring exhilarating energy, warmth, and humor to a tour of live concert shows across the nation as he celebrates over six decades in the entertainment business.

Grammy Nominee Tony Orlando has sold millions of records, including Five #1 hits. He has 2 Platinum and 3 Gold albums and 15 Top 40 Hits. His smash hit (with Dawn) "Tie A Yellow Ribbon Round the Ole Oak Tree" was the Billboard top song of 1973 and became Orlando's theme song. It has grown into an American anthem of hope, homecoming, and renewal.

Tony has performed for our armed services around the globe and raised millions of dollars for veteran organizations. He serves on the Board of Directors for the Eisenhower Foundation as well as Tribute to Valor Foundation, an organization that inspires, impacts, and influences young people.

Tony's musical career has reached the pinnacle of success in recording, television, and the live stage. Tony has performed for five U.S. Presidents. He is the recipient of The Bob Hope Award for excellence in entertainment from the Congressional Medal of Honor Society, honoring his efforts on behalf of our nation's veterans.

Tony was also the General Manager and VP of CBS-Music Division, April-Blackwood Music, from 1966 to 1970. He represented such songwriters and groups as James Taylor, Laura Nyro, and Blood Sweat and Tears. He also signed and produced Barry Manilow's first recording and represented James Taylor's music publishing while working for the legendary Clive Davis.

The enormously popular Tony Orlando and Dawn television variety show ran for four seasons, from 1973 to 1977, on CBS. The singers still rank among the Top 100 Billboard Magazine artists of All-Time.

Tony is a recipient of three American Music Awards and two People's Choice Awards for Best Male Entertainer. Five times he has been awarded the Casino Entertainer of the Year Award, as the "Best All Around Entertainer" in Las Vegas, and received that same award four times in Atlantic City.

Tony has a wife, Francine, a daughter, Jenny, and a son, Jon.

Learn more at TonyOrlando.com.

Gary Sinise. Gary Sinise's stage, film, and television career has spanned more than four decades. For his performance as Lt Dan Taylor in *Forrest Gump*, he received nominations for Golden Globe, Screen Actors Guild and Academy Awards, and earned the Best Supporting Actor Award from the National Board of Review. Other film credits include *Apollo 13*, *Ransom*, *Snake Eyes*, *Impostor*, *The Green Mile*, *Mission to Mars*, *The Human Stain*, and *Of Mice and Men*.

He starred as Jack Garrett on the series *Criminal Minds: Beyond Borders*, and for nine seasons as Detective "Mac" Taylor on the hit series *CSI: NY*, both of which aired on CBS. Sinise is an Emmy, Golden Globe, and two-time SAG Award winner for his roles in *Truman* and *George Wallace*.

Though he has achieved considerable fame as an actor, Gary has also become well known as an advocate on behalf of America's service members. In 2003, after several USO handshake tours, he formed the "Lt. Dan Band" and began entertaining troops serving at home and abroad. Over the years, the band has performed hundreds of shows for charities and fundraisers supporting wounded heroes, Gold Star families, veterans, and active-duty troops around the world. Sinise has contributed his time on over 100 USO tours and in support of multiple veteran nonprofits over the years.

To expand upon his individual efforts, in 2011 he established the Gary Sinise Foundation with the mission to serve and honor America's defenders, veterans, first responders, their families, and those in need.

For his humanitarian work he has received many honors including the Presidential Citizens Medal, the second-highest civilian honor awarded to citizens for exemplary deeds performed in service of the nation. He is only the third actor ever to receive this award.

You can read his personal story in his 2019 autobiography and New York Times Bestseller, *Grateful American: A Journey from Self to Service*. Learn more about Gary at GarySinise.com and his foundation website at Garysinisefoundation.org.

THE N8TRAITS® RELATIONSHIP REPORT

The first goal of the Relationship Report is to help you gain objective insights into who you are and understand your natural **DNA Behavior**. It will dissect the following eight Factors with sixteen Traits of behavior shown below that will help you understand and develop more of the positive aspects of what makes you tick.

As you honestly assess both your natural **strengths** and **struggles** together as a couple, you'll be able to see each others' **strengths** and especially their **struggles** from a more objective and compassionate perspective. There is no hierarchy of talents. They are all valuable and worth celebrating. We each possess many talents—our own unique array—but they're occasionally hidden from view and must be coaxed out.

> *Purchase and take your assessment and instantly get your personalized report at POWRomance.com/Report.*

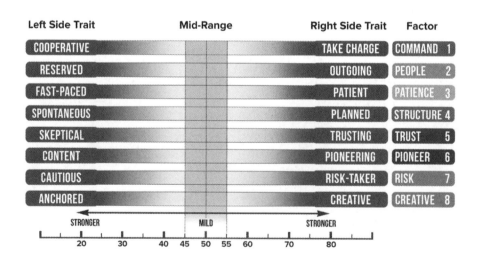

Understand and Celebrate Your Differences with the N8Traits® Relationship Report

Three of the most important aspects are that each person:

- Has natural traits (their natural talents).

- Has strengths and struggles that go with their talents.
  Yes, we all have an equal number of struggles that go along with our talents.

- Likes to be related to, and communicated with, in their unique way—which is often very different from the other.

The N8Traits® Relationship Report provides a scientific explanation of each person's unique talents (strengths and associated struggles) and supporting graphics that make it easy to see areas where the two may be similar or different. Coaching points are also included to help you apply what you've learned.

Purchase and take your assessment and instantly get your personalized report at POWRomance.com/Report.

OTHER BOOKS AVAILABLE FROM FreedomStar Media®

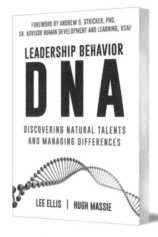

How did American military leaders in the brutal POW camps of North Vietnam inspire their followers for six, seven, and even eight years to remain committed to the mission, resist a cruel enemy, and return home with honor? What leadership principles engendered such extreme devotion, perseverance, and team-work?

In this award-winning, powerful, and practical book, Lee Ellis, a former Air Force pilot, candidly talks about his five and a half years of captivity and the 14 key leader-ship principles behind this amazing experience.

You may have some awareness of the unique differences in people, but do you know how to harness and manage these differences to create a dynamic people culture?

Grounded in statistical research and supported by data from millions of clients and more than 45 years of workplace experience, Lee Ellis and Hugh Massie reveal their personal stories on how they've successfully helped organizations achieve their goals by applying practical insights on human design.

Purchase Copies at Your Favorite Book Retailer or FreedomStarMedia.com

Self-study and online group training materials are also available for these resources. FreedomStar Media resources are available at special discounts for bulk purchases for sale promotions or premiums.

STAY CONNECTED WITH THE AUTHORS!

| Lee Ellis | Greg Godek |

- *Where are they speaking?*
- *Where are they being interviewed?*
- *Where are they publishing articles and videos?*

**Visit POWRomance.com to follow them
on their favorite social media platforms.**